Heinz Kohut and the the Self

Heinz Kohut and the Psychology of the Self examines the pioneering work of the analyst and teacher who became a founder of Self Psychology. A former President of the American Psychoanalytic Association and Vice-President of the International Psychoanalytic Association, Kohut became increasingly alienated from both as he developed his ideas about narcissism and the self. An introductory chapter by Kohut's friend and colleague, Ernest Wolf, provides a psychological portrait of the man and his struggle with the psychoanalytic establishment.

Allen M. Siegel describes Kohut's theoretical development, exploring concepts such as empathy, the developmental line of narcissism, unconscious narcissistic configurations, selfobjects and selfobject transference. Kohut's understanding of the curative elements of therapy was based on the belief that narcissistic vulnerabilities play a significant part in the suffering that brings clients for treatment. The author describes the significance of Kohut's clinical innovations inspired by his rejection of the psychology of drives in favour of his own vision of the vulnerable self, trying to stay safe.

Kohut's often difficult work was written predominantly for a psychoanalytic audience. Using examples taken from clinical practice, Allen M. Siegel shows how Kohut's theories can be used effectively in other forms of treatment.

Allen M. Siegel studied Self Psychology for over twenty years and is now a psychiatrist and psychoanalyst in private practice, Chicago.

The Makers of Modern Psychotherapy
Series editor: Laurence Spurling

This series of critical texts looks at the work and thought of key contributors to the development of psychodynamic psychotherapy. Each book shows how the theories examined affect clinical practice, and includes biographical material as well as a comprehensive bibliography of the contributor's work.

The field of psychodynamic psychotherapy is today more fertile but also more diverse than ever before. Competing schools have been set up, rival theories and clinical ideas circulate. These different and sometimes competing strains are held together by a canon of fundamental concepts, guiding assumptions and principles of practice.

This canon has a history, and the way we now understand and use the ideas that frame our thinking and practice is palpably marked by how they came down to us, by the temperament and experiences of their authors, the particular puzzles they wanted to solve and the contexts in which they worked. These are the makers of modern psychotherapy. Yet despite their influence, the work and life of some of these eminent figures are not well known. Others are more familiar, but their particular contribution is open to reassessment. In studying these figures and their work, this series will articulate those ideas and ways of thinking that practitioners and thinkers within the psychodynamic tradition continue to find persuasive.

Laurence Spurling

Heinz Kohut and the Psychology of the Self

Allen M. Siegel

London and New York

First published 1996
by Routledge
11 New Fetter Lane, London EC4P 4EE

Simultaneously published in the USA and Canada
by Routledge
29 West 35th Street, New York, NY 10001

Routledge is an imprint of the Taylor & Francis Group

Reprinted 1999

© 1996 Allen M. Siegel

Typeset in Times by LaserScript, Mitcham, Surrey
Printed and bound in United Kingdom by
Clays Ltd, St Ives plc

All rights reserved. No part of this book may be reprinted
or reproduced or utilised in any form or by any electronic,
mechanical, or other means, now known or hereafter
invented, including photocopying and recording, or in any
information storage or retrieval system, without permission
in writing from the publishers.

British Library Cataloguing in Publication Data
A catalogue record for this book is available from the British Library

Library of Congress Cataloging in Publication Data
Siegel, Allen M., 1940–
    Heinz Kohut and the psychology of the self/Allen M. Siegel.
        p. cm. – (Makers of modern psychotherapy)
    Includes bibliographical references and index.
    1. Kohut, Heinz. 2. Self psychology. 3. Psychoanalysis.
I. Title. II. Series.
BF109.K617S54   1996
150.19′5′092 – dc20   96–7012
                                                                    CIP

ISBN 0–415–08637–X
ISBN 0–415–08638–8 (pbk)

To Renée

Contents

List of figures	viii
Acknowledgments	ix
Introduction	1

1. The Viennese Chicagoan 7
   Ernest S. Wolf
2. The classical foundation of Kohut's thought 19
3. Early papers: emerging strands of a new cloth 44
4. Toward a psychology of the self 55
5. *Analysis of the Self*: Part I, The idealized parental imago 70
6. *Analysis of the Self*: Part II, The grandiose self 86
7. *The Restoration of the Self*: Part I, Innovations in theory 104
8. *The Restoration of the Self*: Part II, Clinical considerations 118
9. The two analyses of Mr. Z 141
10. *How Does Analysis Cure?*: Part I, Theoretical reflections 153
11. *How Does Analysis Cure?*: Part II, The therapeutic process reconsidered 169
12. Last words 186
13. Critique and conclusions 193

Glossary	203
Chronology	208
Bibliography of the work of Heinz Kohut	210
General bibliography	217
Index	221

Figures

2.1	Freud's topographic model of the mind	24
2.2	Transference's intrusion of the Unconscious into the Preconscious	25
2.3	Freud's schema for neurotic and psychotic symptom formation	33
2.4	Evolution and regression of object libido	39
2.5	Kohut's depiction of Freud's tripartite model	40
4.1	The 'area of progressive neutralization'	57
4.2	Kohut's addition to Freud's developmental line	59
4.3	Developmental line of narcissism	68
4.4	Trauma in the development of the grandiose self	69
4.5	Trauma in the development of the idealized parental imago	69
5.1	Consequences of trauma in the developmental sequence	73
6.1	Types of transference	88
6.2	The vertical split	93
6.3	Vertical split containing disavowed grandiosity	93
6.4	Healed vertical split integrating the disavowed grandiosity	95
8.1	Kohut's characterization of Mr. X's personality and the two phases of his analysis	124
9.1	Kohut's diagram of the two analyses of Mr. Z	151

Acknowledgments

Heinz Kohut asserts that the oxygen of psychological life is to be found in an affirming, supportive and validating milieu and that the need for such an atmosphere exists from birth to death. I have the great fortune to live and work among people who, in their essence, provide such an atmosphere. In these acknowledgments, I wish to thank them with warmest feelings and deepest gratitude for their belief, support, encouragement and friendship.

I wish first to thank Ernest Wolf. It was he who suggested that I should write this book. He came to know my work through a clinical workshop in which we both participated. In the summer of 1991 he invited me to join him and Joseph Lichtenberg in a week-long clinical symposium held at Cape Cod, Massachusetts. That was the beginning of a series of delightful summers on the Cape, filled with intellectual excitement and the treasure of family fun as we came to know each other. Unafraid to speak his mind or stay the course of his convictions, Ernie has been a model of integrity and courage for me. I wish to thank him and his wife Ina for their belief in my abilities and for their unfailing friendship.

Many people have contributed to the story of this book, each in their own way, and I wish to name them all. I wish to thank Dixie Borus, Robert Buchanan, Mark Berger, Henry Evans, Barbara Fajardo, Robert Fajardo, Paula Fuqua, Jill Gardner, Arnold Goldberg, Elin Greenberg, Elaine Hacker, David Hacker, Charles Kligerman, Nicholas Lenn, Rita Lenn, Joe Lichtenberg, Rebecca London, Sheldon Meyers, Thomas Pappadis, Brenda Solomon, Phil Suth, Ruth Suth, David Terman, Marian Tolpin, Paul Tolpin, Gloria Turoff, Jim Wilson, Martha Wood, David Zbaraz and Deety Zbaraz. I extend my deepest appreciation and gratitude to David Solomon. His wisdom, knowledge and courage are an integral part of the evolution of this book. In addition, I am grateful to my stalwart friends Jonathan Borus, Martin Greenberg and Andy Johnson for their unending support. I would like to thank Leonard Rosenbaum for his skill and professionalism in creating the index for this book.

An author writes to an audience, but since the process of writing is solitary, one writes without the benefit of response. I am deeply indebted to my readers, busy people all, who responded unhesitatingly and with unbelievable speed to my request for their comments. I wish to thank Jonathan Borus, Arnold Goldberg, Marian Tolpin, Jim Wilson, Ernest Wolf and Ina Wolf.

I thank also Laurence Spurling for this opportunity to study Kohut's work in depth, for his patience while I did the work and for his suggestions which made this a much better book. I should like to thank the Kohut Archive, located at the Chicago Institute for Psychoanalysis, for access to Kohut's course material. I acknowledge the permission I received from International Universities Press and the University of Chicago Press to quote directly from Kohut's published writings. Every effort has been made to obtain permission to reproduce the cover picture. The publishers would be pleased to hear from anyone who could help trace the copyright holder.

Although the work of a psychoanalyst is rich and fulfilling, it is private and cannot be shared with one's family. I have often felt a sadness that my work was unknown to my daughter. This book has provided a wonderful opportunity to address that situation, for she has been my editor. It is with delight that I express my appreciation to Deborah Siegel for her thoughtful contribution to this book. Her style and sense of prose have added immeasurably to it.

As I note above, an affirming atmosphere is the oxygen of psychological life. In that regard, this book could not have been written without the loyalty of my wife, Renée, who created such an atmosphere for me. At various times she has been my editor, secretary, protector and friend. I thank her deeply.

Finally, since this is a book about selfobjects, I should feel remiss if I did not mention a white-haired, four-legged friend who kept me company for countless hours, abandoning me only once to chase an errant chipmunk across the yard. Thank you, Yoffi.

Introduction

As a candidate at the Chicago Institute for Psychoanalysis, I participated in a course on the theory of Self Psychology taught by Paul Tolpin and Ernest Wolf. Heinz Kohut attended one class session as a guest lecturer. I remember his lament that although he had taken great pains to be as clear as possible in all his writings, it seemed people still misunderstood what he said. He acknowledged that unconscious motivations might have fueled some of the misunderstandings, but more importantly, it seemed to him that people no longer read seriously. His words stayed with me: 'People simply do not read what I have written!'

My goals in writing this book are twofold. One is my wish to stimulate you to read Kohut in the original. To do this I have included Kohut's own assertions, observations, passing comments, explanations and clinical pearls. My hope is that his insights and captivating way of expressing himself will pique your curiosity and kindle a desire to read him directly. I believe it is worth the effort, and I hope this book can be a companion and a guide in that endeavor.

But why should a student of psychodynamic psychotherapy read Kohut, whose writings are addressed to a psychoanalytic audience? Kohut *was* a psychoanalyst and psychoanalysis is what he did; and his observations are certainly about people involved in a psychoanalytic process. But the point of his work is that his observations are about *people*, regardless of what treatment they seek or of whether they are in treatment at all.

Kohut makes major contributions to the understanding of emotional life, and his conceptualizations have far-reaching implications for the understanding and treatment of emotional states. He asserts that narcissism is normal and has a developmental course of its own. He fashions a theory about specific configurations that form as narcissism matures. He teaches that specific needs are related to these narcissistic configurations; that the establishment of a healthy self requires the fulfillment of those needs early in life; and that the maintenance of a stable, lively, productive self requires the continuing nurturance of those needs across the span of life.

This brings me to my second goal: to present Kohut's ideas in a clear and understandable way so that psychotherapists of all inclinations can use his conceptualizations to inform their work. In addition to his theories, Kohut developed a new understanding of the therapeutic setting that is applicable to both psychotherapy and psychoanalysis. I have found Kohut's theories and techniques useful in long-term psychodynamic psychotherapy, brief psychotherapy, couples therapy, consultative work with schools and the clergy, as well as in psychoanalysis.

To study the evolution of Kohut's ideas and the development of his theories, one must know something about the man and the milieu in which he lived, practiced and wrote. Kohut emigrated to the United States from a cultured European background. With a classical education in music and literature, in addition to medicine, he came to Chicago from Vienna in 1940 at the age of twenty-five and pursued training as a clinical neurologist in the Department of Neurology at the University of Chicago. There he was recognized by teachers and peers alike as a brilliant clinician, destined to become a star in the department. Kohut, however, like Freud, left the field of neurology to study the workings of the mind. He trained at the Chicago Institute for Psychoanalysis, where he received an education in classical Freudian theory, the prevailing psychoanalytic theory in the United States.

The first chapter of this book is an essay by Ernest Wolf, Kohut's colleague, friend and collaborator, entitled 'The Viennese Chicagoan.' Dr. Wolf gives us an intimate and evocative portrait of Kohut's personality. He offers penetrating insights into the psychological impact of trauma Kohut sustained as a child. He traces the sources of Kohut's creativity, the origins of his interest in narcissism, and the influence his ideas will come to have on science in general, and on the understanding and treatment of emotional states in particular. Dr. Wolf brings to life the tendentious ambience of the psychoanalytic scene in which Kohut worked and struggled, and gives us a glimpse of the circle of devoted, admiring friends surrounding Kohut during those difficult times. Dr. Wolf brings Kohut to life. I thank him for this major contribution.

In Chapter 2 I describe the course on Freudian theory that Kohut taught at the Chicago Institute for Psychoanalysis. An exceptional student of Freud, Kohut was deeply aware of the origins, strengths and shortcomings of Freud's thinking. He was no renegade; his eventual departure from classical theory grew out of this profound understanding. His course on Freud's theory reveals his mastery of Freud's work better than anything else I have read.

Kohut was an exceptional teacher. His lectures were elegant and ordered, clear and articulate. He spoke without notes, expounding on various subjects with spellbinding ease and fluidity. I have included this course because Kohut's understanding of classical Freudian theory helps make his eventual extension of that theory comprehensible.

In Chapter 3 I consider Kohut's early papers, covering the period from 1948 to 1960. His first paper, written when he was thirty-four years old, is seeded with many of the ideas that were eventually to coalesce and lead him into a psychology of the self. Taken as a whole, these early papers can be seen to contain three major organizing principles that guide Kohut's work. These are his interest in Freud's metapsychology, with particular emphasis on the genetic, dynamic and psychoeconomic points of view, his interest in narcissistic issues, and an epistemologic concern about the methodology of data collection in the analytic situation. Kohut frequently said that his paper dealing with this last concern was his most important contribution.

In Chapter 4 I chronicle the synthesis of Kohut's ideas during the 1960s, when he wrote an integrating series of three papers: 'Concepts and Theories of Psychoanalysis' (Kohut and Seitz 1963), 'Forms and Transformations of Narcissism' (Kohut 1966) and 'The Psychoanalytic Treatment of Narcissistic Personality Disorders: Outline for a Systematic Approach' (Kohut 1968). In these papers he lays out his hypothesis that narcissism has a normal course of development that entails the formation of specific unconscious narcissistic configurations. He describes a new therapeutic approach to the treatment of a particular kind of psychopathology, namely the narcissistic disorders. Although Kohut's ideas grow out of a deep understanding of Freud's work their assertions differ. Fearful that he is treading on sacred soil, Kohut stresses that his ideas are an *addition* to Freud's work. They are not intended to be a replacement. Kohut hoped to remain a traditional analyst, and, anticipating criticism over his effort to extend Freud's theory, cited the evolving nature of theory in science and psychoanalysis to support his work. In the latter part of the 1960s, Kohut began to write his seminal monograph, *Analysis of the Self* (1971). I discuss Kohut's introduction to this monograph in Chapter 4 because it serves as bridge between the papers mentioned above and *Analysis of the Self* (1971), which I discuss in Chapters 5 and 6.

In *Analysis of the Self* (1971) Kohut repeats the hypothesis he presents in the earlier papers, asserting again that narcissism has its own developmental line. The substance of this monograph is Kohut's in-depth delineation of the normal narcissistic configurations and their expression in specific transferences. He describes in detail how narcissism matures from early infantile forms to the eventual establishment of stable mature psychological structures. Kohut asserts that the psychologically attuned responses of a child's caretakers are responsible for the formation of a child's healthy self. Retaining the language of classical psychoanalysis, Kohut refers to the child's caretakers as objects. These objects provide specific psychological functions for the developing self. As such, they are experienced as part of the self and Kohut calls them selfobjects. Kohut describes how the consistently faulty responses of a child's selfobjects can constitute a trauma and abort the normal development of the narcissistic configurations. He asserts that repeated trauma at the hands of a failed selfobject is responsible for a deformed and weakened self. On the basis of this understanding, Kohut proposes a new clinical approach to the psychoanalysis of people with disordered selves. Again, although he is addressing the psychoanalytic situation, the narcissistic configurations he describes and the essential psychological functions provided by the selfobjects extend to everyone. These principles of development, and their implications for treatment, are as useful to the psychodynamic psychotherapist as they are to the psychoanalyst. The cases of two of my own patients serve to demonstrate the applicability of Kohut's ideas.

Kohut's next book, *The Restoration of the Self* (1977), is the subject of Chapters 7 and 8. With this book Kohut makes his break with classical theory and places the self and its vicissitudes at the center of his psychology. He proposes a new definition for emotional health, introduces his new model of the bipolar self and questions the validity of the dual-instinct theory and its manifestation in the oedipal complex as the central motivator for human behavior. He strenuously argues that psychoanalysis is in need of a psychology that considers the self, and attempts to demonstrate the superior explanatory power of such a psychology. *The Restoration of the Self* (1977) marks Kohut's break with what he calls the classical drive–defense, 'mental apparatus', psychology.

I believe Kohut's break with classical theory at this time was influenced by two events, the first of which occurred shortly after he published *Analysis of the Self* (1971). In the fall of 1971 Kohut learned that he had chronic leukemia. The second was that at the same time as he received this news, the ideas he proposed in *Analysis of the Self* (1971) were being severely criticized. I believe that, faced with an early death and surrounded by a circle of supportive friends, he gained the courage to step away from the psychoanalytic establishment and clarify the distinctions between his ideas and classical theory.

In Chapter 9 I review 'The Two Analyses of Mr. Z,' Kohut's 1979 report of two analyses he conducted with the same person at different times in his (Kohut's) development. The first analysis occurred when Kohut was theoretically entrenched in the dual-instinct theory. The second analysis occurred after Kohut worked within the perspective of the self. This intriguing report is part of his continuing argument for the superior effectiveness of his new theory.

Chapters 10 and 11 offer a discussion of Kohut's posthumously published last work, *How Does Analysis Cure?* (1984), edited by Arnold Goldberg in collaboration with Paul Stepansky. Kohut opens this book with a response to the criticisms evoked by *The Restoration of the Self* (1977). He suggests that the idea of a 'complete analysis' is a myth that has more to do with a perfectionistic attitude on the part of the classical theorists than with reality. He re-examines the Oedipus complex and then considers the question of whether 'analytic neutrality' is possible, given the fact that being listened to in a deeply understanding way is a profound experience rather than a neutral one.

The remainder of *How Does Analysis Cure?* (1984) is devoted to Kohut's last thoughts about the processes he believes effect a cure. He dissects the elements of what he considers to be the complete interpretation into an understanding phase, and an explaining phase and discusses the meaning, import and impact of each phase. He elaborates his view of defenses and resistance, a topic of central technical concern for traditional psychoanalysts. Then he describes how this new understanding has changed the ambience in his consulting-room. I conclude the chapter with a discussion of a psychotherapy case from my own practice in order to demonstrate the utility and applicability of Kohut's ideas in the conduct of a psychodynamic psychotherapy as well as a psychoanalysis.

In Chapter 12 I consider Kohut's last publicly spoken words. They are not the last we hear from him since two posthumous publications, *How Does Analysis Cure?* (1984) (which I have already referred to) and a second posthumous address, 'Introspection, Empathy and the Semicircle of Mental Health' (1982), which reflects the issues presented in both *How Does Analysis Cure?* (1984) and 'On Empathy' (the paper I discuss in Chapter 12), appeared after his death. These, however, are Kohut's thoughts three days before he dies. What did he address? What concern merited his last public words?

In fact, Kohut returned to empathy, the seminal topic of 1959. He was drawn back to empathy because he feared that what he has written has been widely misunderstood. He declared, in fact, a feeling of obligation to set the record straight since he feels some responsibility for the misuse of empathy. He then presented a poignant and engrossing extemporaneous discussion of empathy which is preserved on videotape and exists in the library of the Chicago Institute for Psychoanalysis. It merits viewing for its emotional impact.

Chapter 13 contains my critique of Kohut's work. I assume that readers will have questions, arguments, agreements and disagreements as they read. To avoid distracting interruptions as we follow the evolution of Kohut's ideas, I have saved my own thoughts for the end rather than intersperse them as they arise throughout the book.

We turn now to the 'Viennese Chicagoan.'

Chapter 1

The Viennese Chicagoan

Ernest S. Wolf

[P]sychoanalysis, this new sun among the sciences of man, will shed its understanding warmth and its explaining light.
(Kohut 1973, p. 684)

I

I begin these biographical comments with some disclaimers. To write about Heinz Kohut is both easy and exceedingly difficult. Perhaps this is true for any friend who undertakes to tell something of the story of another. It is easy to focus on one's own experiences and let what one knows firsthand be the guide. With a reasonable degree of candor and serious attempts at objectivity one may succeed in painting a lively picture that yet remains a very limited and personal view. Heinz Kohut loved to talk to his friends and students, expressing opinions about all sorts of things. At the same time he remained a very private, even secretive, person, who hid his own past in a fog of generalities. To date no one has published a scholarly biography, nor is the time ripe to reopen old wounds and rekindle the barely banked fires of controversy. The reader of this little essay, therefore, must be satisfied with a quickly passing glance at one of the major innovators of twentieth-century psychological science by someone who was perhaps stationed too close to be able to get a comprehensive overview. In keeping with the spirit of Kohutian self psychological psychoanalysis I will avoid categorical objective judgments in favor of letting the experiencing of evolving interactions prevail.

The first time I met Heinz Kohut I was waiting at an elevator on the upper of two floors occupied by the Chicago Institute for Psychoanalysis. The Institute was still at its old address, 664 North Michigan Avenue, I was still in analysis with Charles Kligerman, so it must have been in the late 1950s. A group of us, patients and candidates, were waiting to leave on the next elevator going down. A youngish man, slim, well dressed, of very serious mien, asked whether we were going to the next floor below or whether we were headed out of the building on the ground floor. He indicated that it would be all right to use the elevator to go to the ground floor but to descend just a single floor one should walk via the stairway. I was taken aback. I had never met Heinz Kohut before but knew who he was and of his reputation as one of the best teachers at the Institute. 'Who is he to tell us whether we can use the elevator or not?' I thought. I did not like this man who seemed so ascetic and disciplined, so Teutonic and commanding. At the time I was deep into my second analysis but still recovering from the painful humiliations suffered at the words and silences of Maxwell Gitelson, my first analyst.

In retrospect, my initial response to Kohut was colored both by some residual transference to Gitelson and, as a refugee from Hitler's Reich, by a gut reaction of anxiety toward and hatred of anything German. And that included Austrian. At the time I had not yet fully recovered from the experience of growing up as a Jew in Hitler's Germany and I was still neurotically afraid of anything German. I did not know then that both Kohut's parents were Jewish, albeit secular. Indeed, though Heinz and I later became good friends, especially after I joined the circle of admiring students of self psychology in the late 1960s, I did not learn about his Jewish ancestry until later. Over the years I got to know him very well but I never thought of him as Jewish. Jewish culture, Jewish food, Jewish jokes were alien to him. Growing up in a family that had been totally assimilated, he did not think of himself as a Jew. But the Nazis did, and that forced him to leave Austria. Even though my own Jewish identity has never been questioned by myself or by others, it has presented me with enough serious problems to make it quite easy for me to understand that one might not want to call attention to one's Jewish lineage.

When Kohut arrived in Chicago he already had a medical degree from the University of Vienna. At the University of Chicago Hospitals he began a residency in neurology under Richard Richter, who was the renowned chairman of the department. To be one of Richter's residents was a recognition of achievement and of great promise. It is understandable that some of Kohut's friends shook their heads in sad disappointment when he left this position to become a candidate at the Institute for Psychoanalysis.

Kohut seemed a strange mixture of aloof, aristocratic and almost puritanical austerity in a warmly responsive and considerate person. He was a very private person and was careful how he let himself appear in public. I never saw him sloppily dressed and I know that he corrected and edited his writings again and again before he was satisfied to release them for publication. He was properly discreet about his health, and few of his friends knew that during the last decade of his life he was suffering from a chronic leukemia in remission. Long before the contemporary popularity of exercise and jogging, Kohut ran, not jogged, his prescribed miles several times a week. He ate sparingly to maintain a trim figure.

Yet dinners at the home of Heinz and Betty were grand celebrations of gourmet cuisine. Heinz was a connoisseur of fine wines. The evening usually began with some special Moselle while chatting before dinner, sometimes by a crackling fire in the living room. Dinner itself was graced by a vintage Burgundy or Bordeaux that fitted the occasion. For dessert he might serve a vintage Sauternes or a Spätlese Rhein or Moselle. Betty was famous for her delicious Sacher Torte, prepared according to a secret recipe which she never divulged. However, the wines were what mattered most to Heinz. He taught me to be careful when pouring into a wineglass, not too much, just about half full. He proudly showed me a letter from his good friend Heinz Hartmann, in fact Hartmann's last letter to Kohut, written shortly before Hartmann died. In this letter Hartmann laments the discomforts of aging but then points out that there are pleasant compensations when growing old: the wines one drinks get better and better. Kohut's ardent appreciation of wine helped, also, in making me feel more at home when a guest at Heinz and Betty's. Having grown up in the Rhineland I was used to a glass of good Rhine or Moselle wine on most festive occasions at home. Even as children we were allowed a little sip of wine, which made us children feel part of the whole warm family ambience, even though we did not really like the taste.

Dinners at the Kohuts' were a little like that. Heinz had collected around himself a group of younger colleagues whom he met regularly for discussion of his work in progress and sometimes for dinner. In part the formation of this group was a reaction to Kohut's experience of being cold-shouldered by his former friends and colleagues, especially the leadership of the American Psychoanalytic Association, as he began to talk about and publish his ideas about narcissism and the self. He mentioned to me some colleagues who knew him well but who ignored him now when he met them walking through the hotel lobby at some national meeting. Old friends suddenly looked past him or answered his greetings only coldly and curtly when crossing his path. He felt hurt and angry. Kohut had been a President of the American Psychoanalytic Association and a Vice-President of the International Psychoanalytic Association. He had been part of the circle around Anna Freud and Heinz Hartmann, and for a time he was expected to be the next President of the International. Among the candidates at the Chicago Institute he was highly respected for teaching the best theory course and writing the most interesting papers. I recall, when I was still a candidate, hearing him discuss with our class his recently published 'Forms and Transformations of Narcissism' (1966), which opened new psychoanalytic vistas for many of us. Almost all candidates thought that he was one of the best teachers at the Institute. His course in psychoanalytic theory was conducted by him at the most sophisticated level. We had our reading assignments and he would start by asking us a few questions about our understanding of what we had read. A few questions back and forth between Kohut and the class and then he would be off on a lengthy discussion of some point that had just been raised. We then sat there, listening, all ears, as the intricate theoretical mysteries of psychoanalysis were revealed to us. Once started on such a topic he could go on and on, maybe for half an hour or more, and he did not like to be interrupted. I was both fascinated and astounded by his tremendous knowledge. In short, he was thought by all of us as the intellectual leader of modern psychoanalysis, as Mr. Psychoanalysis.

All that respect and admiration changed rather suddenly with the emergence of self psychology. For example, after a scientific meeting at which Kohut had emphasized Breuer's and Anna O's great contribution to the creation of psychoanalysis by Freud, he was condemned for not being properly laudatory of Freud, and, within a few weeks, he was removed from the Psychoanalytic Education Council of the Chicago Institute by a vote of his colleagues! He began to feel professionally isolated. Psychologically he needed an affirming responsiveness. Earlier, after he had begun writing his first book, *Analysis of the Self*, he started to have meetings with a number of interested young analysts to discuss the emerging book chapter by chapter. I believe that initially the group consisted of Michael Basch, John Gedo, Arnold Goldberg, David Marcus, Paul Tolpin and, from Cincinnati, Paul Ornstein. Later I was asked to join in, and then also Marian Tolpin and Anna Ornstein.

I was both awed and excited by the privilege of being present during the creative spurts of a genius. I thought of Heinz Kohut as the new Freud and of our meetings as worthy successors to the Wednesday night meetings of the early Vienna group in Freud's house. Looking around the room I would fantasize that so-and-so was the contemporary Abraham, the other was Ferenczi, and so on. John Gedo was a leading spirit among us, and he also seemed closest to Kohut. After the publication of *Analysis of the Self* in 1971 there had not been a public lecture by Kohut for some time and John and I wondered about an appropriate forum for a lecture-presentation for him. Kohut would be sixty years old in another year and, in my naiveté, I assumed that the psychoanalytic community would wish to honor him by celebrating the event. Fools rush in where angels fear to tread. At the time I happened to be on the Program Committee of the Chicago Psychoanalytic Society. When the Committee met I therefore proposed that the Society sponsor a scientific meeting to honor our renowned colleague Heinz Kohut on his sixtieth birthday. This was not received with great enthusiasm but it was decided to bring up the suggestion at a regular meeting of the whole Society. Colleague after colleague got up to denounce my proposal. Indeed, there was no precedent for anyone's birthday being honored by the Society and my initiative was soundly and, as I now see, justifiably rejected. Even in retrospect I do not clearly understand what made me expect the members of the Society to wish to honor someone whom they envied and whose ideas threatened them in their comfortable certainties.

However, I was not ready to give up and I felt righteously outraged at the shortsightedness of my fellow Society members. Carried forward by my enthusiastic idolization I decided to organize with my friends a scientific meeting to honor Heinz Kohut. Together with Paul Tolpin and George Pollock, who as Director of the Institute gave us his blessings, we formed a committee (well assisted by my wife Ina) to arrange the Birthday Conference. Since we needed seed money to get started I personally importuned a dozen or so friends for a loan of about $150 each with the promise that, if possible, they would be repaid after the Conference. We engaged space for scientific presentations and for a banquet at a local hotel. We planned a high-level scientific program with speakers from Europe as well as North America. Heinz took an active part in planning the program. I cannot remember all the invitees nor their topics but among them were the historian Carl Schorske from Princeton University, who spoke about Freud's Vienna; Paul Parin, psychoanalyst and anthropologist from Switzerland; Lawrence Friedman from New York, who spoke about psychoanalytic theory; Mary Gedo, who spoke on art and psychoanalysis; Alexander Mitscherlich, leader in the postwar revival of psychoanalysis in Germany, from

Frankfurt. John Gedo gave the laudation at the banquet. The Kohut Birthday Conference was a great success scientifically and personally. Nearly 600 people, friends and colleagues, from all over the world attended. René Spitz came from Denver. Anna Freud, who was unable to attend, sent a warm letter of congratulations from London. She was among the honorary sponsors, who included also the Mayor of Chicago, Richard Daley. Even after repaying the seed money loans, the conference had a surplus that was donated to the Institute.

The Kohuts had a warm ongoing friendship with Anna Freud. When visiting Chicago Anna Freud would stay with Heinz and Betty. On one of these occasions Betty Kohut admired an amber necklace worn by Anna Freud. On the last day of her visit, just before leaving the Kohuts, Miss Freud took off her necklace and put it around Betty's neck as a gift. Later, when Heinz had sent a copy of the manuscript of *Analysis of the Self* to her in London, he received a somewhat equivocal but encouraging reply. The friendship survived the strains introduced by Kohut's theoretical innovations, as did the friendship with K.R. Eissler. There were frequent exchanges of gifts around birthdays and holidays but as time went on there was no longer any mention of psychoanalysis or Heinz's newer contributions. His work had become taboo among his closest friends.

Some decades earlier, when the Eisslers were still in Chicago, Heinz had been in analysis with Ruth Eissler. His first analysis, in Vienna, had been with August Aichhorn. He always spoke warmly about Aichhorn. After I published one of my early self psychologically influenced papers, 'Ambience and Abstinence', in 1976, I was rewarded by Heinz with the gift of a photograph of a very young Heinz Kohut sitting at a desk with Aichhorn, the two looking at a manuscript together. The inscription on the back of the photograph reads 'With Aichhorn in 1937 – lots of ambience and little abstinence. For Ernie from Heinz, October, 1976.' Aichhorn, the author of *Wayward Youth*, was one of the very first analysts who was able to understand and therefore to deal successfully with the delinquency of adolescents. When treating young people he fostered their idealization of himself and then used this intense idealizing transference as a lever for exerting psychotherapeutic influence. I have always wondered whether Kohut derived some of his own ideas about the importance of the idealizing transference from his contact with Aichhorn, though of course Kohut did not manipulate the idealizing transference, he analyzed it. He told one anecdote from his own treatment with Aichhorn. Apparently as a youngster Heinz had been a very well-behaved, 'good' boy, and in his analysis his 'goodness' somehow drove Aichhorn into impatient irritation until he finally burst out, 'Heinz, I wish I could inject some delinquent's serum into you!' Though Kohut never mentioned her to me, another patient of Aichhorn, Margaret Mahler, also became a leader and innovator in psychoanalysis.

When Kohut heard that Freud was leaving Vienna he went to the station to wave good-bye and he was rewarded by Freud tipping his hat to him. I think that was the only time Kohut saw Freud, but he loved to tell the story. I believe he felt in Freud's gesture a symbolic passing of the torch. Sometime in 1938, after Freud's leaving, Kohut also left Vienna. After a year in Britain he came to Chicago, encouraged by his good friend Siegmund Levarie, the music scholar, who was then at the University of Chicago. Kohut greatly enjoyed music and was a regular at Chicago symphony concerts as well as the opera. His father had been a fine pianist who had contemplated a concert career until military service during World War I put an end to his musical ambitions. Heinz's fondness for and involvement with music was well known to us. On one occasion, we, the group of his younger colleagues, gave Heinz a set of the complete recordings of the Bach cantatas which he then listened to, one by one, a cantata every evening.

Despite the cold rejection of Kohut's ideas by most of his generation of psychoanalysts there was a beginning burgeoning of interest in self psychology among younger psychoanalysts and among analytically oriented psychotherapists. Kohut believed that his theoretical writings, though amply provided with case vignettes, needed to be supported by a collection of extensive illustrative case histories. All of us in the circle of colleagues around him were accumulating clinical experience. Under the leadership of John Gedo we organized ourselves into writing a book consisting of case histories and their full discussion within the new frame of self psychology. We met at regular intervals at the Institute with Kohut and discussed our cases with his participation. It was a unique and most valuable learning experience for every one of us, truly a masterclass at the feet of the master. Each case was discussed at length so that we could decide about its possible inclusion in the forthcoming casebook. Being scrutinized by one's closest colleagues is not a pleasant experience and it led to some tensions within the group. Usually these were dissipated by Kohut's summarizing comments, but in one instance there was no possibility of resolution and, as a consequence, John Gedo withdrew from the group. The casebook project was continued under Arnold Goldberg's energetic leadership and published under the title *The Psychology of the Self: A Casebook* (1978).

The last decade of Kohut's life was characterized by both professional satisfaction and the anguish of personal affliction. The first Annual Self Psychology Conference in Chicago in 1978 was well attended, with over 500 registrants. It set a pattern for an unbroken series of annual Self Psychology Conferences with high-level scientific programs. At the time of this writing I am looking forward to the Eighteenth Annual Conference to be held in San Francisco in October 1995. Heinz was an active participant until his death at age sixty-eight in 1981. He died in Chicago just three days after giving his final address, which was to the Fourth Self Psychology Conference at Berkeley.

In retrospect one wonders about the wellspring of Kohut's originality and its final focus on narcissism. I would speculate that his creativeness was a compensatory response to some early deprivations that had threatened the cohesiveness of his budding self. One major deprivation was the absence of his father during World War I. I do not know the exact dates for his father's military service, but Kohut had been born in May 1913. For Kohut's father the war had been a catastrophic interruption of his career as a concert pianist and he was unable to pursue his musical aims after he returned. One can easily imagine the father's depression and the son's disillusionment in the now returned father, who must have been a distantly admired hero during his military service. But the father's musical interest was reflected many decades later in some of the most original essays on music written by Kohut together with his friend Siegmund Levarie.

Little Heinz was close to his mother and he remained so for many years. Yet certain remarks that he made at times left me with the impression that his mother was a somewhat distant woman who was overly involved with her social life, leaving Heinz in the care of servants and tutors. I speculate that his parents must have had some social aspirations that included melding into the upper bourgeoisie. We know now that the Wittgensteins and others had accomplished assimilation into the dominant culture with remarkable success, and I wonder whether the Kohuts had similar aims. (It may be that the remarkable flowering of individual creativeness within the newly assimilated group may well be a self-assertion; that is, an expression of the individual's roots, ambitions and ideals, to compensate for having had to give up self-sustaining aspects of their prior identity as belonging to the old pre-assimilated group.)

Heinz was an only child, and I have heard him complain that his isolation from other children of his own age robbed him of certain socializing experiences. He was not sent to public school but privately tutored at home, which later made it difficult for him to feel at ease in large groups even as an adult. I must add that he certainly seemed to me to be able to hide whatever uneasiness he was experiencing.

One can speculate on basic psychological traumas sustained during Heinz's childhood. Add to that the trauma of suddenly being torn out of his circle of non-Jewish friends during late adolescence and young manhood as a result of the growing nazification of Austrian youth. He must have been a troubled young man when he saw August Aichhorn for his analysis.

Aside from all these factors that made him develop into the person we knew, what caused Kohut to break out of the mold of 'Mr. Psychoanalysis' into becoming the creator of psychoanalytic self psychology? He himself has written about analysands who taught him to stop making stereotyped oedipal interpretations and told him to really listen to what they were saying. Another precipitating factor was his experience as President of the American Psychoanalytic Association. Apparently he was exposed to the self-serving political maneuvering of respected colleagues. It was an education in the narcissism of politics and it set him searching for a better psychoanalytic understanding of the unanalyzed remnants of narcissistic character disorder in supposedly well-analyzed analysts.

I believe the circle of younger analysts who formed around Kohut – Gedo, Goldberg, Basch, Paul and Anna Ornstein, Paul and Marian Tolpin and myself – had an impact upon his emerging thinking that is difficult to define but nevertheless made itself felt. Not that Kohut got his ideas from his followers. What he needed was a sounding board, preferably one with a positive, harmonious resonance. Thus it was a group selected by him personally that had the privilege to listen to him read his writings as they came out of his study, so to speak. Yet inevitably there was some discussion as the group responded enthusiastically to some ideas, less so to others. Some of us were more clinically inclined in our responsiveness, others were more fascinated by the audacious theoretical innovations. No one rejected his ideas outright, even if they harbored some skepticism, because sitting at the feet of the master as he displayed an astonishing erudition, brilliantly reinterpreting clinical data, and boldly putting forth near-heretical thoughts, was such a satisfying and exciting experience for every one of us. We were all recent graduates of the Chicago Institute for Psychoanalysis, and, let me add without undue modesty, the best of the lot. We admired him and we provided a good selfobject experience for Heinz Kohut that enhanced his creativeness.

II

How is one to evaluate the impact of such a giant as Heinz Kohut on psychoanalysis and on oneself? Clearly, I am not unbiased, nor do I need to be. The heat of current controversies in psychoanalysis probably makes it impossible to be evenhandedly free of prejudgments. One of my biases comes out of the medical tradition and my training as a physician: I value healing more highly than precise theoretical formulations. It is an important judgment of priorities that puts me at odds with many colleagues and also with Freud. Freud disliked being a physician and put the advancement of scientific knowledge, particularly the knowledge gained by the psychoanalytic method, ahead of therapeutic ambitions. When I first began to read Freud and became a candidate at the Chicago Institute for Psychoanalysis I adopted Freud's value system, more or less consciously. Yet I was never very happy with the therapeutic results obtained in my analytic work. Most of my patients did get better; perhaps two-thirds or three-fourths of them improved markedly. That is not a bad record and stands well in comparison to the results of other medical specialties. Still, I always thought it was too easy a way out to blame the patients' 'resistances' or 'unanalyzability' when they failed to live up to what I thought were their potentials.

Heinz Kohut did not take such an easy way out. One of his patients, a clear case of oedipal psychopathology, did not respond to his interpretations of her oedipal transferences in the way she was expected to. Again and again he made the interpretation, and each time the patient rejected it. Resistance? Data and theory fitted each other well. Unanalyzable? Finally, Kohut decided to listen to what the patient was telling him, listen openly and empathically, listen for what this patient was experiencing inside herself. Thus was self psychology born. Eventually Kohut was able to formulate his value system: empathy values are higher than truth values. I was deeply shocked when I first heard him say this. It took me a long time to really understand what he meant. He was not devaluing truth, he was not neglecting the accomplishments of hundreds of years of science. Let me quote from Kohut's presentation at the banquet honoring him on his sixtieth birthday, May 1973:

> But now I must leave generalities behind and reveal the specific change in the hierarchy of values that will, I believe, occur in psychoanalysis. The full integration of his ideals may allow the analyst of the coming generation to become the pacesetter for a

change in the hierarchy of values of all the branches of science concerned with man, through a shift of emphasis from a truth-and-reality morality toward the idealization of empathy, from pride in clear vision and uncompromising rationality to pride in the scientifically controlled expansion of the self . . . scientific empathy, the broadening and strengthening of this bridge toward the other human being, will be the highest ideal.

(Kohut 1973, pp. 676–98)

Psychoanalysis has always entailed this revolutionary program for the recasting of our moral priorities. Freud may or may not have seen clearly the pivotal role of empathy in defining psychoanalysis as a field delimited by its method of data collection; that is, by empathy. He mentioned empathy not more than a dozen times in his whole opus, yet he said, 'A path leads from identification by way of imitation to empathy, that is, to the comprehension of the mechanism by means of which we are enabled to take up any attitude at all towards another mental life' (Freud 1921, p. 110f). In the original German the meaning is even clearer: without empathy there can be no opinion (*Stellungnahme*) about another's mental life. This footnote is the only explicit acknowledgment by Freud of what became for Kohut the central focus of the psychoanalytic method. But even for Freud, empathy is implicit in his inferences and his interpretations. Kohut's explicitly positing the participation of empathy in the collection of data as the *sine qua non* for making data psychoanalytic leads, inevitably, to placing the self at the center of any theorizing about human inner life. That, in Kohut's view, is psychoanalysis, and it advances the psychoanalytic revolution started by Freud. It is this explicitly empathic stance that made a most lasting impression on me and that has been the most important factor in making me a self psychologist.

What about the impact of self psychology on psychoanalysis? In my view Kohut's thought and clinical practice corrected the mainly post-Freudian distortion of psychoanalysis that had transformed a humanly scientific endeavor into a mechanistic, non-human system, ego psychology which was no longer compatible with contemporaneous science and philosophy. If we confine our inquiry to the activity practiced by psychoanalysts who are recognized and certified as such by the American Psychoanalytic Association, then how can we evaluate Kohut's influence on their technique? Perhaps most analysts no longer practice what was called the Standard Technique the way I and most of my contemporaries experienced it thirty to forty years ago. The long periods of silence and the destructively unresponsive or hostile interventions of those days are, I believe, largely a thing of the past. The interpretation of selfobject transferences that were unknown then, like the mirror transference or the idealizing transference, has now become a part of the therapeutic armamentarium of most analysts. But a comprehensive understanding of self psychology remains an accomplishment for future generations of analysts. It is difficult to unlearn years of working within the frame of libido and instinctual drives, or to stop thinking automatically in terms of id, ego and super-ego. Most analysts have not yet grasped that the function of a verbal interpretation is not to convey information for purposes of providing insight but to evoke an experience with therapeutic potential within the analytic dyad. Such an experience may sometimes entail cognitive aspects that the analysand can conceptualize verbally. Yet we also know former analysands who by criteria of functioning were well analyzed without having learned the proper words to label the dynamic changes within. One might say that they have had a curative analysis without many conscious insights. Finally, we know former patients who gained a great many insights and who can tell us in detail what they have learned during their treatment about their conscious and unconscious dynamics but whose mental functioning has not improved in spite of all their hard-won knowledge. Shall we say about them also that they have been well analyzed?

I realize, of course, that colleagues working in the traditional mode would probably dismiss our work as not really being psychoanalysis, but they might allow that maybe it is good psychotherapy. Or, perhaps, I have judged wrongly and my views of the traditional approaches are distorted by my fixation on a past that is long gone. What I understood to have been traditional practice may represent only a caricature of what really goes on in other analysts' consulting-rooms nowadays. I do know how the ambience in my consulting-room has changed over the past decades as a result of my exposure to Heinz Kohut and his ideas. Like Kohut I am very optimistic about the future of psychoanalysis. As reflected in registrations at self psychology conferences and seminars, both in the United States and overseas, there is a steadily increasing interest, knowledge and sophistication on the part of those attending. There is reason to hope that the psychoanalyst of the future will be trained in and familiar with all the various mainstreams of psychoanalytic thought, including self psychology, and that psychoanalysis will become the basic science and language of all mental health professionals from all the various disciplines involved in the study of humankind.

Chapter 2
The classical foundation of Kohut's thought

To comprehend fully the evolution of Heinz Kohut's ideas, psychotherapists and analysts alike must understand classical Freudian theory as Kohut had learned, integrated and eventually extended it. To this end I present the classical Freudian foundation of this pioneering thinker through a discussion of the Freudian Theory course he taught at the Chicago Institute for Psychoanalysis. In my effort I hope to provide a glimpse of Kohut's style as a teacher. Missing, of course, will be his spontaneity and erudition, not to mention his charisma. Present, I hope, will be the clarity, order and organization that were the hallmarks of his teaching.

All that follows in this chapter draws upon extensive notes compiled by Phillip Seitz, MD, Kohut's co-instructor in the two-year course. The notes, unpublished, are stored in the Kohut Archive at the Chicago Institute for Psychoanalysis (see Kohut and Seitz, 1960, for 'Kohut's unpublished course'). I have included a glossary at the end of the book to serve as an aid in the study of this material.

THE COURSE: YEAR ONE

Introduction

Kohut introduces his two-year course, which he taught from 1958 through the late 1960s, by emphasizing the evolving nature of theory-building in psychoanalysis. In his introductory comments, Kohut stresses that his discussion of Freud's work will be colored by the advances in psychoanalytic thought that have occurred since the time Freud wrote. Kohut's opening statement is a response to the dogmatic stance of the many contemporaneous North American psychoanalysts who adhered to Freud's work with unchanging certainty. At that time, nearly every analytic paper began with a citation of Freud's work, an invocation intended to endow the ensuing presentation with credibility. Ideas that suggested change were treated as deviant; innovative suggestions that differed from Freudian thought were often met with interpretations about the author's unconscious. Since Kohut had not formally developed his own theories when he began to teach his course, this opening move is not an attempt to lay the ground for his own new ideas. Rather, it is a teacher's call to his students for an open-minded scientific attitude.

Kohut asserts that analytic theory is not a fixed body of knowledge, as some in the analytic community implied, but one that has, in fact, undergone continuous change. Kohut cites Freud's evolution as a prime example of the evolving nature of psychoanalytic theory, noting that over time Freud developed new models of the mind and rejected old ideas in favor of the new.

History of psychoanalysis

Kohut follows his introductory statement with a review of the history of psychoanalysis, noting that the field has traversed three distinct phases since its inception. The first phase of psychoanalysis began during the last decade of the nineteenth century when Anna O, the first analytic patient, came to Freud's colleague Joseph Breuer for treatment. When Breuer withdrew from her because their relationship had become too intense for him, Anna O became Freud's patient. Anna O was credited with inventing the method known as free association when she told Freud to stop interrupting the free flow of her thoughts. Freud developed his basic ideas during this first phase, which extended through 1920. The first year of Kohut's course was devoted to the first period in psychoanalysis and emphasized the topics of the id, the Unconscious and infantile sexuality. During this portion of the course, Kohut teaches Freud's basic concepts without extending any of Freud's ideas. The second and third phases of psychoanalysis are the subjects of the second year of Kohut's course.

The second phase of psychoanalysis (1920–37) was dominated by an interest in the structural point of view, illustrated by the tripartite model presented by Freud in 'The Ego and the Id' (1923). This second phase of psychoanalysis was characterized by a study of the id–ego–superego and their interrelationships.

In his discussion of the third phase of psychoanalysis, a period that extended from 1937 to the time when Kohut began teaching his course in 1958, Kohut notes that psychoanalytic interest focused on the ego. This was the period of ego psychology, a period in which the ego was studied as a structure in itself and the ego's functions and defenses were of predominant interest.

Ordering principles

After presenting his historical overview Kohut engages the pedagogic problem of how to enter Freud's complex psychology. He approaches this problem by demonstrating how Freud, faced with the problem of bringing order to the maze of psychological data, developed a set of five ordering principles. We will follow Kohut's explication of four of these five principles in detail so that we, like his students and Freud as well, will have tools to order the clinical data that confront us. Freud's five ordering principles are:

1 the principle of a hierarchy of mental functions with differing levels of mental functioning;
2 the dynamic point of view;
3 the topographic point of view;
4 the economic point of view; and
5 the genetic point of view.

Kohut omits the structural perspective at this point because Freud had not developed it during the period of time covered by the first year of the course.

Dynamic point of view

Kohut opens this discussion with a consideration of the 'dynamic point of view.' He does this because the dynamic perspective enables him to engage and discuss the central concept in Freud's psychology, namely that a portion of the mind, unavailable to conscious thought, holds mental phenomena such as wishes, memories, fantasies and prohibitions. Freud hypothesized that some of these phenomena had force and intensity aimed at objects (Freud's term for people). In his diagrammatic models, Freud used vectors to portray internal forces and to demonstrate that forces clashed within the mind. The clash of opposing forces is an important element in Freud's theory, for Freud conceived of the mind as having an innate tendency toward conflict.

Kohut celebrates the genius of Freud's capacity to conceptualize an internal world, without, of course, having an ability to view it directly.

Kohut emphasizes that the essence of Freud's theory is that psychological dynamics are not available to conscious thought. They are contained within the portion of the mind Freud called the System Unconscious. The contents of the System Unconscious are experienced by the person as a driving force, and Freud, in fact, referred to the mental contents as expressions of 'the drives.'

Because conflict was *the* central organizing idea among psychoanalysts in North America at the time of Kohut's training and teaching I will deviate momentarily from Kohut's material to discuss the concept. Conflict was the conceptual context in which Kohut originally thought. It is also the concept from which he eventually freed himself.

To understand the origins of the concept we must be aware of the influence the prevailing scientific theory and language of Freud's time had upon the metaphors of his psychology. In an effort to lend credibility to his new and revolutionary science Freud borrowed language and concepts from the well-established sciences of biology and physics. From physics he borrowed the concepts of mechanics and hydrodynamics. He conceived of the mind as a mechanical apparatus that processed forces. These forces had energy and behaved much like a fluid in a contained system. When energy was blocked it created pressure that pushed for release. Freud conceived of elaborate ways in which the mental apparatus managed this energy.

Freud borrowed biological concepts to explain the origin of the energy. In 1859, forty-one years before Freud published *The Interpretation of Dreams* (1900), Darwin had postulated that organisms sought to preserve themselves and their species. Freud applied Darwin's biological postulates and inferred that two instincts provided the energy and motivation for human behavior. For Freud a sexual instinct preserved the species and an aggressive instinct preserved the self.

Kohut eventually grew critical of the intrusion of biological principles into the science of psychoanalysis (1959). In time he came to feel that such ideas are out of place in the psychoanalytic endeavor and that they lead to misguided speculations that take psychoanalysis far afield from actual human experience. This is a theme that Kohut emphasizes with growing strength as he moves through his life and work.

Since Freud hypothesized that the instincts provide motivation for human experience, Freud's theory is referred to as an instinct or drive theory. The terms are synonymous; each alludes to the biological origin of motivation. Freud coined the term 'libido' to describe the energy he believed was associated with the drives. He suggested that there are two types of libido: sexual libido (sometimes referred to simply as libido) and aggressive libido. Freud maintained that open expression of the drives is antithetical to the maintenance of civilization. In his monograph *Civilization and Its Discontents* (1930), Freud describes how cultures prohibit the expression of sexual and aggressive impulses. These prohibitions make it possible for people to live together but, Freud argued, members of a culture pay the price of neurotic suffering for the gain of social harmony. Neurotic suffering is the result of a conflict between the drives that push for expression and internalized cultural prohibitions. To protect itself, the mind establishes defenses against an awareness of the prohibited drives. Understanding this tension between drive and prohibition is central to understanding Freud's psychology. With this concept in mind I return to Kohut's course.

Topographic point of view

Freud's awareness of the Unconscious led him to consider his next ordering principle, the 'topographic point of view,' which describes the conceptual topography of the mind. In this topography Freud conceived of the mind as having three layers, as indicated in Figure 2.1:

1 the System Conscious, the most superficial layer, the contents of which are conscious;
2 the System Preconscious, the middle layer, which has access to the conscious layer above as well as access to the unconscious layer below; and
3 the System Unconscious, the deepest layer, the contents of which do not have access to consciousness.

Freud called this the topographic model and used it to present a picture of how one system influences another. Kohut notes the dynamic nature of this model and its usefulness in describing the relationship of one system to another. For example, this model describes how dreams, slips of the tongue and forgettings are the result of one system, the System Unconscious, intruding into another system, the System Preconscious. Freud gave the name 'transference' to the intrusion of the System Unconscious into the System Preconscious.

Kohut calls attention to the fact that the term transference has come to be greatly misunderstood and misused. Over time, transference has come to describe an aspect of the patient's relationship with the therapist. Kohut calls this 'technical transference' and notes that it is a

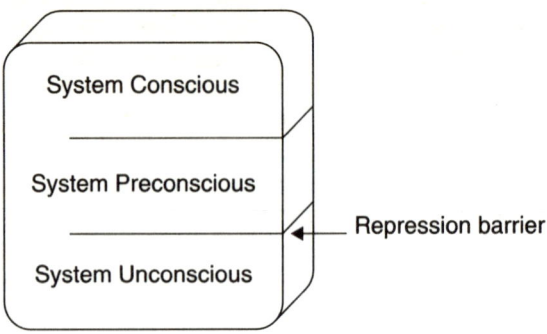

Figure 2.1 Freud's topographic model of the mind

special form of the transference phenomena that Freud developed later (1905b). Kohut prefers the precision of Freud's original definition, the intrusion of the Unconscious into the Preconscious.

Freud developed a psychology that describes the qualities of the Systems Unconscious and Preconscious. He called his a 'metapsychology' since it went beyond the simple phenomenological descriptions of the psychology current in his day. Freud's metapsychology has a specific language and Kohut is painstakingly precise as he presents Freud's metapsychological language. Kohut defines each term clearly and uses it repeatedly in its appropriate context. He looks at it first from one position, then from another until, like any teacher of a foreign language, he feels certain that his students have grasped the essential connotations of the new term.

Kohut scrutinizes the Systems Unconscious and Preconscious in an effort to reveal Freud's concept of the mind and how it functions. Specifically, he examines the functional processes within each system. He approaches Freud's model as one might if one were looking at the individual parts of an engine to see how they functioned independently and in relation to each other. Freud named the processes within each system. The processes in the System Unconscious are the 'primary processes' and the processes in the System Preconscious are the 'secondary processes.' Freud hypothesized that the secondary-process thought of the Preconscious is rational and is responsible for the ordered thought and speech present during the wakeful state. In contrast, the primary process is irrational and is responsible for

Classical foundation of Kohut's thought 25

thoughts found in dreams, where the rules of daytime logic do not apply, where one thing represents another, where impossible things are possible and inconsistencies are not troublesome. Because the primary process occurs within the System Unconscious, it is not conscious and can be known only by inference. Such inference can be made when the primary process invades the secondary process with a force that overwhelms the barrier separating the two systems. It also can be inferred when a clever psychological trick 'fools' the separating barrier.

The mechanism behind this trick lies in Freud's hypothesis that forbidden unconscious wishes attach to insignificant contents. These insignificant contents are 'day residues' and it is their insignificance that makes them ideal for the transference of unconscious wishes across the separating barrier and into the System Preconscious. The day residues act like a Trojan horse. They fool the censor that prevents threatening wishes from invading the Preconscious. Freud called the barrier that exerts this censor-like function the 'repression barrier.'

Figure 2.2 illustrates the intrusion of primary process across the repression barrier and into the secondary process. This transference mechanism is responsible for slips, dreams and neurotic symptoms.

Kohut repeats and emphasizes this definition of transference. It is important for him because it allows him to distinguish situations in which the relationship with the analyst is a transference from those in which the relationship with the analyst expresses other qualities. Kohut applies Freud's definition of transference to the clinical situation, where Kohut notes that the analyst is ideally suited to be a transference object

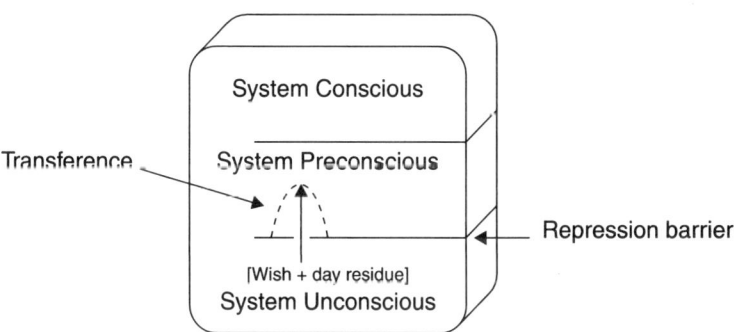

Figure 2.2 Transference's intrusion of the Unconscious into the Preconscious

because he or she does not have 'real' significance in the patient's life. Kohut suggests that the analyst is like a day residue for the patient when he states, 'If he were to become the supporter, helper, friend, gratifier of the patient, then he would not be as readily useable as an object of transference' (1960, p. 14).

Kohut uses the topographic perspective to elaborate Freud's ideas. Remember that conflict is a central concept in Freud's theory. Conflict, according to Freud, exists not within a single system, but between the two systems. Kohut describes the seeds, embedded within the System Unconscious, that are responsible for this intra-systemic conflict. He notes that infantile sexuality (the pleasure arising in the child from stimulation of the mucous membranes, which is not the same as adult sexuality) is one such seed. According to Freud, infantile sexuality, whose origin lies in the primordial sexual instinct, exists within the System Unconscious as an intense pleasure-seeking set of drives experienced as wishes that push for instant gratification. Pressure for immediate gratification is a governing principle of the System Unconscious that Freud called the 'pleasure principle.'

Kohut stresses the wish-fulfilling nature of the primary process. He maintains that comprehension of this essential concept is predicated upon the understanding that an individual's experience constitutes the center of his or her psychic world and emphasizes repeatedly that internal experience is the definer of psychic reality. Kohut also emphasizes the dynamic relationships of the two systems but leaves the elaboration of the specific contents of the System Unconscious to other courses. He refers generically to the contents of the Unconscious as 'unconscious wishes, drives and impulses.' For our discussion, however, I will briefly outline the hypothetical contents of the System Unconscious.

In Freud's theory, sexual and aggressive instincts are expressed through the childhood wish for an incestuous relationship with the parent of the opposite sex and a murderous wish toward the rivaled parent of the same sex. Awareness of these wishes creates an intense anxiety because the wish carries the fantasy of retaliation from the rivaled parent. The constellation of unconscious murderous and incestuous wishes and the fear of retaliatory retribution constitutes the conceptual configuration that sits at the heart of Freud's theory, the oedipal configuration.

Whenever Freud wrote of wishes in the Unconscious, it was the sexual and aggressive wishes to which he referred. For Freud, sexual and aggressive wishes are the seeds of conflict. As I mentioned, they carry the fantasied threat of retribution from the offended parent. For boys the retribution is in the form of castration by the father, for girls (who, according to the theory, experience themselves as already castrated) it is the fear of abandonment by the mother. According to Freud, so terrifying is the anxiety over retribution that defense mechanisms are mobilized to protect the psyche from the invasion of an unconscious wish into the Preconscious. Action in the external world is experienced as dangerous because of its unconscious link to the sexual and aggressive instincts. Assertiveness is psychologically dangerous and must be inhibited. Consequently, protective mechanisms take the form of broad inhibitions that prevent action in the external world.

Freud asserted that all activity (walking, looking, talking, thinking, writing) begins as an expression of the sexual instinct. To function normally and without inhibition, activity must be free from an attachment to the conflict-inducing sexual wishes. The secondary process of the System Preconscious must keep these activities desexualized. When activities become resexualized, they carry derivatives of the unconscious wish, which causes the mental apparatus to erect its defenses. These often take the form of inhibitions. One such example is the writing block experienced by an author who sees success upon the horizon. Freud had not yet conceptualized an agency that explained guilt over forbidden wishes. Such an agency had to wait until he presented his concept of the superego in 'The Ego and the Id' (1923).

Kohut next addresses Freud's concept of emotional maturation. For Freud, the maturing child faces the task of developing a capacity to distinguish between hallucinated wishes and real satisfactions. Freud asserted that experiences of 'optimal frustration' are responsible for the differentiation between a wish and reality. An optimal frustration is the period of delay a child experiences before a particular wish can be satisfied. Through the delay the child comes to realize that active steps must be taken in order to satisfy the wish. According to Kohut, Freud suggested that it is only through an *optimal* frustration, a frustration that is neither so intense as to be traumatic nor so minimal as to be insignificant, that wishes can be differentiated from reality. Freud called the capacity to comprehend reality and delay gratification the 'reality principle,' which is a quality of secondary-process thought. It operates within the System Preconscious and differs from the primary process, the pleasure principle of the System Unconscious, which assumes satisfaction of a wish as soon as it appears.

Kohut's discussion of optimal frustration draws upon his early sensitivity to narcissistic issues. He teaches:

If the child is over-spoiled (not optimally frustrated), it retains an unusual amount of narcissism or omnipotence; and at the same time, because it lacks actual skills, feels inferior. Similarly, overly frustrating experiences make it difficult for the Unconscious to differentiate into Preconscious; and experiences of this kind lead to retention of narcissistic omnipotence fantasies.

(Kohut and Seitz 1960, p. 20)

At this point, Kohut already conceptualizes narcissism within a developmental context. He asserts, 'In persons who tend to be "spoiled" one finds fixated primary process omnipotence delusions, which are not simply defensive overcompensations' (1960, p. 19). He conceives of a narcissistic omnipotence due to a developmental defect and differentiates it from the psychoanalytic understanding, prevalent during the 1950s and 1960s, that conceived of narcissistic omnipotence as a defense. Eventually Kohut will conceptualize a distinct developmental line for narcissism.

Because his is a conflict psychology, Freud developed a language that describes two systems at odds with each other. Using Freud's terms, Kohut carefully groups the qualities and characteristics of each of the two systems. He teaches that primary process, pleasure principle, wish fulfillment, infantile sexuality and infantile aggression are all part of and synonymous with the System Unconscious whereas secondary process, reality principle and rational thought are all part of and synonymous with the System Preconscious.

Kohut describes the relationship of the two conflicting systems when he explains, 'If one thinks of a continuum from Unconscious to Preconscious, one may then conceive of a gradual change from primary process to secondary process, from pleasure principle to reality principle' (1960, p. 20). He describes what he believes is a key to understanding the Unconscious when he says:

> One of the most difficult emotional feats one has to make in understanding the pleasure principle is to be able to imagine, as Freud could, that the primitive Unconscious contains nothing but wishes fulfilled. All there is in this primitive layer of the psyche is hallucinations.
>
> (Kohut and Seitz 1960, p. 20)

Kohut summarizes his understanding of the topographic model as follows:

[T]here are two parts of mental functioning, Preconscious and Unconscious, which are not directly connected with each other but have a barrier between them; . . . optimal frustration leads to maximal differentiation of Unconscious into Preconscious, of primary process into secondary process, and . . . over or under-frustration leads to fixation upon unconscious–omnipotent–pleasure principle–infantile sexual-wishfulfilling–primary process functioning.

(Kohut and Seitz 1960, p. 21)

Psychoeconomic point of view

Kohut turns to the psychoeconomic point of view, a perspective that holds special interest for him. I believe it functions as a bridge between his theoretical abstractions and his clinical experience. Kohut has an overriding concern about the psyche's capacity to experience intense affects and remain intact. He is sensitive to the tendency of the psyche to fracture under the burden of unmanageable affects. He is keenly aware that this tendency is relative and depends upon the nature of the traumatic affect, the timing of the affect in relation to development, the relative strength of the psyche at the time of the trauma and the milieu in which the traumatized person lives. The psychoeconomic perspective speaks to the issue of affect management and tension regulation. It does not focus on specific contents of the Unconscious, rather it focuses on the intensities of feelings and the nature of emotional states. Trauma, a concept central to the psychoeconomic perspective, occurs when an affect overwhelms the mind's capacity to maintain its balance. Kohut teaches that trauma refers to the intensity of the affects surrounding an event rather than to the content of the event itself. Trauma is relative to the nature and maturity of psyche. Timing is crucial, since the intensity of a trauma depends upon the vulnerability of new structures at the time of the traumatic event, both in childhood and in the course of an analysis. Kohut teaches that

> An immature, vulnerable ego will be easily overstimulated and hence traumatized. It is the intensity of early infantile primary process in the presence of an immature, vulnerable, easily overstimulated ego that is responsible for so many early wallings-off or primal repression. Trauma is always relative to the degree of (im)maturity at any given time.
>
> (Kohut and Seitz 1960, p. 22)

He insists that trauma cannot be defined objectively since it is relative to the experience of the person. From this perspective trauma can be known by an observer only through the report of the traumatized person or through the observer's empathic immersion into the traumatic state. Kohut's emphasis on empathy, evident here, will become a cornerstone for his clinical method of investigation (1959).

Kohut returns to Freud's topographic model and uses the experience of trauma to demonstrate how the topographic model works. He asserts that traumatic experiences cannot be integrated into the Preconscious because the intensities of the trauma are unmanageable and must be walled off in the Unconscious. The walling off of unmanageable intensities within the Unconscious (whatever their nature) is called 'repression.'

Kohut uses the language he has taught his students in order to expand upon the concepts of trauma and repression. He describes the psychoeconomics of the primary and secondary processes and explains that under normal circumstances, secondary process exerts control over primary process. Secondary process deals with small quantities of energy whereas primary process deals with large quantities of energy. The source of the large quantities of energy is the residue of the pleasure-seeking infantile wishes, contained in the Unconscious, that push for immediate gratification. Because of their traumatic nature, infantile sexual wishes cannot be integrated into the secondary process. Instead, they are walled off by forces of repression and retained unmodified in form within the Unconscious.

Genetic point of view

The genetic perspective was used by Kohut to explain the shape of a particular psyche. He felt that the genetic point of view embodies the essence of psychoanalysis. From this perspective one speculates about the origins of the patterns in a person's life and places the form and content of a particular mind within a historical context.

Kohut disagreed with Freud, who abandoned his interest in the effect of the environment upon the psyche when Freud conceived of the drives as the sole source of motivation in the mental apparatus. From his own clinical experience, Kohut felt that the environment does indeed have an impact upon the child's development and capacities. His interest in the effects of the environment upon the psyche, however, became the target of severe criticism by the North American psychoanalytic establishment. Such critics charged that Kohut acted like a sociologist, rather than as a psychoanalyst, when he paid attention to the environment. Proper psychoanalysts, the critics contended, were solely concerned with unconscious internal issues. The criticism, however, was based upon a misunderstanding of Kohut's position, for he emphasized that his focus was not on the environment but upon the *experience* of the environment, and the effect, healthy or toxic, that the environment has upon developing psychic structures during childhood.

Symptom formation

At this stage of the course, Kohut has clarified Freud's metapsychological language and has offered ordering principles to help organize clinical data. With this work as a preliminary, he is in a position to discuss symptom formation, a concept he holds to be central to Freud's early approach.

Neurotic symptom formation

Kohut begins this discussion with Freud's idea that neurotic symptoms are actually transference phenomena, the result of something in the Unconscious that threatens to invade the Preconscious. Neurotic symptoms are similar to the formation of dreams.

Although Freud rejected the idea that the external world influences the contents of the Unconscious, he did assert that neurotic symptom formation begins with a reality-based frustration. Events such as a disappointment in love, failure in work, loss of a business, serious illness, etc. initiate the process of symptom formation. Freud contended that although the frustration does not produce the neurotic symptom, it is the indispensable first step. According to Freud, the psyche reacts to frustration with an increase in the preconscious activity of daydreaming which, Kohut asserts, when limited and elastic, is a healthy attempt at softening the blow of reality. Daydreaming is a regression in the service of the ego where one turns away from a painful, frustrating reality and moves toward a fantasied restoration of the previous non-disrupted state. Daydreaming is a refreshing interlude before the necessary return to reality. Freud called this state of daydreaming a 'manifest regression.' In the formation of a neurotic symptom, however, this restorative attempt fails and the process of regression continues to what Freud called a 'regression proper.'

Libido, let us recall, is the energy attached to the sexual and aggressive instincts. To explain regression proper, which is the retreat of libido from a mature position to earlier developmental points, Freud drew an analogy to the deployment of troops by an army on the move. He noted that as an army advances, it leaves behind small numbers of troops at the sites of earlier skirmishes. If the skirmish is minor, it leaves few troops behind; if the battle is major, it leaves a larger contingent to protect the vulnerable area. As a consequence, the army advances with ever-decreasing numbers and, when eventually confronted by an overwhelming force, it retreats to the area where it had left the bulk of its force. Similarly, Freud suggested that traces of libido are left behind at earlier fixation points as libido moves forward along its developmental path. For people who have experienced early developmental traumas, significant quantities of libido have been left at the fixation points. Freud hypothesized that such people have a diminished capacity for healthy manifest regressions and are prone to retreat into regression proper.

In regression proper the rush of libido back to the early fixation points revives the incestuous feelings of childhood that had been put to rest. Interest in present-day people and reality diminishes and a regressive interest in the unconscious incestuous love of childhood returns. Prior to the frustration, the unconscious incestuous love had been countered by a balancing repressive force. The forces that were in balance like this ✛ move out of balance like this ⚹. The System Preconscious is threatened by the intrusion of contents from the System Unconscious. The economic balance is upset and the fourth step in the process, the increase in 'repressed object libido,' begins. Freud called this economic imbalance an 'actual neurosis' and considered it to be the core of a neurosis.

The actual neurosis is a psychoeconomic concept. It is the result of an imbalance of forces that threatens the 'second system,' the System Preconscious, with disorganizing anxiety. Formation of the neurotic symptom is the psyche's attempt to protect the System Preconscious from the anxiety. If the neurotic symptom is removed, without resolving the underlying conflict, the anxiety will return. If the neurotic symptom stays in place, the anxiety will remain at bay.

The last step in the symptom formation process is the compromise formation. Freud asserted that the form of a symptom is a compromise between the forbidden unconscious drives and opposing unconscious forces. This compromise occurs within the System Preconscious and is responsible for the actual symptom. Oedipal phobias, with their classic inhibitions, are examples of compromise formations. The upper diagram in Figure 2.3 shows Kohut's presentation of Freud's schema for neurotic symptom formation.

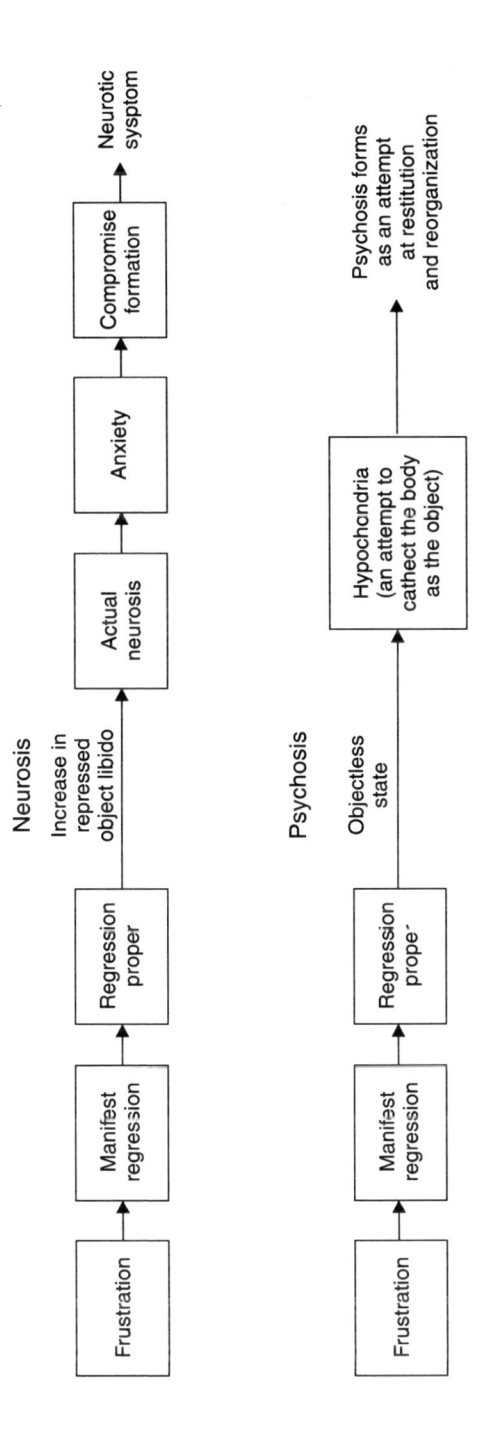

Figure 2.3 Freud's schema for neurotic and psychotic symptom formation

Psychotic symptom formation

Kohut suggests that whereas Freud's early interest lay in neurotic symptom formation, Freud eventually became more interested in what Kohut calls the 'deeper levels of pathology.' Kohut's own special sensitivities to these issues are revealed in his discussion of symptom formation in the psychoses. Citing Freud, he notes that the regression in psychotic symptom formation begins with the same sequence of events as in neurotic symptom formation. The process is initiated by a frustration followed by a manifest regression. In the psychoses, however, the regressive process takes a different turn at the point of regression proper, as in the lower diagram in Figure 2.3.

Unlike the regression to incestuous infantile objects that characterizes neurosis, the regression in psychosis moves toward a pre-object state that contains no libidinal attachments to objects. It is a state in which the unconscious tie to objects is lost. Emphasizing the nature of the object ties, Kohut states: 'even a Robinson Crusoe can have the *feeling* of object experience all about him because the experience of objects is fundamentally an inner experience' (Kohut and Seitz 1960, p. 38). Kohut notes that regression to an objectless fixation point is threatening to the personality because without internal object ties a sense of nothingness, of annihilation and of drifting in space ensues.

Freud suggested that this profound regression leads to hypochondria, a state where the libido searches for an object and, finding none, takes the body as its object. For the person in such a psychotic regression, the body feels as though it is falling apart and the world seems to be slipping away. In Kohut's view what is lost is neither the body nor the external world but the inner core of objects. The loss of unconscious objects produces a pre-object, autoerotic, narcissistic tension. The delusion of the body falling apart, as well as of the world coming to an end, is an expression of the sense of the inner world collapsing. Hypochondria is the psychotic person's attempt to articulate the experience of the objectless state. Kohut describes the psychotic state in the following way:

> This state is very painful because the healthy residue of the ego observes itself losing its equilibrium, its organization, its inner objects. Experienced schizoid characters protect themselves from this pain by walling themselves off from the world. They know their sensitivity and know that if they make contact with people and get

hurt they will regress to an objectless–narcissistic autoerotic state, which is so painful to their remaining ego.

(Kohut and Seitz 1960, p. 39)

In an effort to lessen the unbearable narcissistic tension, the psychotic person attempts to make contact with unconscious internal objects. This restitutive attempt results in psychotic symptom formation. The creation of neologisms is an example of such an attempted restitution. It is an attempt that is doomed to failure, however, because once the unconscious objects have lost their libidinal investments, a connection between the objects in the System Unconscious (primary process) and their representation by words in the System Preconscious (secondary process) no longer exists. As a result, words are taken as objects in themselves. They no longer serve the function of symbolic connection, but are played with and loved for themselves. Neologisms are the result of a failed attempt to connect with the preconscious symbols of words.

Kohut understands psychotic symptom formation as a comparatively healthy attempt to regain contact with objects. He respects the symptom as the most efficient effort available in dealing with an overwhelming psychoeconomic imbalance. His attitude represents a subtle shift in understanding psychopathology, and is in marked contrast to the then prevailing attitude among North American psychoanalysts. In considering psychotic symptoms to be a restorative response, Kohut departs from the view that symptoms are obstacles to the unearthing of unconscious infantile drives and their derivatives.

Phobias

The next symptom Kohut addresses is phobias. He notes that whereas the oedipal phobia constitutes the nucleus of the neurosis, the pre-oedipal phobia is the nucleus of the psychosis, for in the pre oedipal phobia, control over the drives is embryonic and not yet secure. Here he touches upon a repeating theme: the fragility of new structures. As we saw earlier, Kohut feels that newly formed structures are vulnerable to trauma because they are not yet securely established and integrated into the fabric of the psyche. Trauma is relative to the capacity of the structures to manage affects.

As an example of the pre-oedipal phobia, Kohut cites the two-year-old child who is frightened by the hum of a bee. He explains the basis of the child's fright as the threat of unmastered drives breaking through newly acquired defenses. The threatened breakthrough occurs because the skills in the area of mastery over the drives are not yet firmly established. The unmastered drives are projected onto the world, in this instance onto the hum of the bee, and are experienced as dangerous. Kohut suggests that 'At such times a child needs the parent nearby to calm him and to feel reassured that the drive control is secure' (Kohut and Seitz 1960, p. 43). Freud had focused solely upon the internal world and had excluded the effects of the environment upon the developing child. Kohut, however, understands that the parent provides missing psychic functions for the child. Kohut was eventually to develop this understanding into the concept of the selfobject, which I discuss in Chapters 4 and 5.

Kohut is fond of comparing and contrasting mental phenomena that have the same manifest appearance but differ in their meanings because of origins that lay in different developmental eras. He brings this penchant to his discussion of neurotic and psychotic phobias when he distinguishes between, on the one hand, the movement of forbidden drive derivatives across the repression barrier in the neurotic phobias and, on the other, the projections of an insecure and crumbling ego in pre-oedipal phobias.

Kohut summarizes his discussion of symptom formation by noting, first, that psychotic delusions are theories formed by a traumatized person about the experience of the objectless state; second, that hypochondriacal symptoms are theories formed by a traumatized and isolated person about body experiences; and third, that the child's pre-oedipal phobias are theories about his or her disturbing drives.

Kohut and his students spent the remainder of the first year of the course studying Chapter 7 of Freud's *The Interpretation of Dreams* (1900). I refrain from pursuing that discussion since the essence of the material has already been covered and the additional material furthers neither our understanding of Freud's theory nor our appreciation of the evolution of Kohut's ideas. During one particular class session, however, in response to a student's question, Kohut does reveal ideas he will develop later. Kohut had been discussing the pleasure principle when the student asked, 'What is the purified pleasure ego?' Kohut responds with the following:

> [O]ne of the devices that the developing psyche uses to protect itself from disturbances is in its pleasurable narcissistic state. Anything unpleasant is attributed to the outside; anything pleasurable is attributed to the self. When this device is used, the psyche is already differentiating between a self and a not-self: the ego attempts to

claim everything pleasurable as part of the self and attempts to differentiate the unpleasant as the not-self or outside. Controlling, owning, etc. are not yet differentiated from being. Later, when the narcissistic state is disturbed still further, the parents will be invested with qualities of omnipotence. Still later, some of this narcissism projected upon the parents will be re-introjected by the child to form that part of the superego called the ego-ideal.

(Kohut and Seitz 1960, p. 75)

Kohut's response to his student contains the seeds of ideas he will develop more fully into a psychology of the self. We will follow his elaboration of these ideas, which include the concept of the grandiose self, the developmental track of idealization, the accretion of structure through transmuting internalization, and the formation of a superego that is exalted.

THE COURSE: YEAR TWO

Whereas the topographic model dominates the first phase of psychoanalysis, the second phase of psychoanalysis and the second year of Kohut's course is primarily concerned with the structural theory that Freud introduced in 1923. This period in psychoanalytic thought emphasizes the differentiation of the psyche into the structures ego, id and superego. Kohut believes that the second theoretical period grew out of Freud's turn away from the study of transference and toward an interest in narcissism (the libidinal investment of the self) and the psychoses.

In narcissism and the psychoses, Kohut suggests, Freud found a series of clinical phenomena that he could not explain using his elegant, albeit limited, topographic model. Transference, which the topographic model aptly describes, is present in the psychoses but is not at its core. In Kohut's opinion, Freud's interest in narcissism and the psychoses prompted him to write 'On Narcissism' (1914), 'Psychoanalytic Notes on an Autobiography of a Case of Paranoia (Dementia Paranoides)' ('The Schreber Case') (1911) and 'Mourning and Melancholia' (1917). According to Kohut, these papers constitute Freud's attempt to understand regression to the narcissistic, objectless state. Kohut further suggests that Freud's study of the deeper forms of pathology led him to study ego functioning, which in turn led him to the development of structural theory.

Kohut returns to the discussion of psychotic symptom formation, addressing it now from the perspective of narcissism. He does this to demonstrate how Freud's interest in the archaic states helped move Freud from his earlier topographic model to the tripartite model. Kohut begins his discussion with the Schreber case (Freud 1911), one of the five case studies Freud described. Schreber was not a patient of Freud's, but a judge who wrote a diary in the midst of a psychotic episode. Freud used the diary, which describes Schreber's paranoid delusional system, to study the processes involved in a psychosis. Freud believed that the central pathology in Schreber's psychosis was a regression to a narcissistic state, where there was no attachment to objects. Freud constructed a developmental continuum for object attachments that begins with an objectless narcissistic state and moves toward the state of object love, a state where objects are loved and experienced as distinct entities that possess unique qualities. The upper diagram of Figure 2.4 demonstrates this continuum.

In Freud's model, regression occurs when the movement along the continuum is reversed. For Freud, homosexuality is a way-station on the regressive path from object love to narcissism and a restitutive attempt to reconnect with objects, although the objects are like the self. Psychosis occurs when the regression proceeds beyond the homosexual position and moves toward a narcissistic, objectless state as shown in the lower diagram of Figure 2.4. Returning from psychosis, Freud suggested that the restitutive homosexual relationships are the first to be recathected since they are closest to the narcissistic state. Kohut articulates a different understanding when he suggests that symptom formation in psychosis occurs when regression moves beyond the infantile objects to an earlier narcissistic state where object strivings have not yet occurred.

For Kohut, not all regressions are identical. Since similar symptoms appear in both neurosis and psychosis, he believes that it is essential to determine the latent nature of a particular symptom in order to understand the true nature of the regression. He argues that the clinical management of a regressed state depends upon this important distinction. What differentiates psychosis from neurosis is not the nature of the behaviors, but what the behaviors protect against. If a compulsive symptom protects against object-libidinal strivings it is a neurotic symptom; if it protects against regression to an objectless state, then it is a psychotic symptom.

Freud's concept of the evolution of object libido from narcissism to object love

Narcissism → Homosexual object → Heterosexual object → Object love

Freud's concept of regression from object love to psychosis

Object love → Heterosexual object → Homosexual object → Narcissism

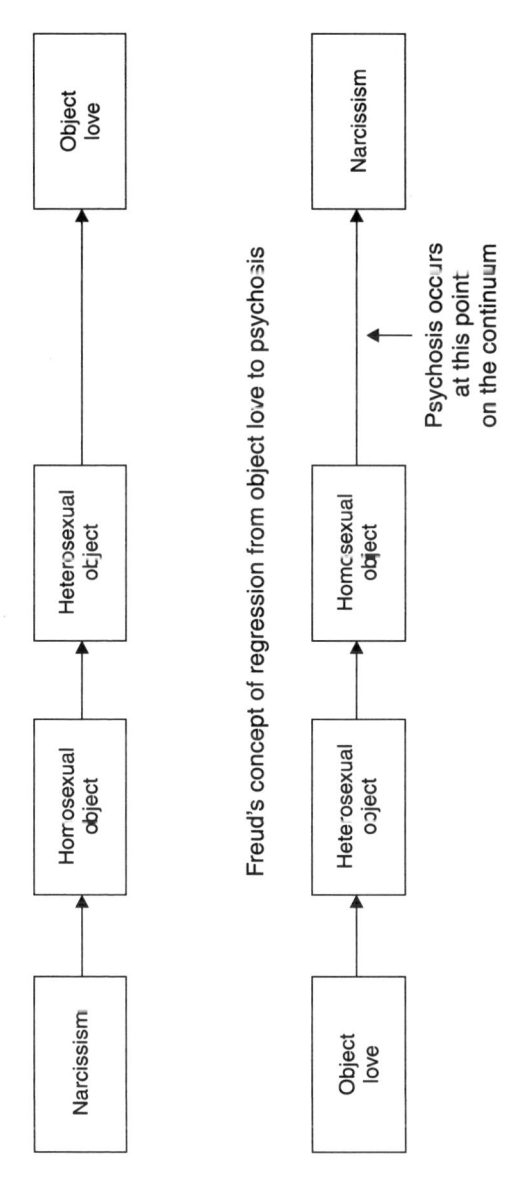

← Psychosis occurs at this point on the continuum

Figure 2.4 Evolution and regression of object libido

Structural theory and the tripartite model

In 1923, Freud crystallized his developing ideas into his structural theory. He created a new model, the tripartite model, to demonstrate the relationships between the three agencies of his new conception: the ego, id and superego. Kohut believes that Freud's interest in the deeper, more archaic forms of pathology brought him to consider the executive agency, which Freud called the 'ego.' In his new model, Freud assigned the censorship function, previously assigned to the repression barrier, to the structure he called the 'superego.' Figure 2.5 is Kohut's rendering of Freud's tripartite model. It should be noted that in his rendering, Kohut emphasizes the repressive forces of the ego rather than the offending forces of the id.

Non-transference area of neutralization

At this point in his course, Kohut makes an important observation. He notes that within Freud's tripartite model there is an area where the repression barrier does not separate the ego from the id. Borrowing language from the earlier topographic model, Kohut notes that there is no separation between Preconscious and Unconscious in this area of the model. Kohut adheres to Freud's definition of transference as the intrusion of the Unconscious across the repression barrier and into the Preconscious. Kohut observes that, by definition, the tripartite model has a non-transference area.

Although Freud did not develop his ideas about the non-transference

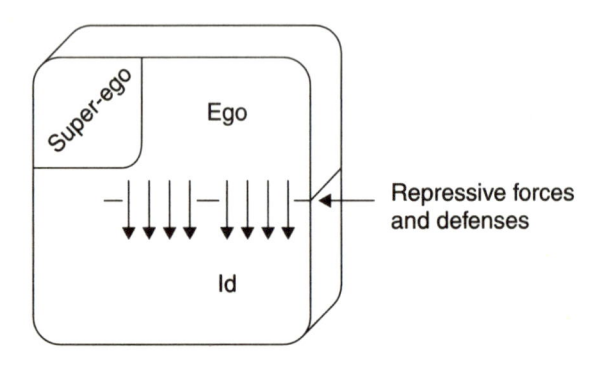

Figure 2.5 Kohut's depiction of Freud's tripartite model

portion of the model, Kohut is intrigued by its potential meaning. He extends Freud's thinking and conceptualizes this non-transference area as a sector of the psyche where optimal frustration (the experience responsible for the accretion of non-conflicted, non-sexual structures and skills) occurs. To illustrate this point, Kohut presents the situation of a parent's management of his or her child's fecal smearing. He suggests that the child develops a capacity for desexualizing its drives when the smearing is responded to in a gentle manner that provides substitutes for the smearing and teaches the child other modes of behavior. Kohut suggests that this situation represents a manageable frustration that allows for growth within the child. It differs from the situation where parents, in an attempt to stamp out and control the unpleasant behavior, respond harshly to the child's smearing. In such cases the frustration is traumatic, rather than optimal. According to Kohut, such traumatic frustration encourages repression by forcing the drives under the repression barrier, where they then provide the seeds for symptom formation. He amplifies these ideas as he teaches his course, and asserts that neutralization or desexualization of the impulses occurs when the correcting parent lovingly counters the child's aggression.

Kohut teaches that neutralization, the knitting of the drives into the fabric of the ego, is a result of the child's identification with the parent's loving management of the child's aggression. Through identification the child eventually responds to its own rages in the same firm, but loving, manner as its parents. If the child's rages are met with a counter-rage by the parents, the child identifies with a rageful way of responding to its own aggression. Kohut contends that this child, when rageful, has a harsh, sadistic attitude toward him- or herself. Repression and other defenses eventually force this dynamic under the repression barrier, away from the non-transference area where Kohut believes neutralization occurs. Kohut, again in contrast to Freud, acknowledges the influence of the environment on the formation of psychic structure.

Superego

Kohut next addresses Freud's concept of the superego and does so by citing Freud's description of superego development. According to Freud, the superego forms as a result of the introjection or 'taking in' of moral aspects of an important person following frustrating experiences with that person. The concept of introjection following loss was important to both Freud and Kohut. It becomes the basis for Kohut's concept of transmuting internalization, an idea which he was to develop later (see Chapters 4 and 5).

The developmental line of narcissism

Kohut's interest in the non-transference area of Freud's tripartite model facilitates Kohut's thinking about narcissism. He hypothesizes that narcissism has its own line of development that begins with primary narcissism and culminates, not in object love as Freud had asserted, but in the development of the ego-ideal portion of the superego instead. After discussing his ideas in class, Kohut publicly presented this extension of Freud's thinking in his paper 'Forms and Transformations of Narcissism' (1966).

Because Kohut's ideas about narcissism, expressed as early as 1960, are of interest as we follow the evolution of his thinking, let us look at some of his classroom thoughts about the vicissitudes of narcissism:

> The next [developmental] phase is one in which the omnipotence is projected to the parents; idealization of the parents, which the child then participates in or shares, as a recipient of the parents' fantasied omnipotence. This stage comes about because, eventually, the reality of the child's actual weakness can no longer be denied. To save what he can of his fantasied omnipotence, the child projects the narcissism to his parents, looks upon them as god-like, and attempts to 'regain' his earlier feeling of narcissistic perfection by closeness to the parents.
>
> The narcissism projected to the parents is then lost. Once again, reality brings this about. Consider, for example, the child's reaction to his first successful lie – his surprise that the parents cannot actually read his thoughts. The wish to have omnipotent and omniscient parents is thus frustrated, and the image of the (lost) perfect parent is (re)introjected, becoming that part of the superego that is called the ego-ideal.
>
> The ego-ideal develops as a reaction to *frustration*: to avoid the loss of the 'perfect' parents, the image of the 'perfect' parents is introjected as the ego-ideal. The ego-ideal achieves its positive emotional quality through the projections of the child's original narcissism upon the parents.
>
> (Kohut and Seitz 1960, pp. 95–6)

Though innovative in his ideas, Kohut is still bound to the drive–defense model and language. This is apparent as he continues his thought:

The original narcissism was associated with the omnipotence of the child's wishes. In this later phase, however, the drive prohibiting parents are seen as omnipotent. Thus the narcissistic balance now depends not on successful wish fulfillment but on the successful curbing of the drives. If the child lives up to the parents' demands for the curbing of the drives he remains in their 'good graces': i.e. he participates in their all-powerfulness and thus retains or regains a positive narcissistic balance. After the re-introjection of the morally perfect parent the same tensions continue in the relationship between the ego and the ego-ideal.
(Kohut and Seitz 1960, pp. 96–7)

Kohut concludes that the exalted nature of the ego-ideal is due to the re-introjection of the child's original narcissism after it has been modified by projection onto the parents:

The powerfulness of the ideal, however, its moral 'perfection', is an expression of the projected and re-introjected narcissism. One could say that the ego-ideal is one's own narcissism that has been modified in specific ways by its 'passage through the parents.' . . .

The development of the neutralized superego structure is dependent upon this passage of the child's narcissism through the parents. If the parents' demands are reasonable, then when the child re-introjects his narcissism it will come back more neutralized than before. If the parents' own ego-ideal is made up largely of un-neutralized structure, then in the passage of the child's narcissism through the parents it will not undergo as much neutralization, but will be re-introjected in an unmodified form, betraying its oral genesis by its impatience and its narcissism by its uncompromising attitude of self-righteous perfection.
(Kohut and Seitz 1960, pp. 96–7, 99–100)

Thus Kohut first creates the term 'passage through the object', which foreshadows his later concept of transmuting internalization, in this course; he was later to discuss it in his paper 'Concepts and Theories of Psychoanalysis' (Kohut and Seitz 1963).

Kohut completes his course with a discussion of Freud's thinking about the changed meaning of anxiety, dual-instinct theory and ego autonomy. Because these constructs do not add to our appreciation of the evolution of Kohut's thought, I will not pursue this discussion. Rather, I turn now to a series of Kohut's early papers, which harbor the seeds of ideas that later germinate more fully into the psychology of the self.

Chapter 3

Early papers
Emerging strands of a new cloth

As we have seen, Kohut was a serious student of Freud, and his early papers, as well as his course, reveal the classical grounding that support the structure of his later work. Interwoven within the fabric of Kohut's early work are strands of subtle texture and tone that he eventually weaves together to form the new cloth of a psychology of the self. His early papers contain repeating themes. The first is his intense interest in Freud's metapsychology, with a particular focus on the genetic, dynamic and psychoeconomic points of view. A second theme is Kohut's interest in narcissistic issues, expressed in his concern about vulnerable people and their struggle to regulate tension and maintain psychic cohesion. A third theme concerns the method of data collection in the analytic situation. I believe that this triad of themes – metapsychology, narcissism and method of investigation – holds the major organizing principles Kohut employed when he entered a psychological field.

Paul Ornstein, in *The Search for the Self* (1990), organizes Kohut's early papers along the lines of Kohut's three major areas of interest: applied psychoanalysis; the psychoeconomic point of view and method; and clinical theory and metapsychology. My observation differs slightly from Ornstein's. I believe the triad of metapsychology, narcissism and method of investigation that I present differs in that it characterizes Kohut's *mode of entry* into any psychological field, be it clinical or applied psychoanalysis, rather than reflecting his separate interests.

THE FIRST PAPER: AN ANNOUNCEMENT OF IDEAS TO COME

Kohut's first paper was '*Death in Venice* by Thomas Mann: A Story about the Disintegration of Artistic Sublimation' (1957a). Though he wrote this paper in 1948, at the age of thirty-four, Kohut withheld it from publication until after Mann's death. In the paper, published in 1957, Kohut discusses Mann's novella, the story of Aschenbach, an acclaimed writer, who experiences an emotional deterioration. Like the overture to an opera, Kohut's paper contains suggestions of themes he was to develop in coming years. His discussion addresses Aschenbach's deterioration. Although Mann did not describe the precipitant for Aschenbach's deterioration, Kohut interprets the deterioration as having a classical oedipal core, centering on an internal conflict with Aschenbach's overpowering father. The result of the conflict is a castration anxiety of disorganizing intensity. Aschenbach unconsciously attempts to protect himself from deterioration by developing an intense infatuation with Tadzio, a fourteen-year-old boy, whom he yearns for from afar. Mann places this infatuation at the heart of his story and in doing so recognizes, as does Kohut, that an infatuation, through its idealizations, has a restitutive quality.

Let us return for a moment to Mann's story. Aschenbach has fallen helplessly in love with the boy Tadzio's beauty, yet this unconscious attempt at restitution ultimately fails. Aschenbach, an acclaimed writer, attempts to protect himself against further deterioration through the defense of artistic sublimation by writing an essay on the question of art and taste. To understand this defense let us recall what we learned from Kohut's course. Remember that Kohut demonstrates how classical Freudian theory explains anxiety as the result of unconscious drives that threaten to break through the repression barrier and invade the System Preconscious. In an effort to bind and control the anxiety, unconscious defenses are mobilized. The act of writing is such a defense. Through this intellectual act, attention is focused on ideas and words rather than upon the offending drives and affects. In Mann's story, however, this defense also fails and Aschenbach's deterioration continues. Toward the end of the story, Aschenbach has a dream in which order deteriorates into chaos. Kohut understands the dream as the unconscious expression of a disintegrating ego, unable to retain its cohesion. This dream is the forerunner of what Kohut later conceives of as a self state dream.

Although Kohut's formulation of Aschenbach's story centers around the oedipal configuration, his primary interest seems to lie in Aschenbach's narcissistic vulnerability and the experience of Aschenbach's emotional deterioration. Kohut's early awareness of the yet-to-be-named selfobject tie appears in a footnote where he discusses Aschenbach's progressive deterioration. Kohut writes that Aschenbach 'had no object-libidinal ties to reality. This may have served as a reassurance to Mann, who despite temporary loneliness, felt that he had sufficient emotional closeness to his family to preserve him from Aschenbach's destiny' (1957a, p. 210). Here, in Kohut's first psychoanalytic paper, is the seed of the selfobject concept. I note it for its historical interest and will discuss the concept at length when considering Kohut's later work, after he had more fully developed his thoughts about the selfobject. For now, I refer the reader to the glossary for its definition. It should be noted that Kohut presents his early ideas in the language of drive–defense psychology, the prevailing theory of that time. He was to articulate them differently later.

Kohut's sensitivity to the rage that grows out of narcissistic wounds becomes clear when he considers whether Aschenbach had a destructive impulse toward Tadzio. Aschenbach had loved Tadzio just as Aschenbach had wished his own father could have loved him. Kohut writes, 'It remains true that the destructive impulses toward Tadzio are secondary, arising only insofar as the narcissistic identification with the boy and the enjoyment of the love by proxy are not entirely successful' (1957a, p. 222).

Fragmentation, another concept central to Kohut's later work, is a pronounced theme throughout this paper, although it is expressed here in drive–defense language. Kohut reveals his interest in Aschenbach's fragmentation in statements such as: 'The reader is given the impression that reason is helplessly succumbing to infinitely stronger irrational forces' (1957a, p. 211) and 'with the crumbling of his moral and rational defenses there is . . . no need nor possibility of deluding himself about his true motivations' (1957a, p. 214).

Kohut's nascent interests are apparent in his choice of Mann's novella as the frame for his first psychoanalytic paper. The paper is remarkable in that it reveals concepts that Kohut will later articulate such as selfobjects, restitutive idealization, narcissistic rage, self-state dreams, fragmentation states and self-cohesion.

ON MUSIC: EARLY THOUGHTS ON DISRUPTION AND REPAIR

Kohut's second paper, 'On the Enjoyment of Listening to Music' (1950), was co-authored with Siegmund Levarie and published in 1950. Levarie, a musical scholar and a friend from Kohut's youth, had immigrated to Chicago during the 1930s. Kohut went to Chicago because Levarie was there. In this second paper, also in the field of applied psychoanalysis, Kohut explores the quality in music that creates pleasure for the listener.

Voicing the classical psychoanalytic position of the 1950s, Kohut and Levarie write that the pleasure in listening to music comes from 'energy that is liberated through mastery of the musical task' (1950, p. 77). They define the 'musical task,' however, as mastery, through recognition of the musical organization of what otherwise would be chaotic sounds. The listener's recognition of the musical organization, they feel, relieves the momentary disruption that occurs when the sounds are not recognized, and they suggest that composers intuitively understand the listener's experience of disruption and relief. They assert that composers purposefully create tension in their music by moving from consonance to dissonance and then resolve the tension by returning to consonance.

Although Kohut expresses his understanding of the pleasure that comes from listening to music in the energy language and theory of the 1950s, his descriptive thrust focuses on mastery of the disruptive experience rather than on the release of energy. He implies that a restorative mechanism containing elements of both disruption and repair lies at the core of musical pleasure. The listener voluntarily exposes him- or herself to the momentary tension of disruption in order to experience the pleasure of resolution. Kohut notes a parallel between the musical listener's experience and the experience of the child who 'plays "being gone" in an effort to master the painful experience of its mother's absence' (Kohut and Levarie 1950, p. 81).

Kohut's perspective in this paper is a psychoeconomic one. His interest is in the affects associated with the experience of a disruption and the need for repair. His conceptualization is couched in the experience-distant language of that time, but his interest addresses the experience-near issues of affect management and tension regulation.

EARLY CONSIDERATIONS OF THE TRANSFERENCE: DEFENSE VERSUS NEED

In a discussion of a paper by Samuel Lipton entitled 'The Function of the Analyst in the Therapeutic Process,' Kohut addresses the issue of transference in borderline patients by asking the question, 'Is the immediate overwhelming reaction these patients experience really transference?' (1951, p. 162). Kohut's response to the question reveals his ability to deal creatively with observations that do not fit established explanations as well as his deep grasp of Freud's metapsychology. It demonstrates his capacity for clear thinking and for these reasons I present it in its original form:

> Clinically, these 'borderline' patients are characterized by the consistent combination of greater ego defect and intense protective secondary narcissism. Their immediate interpersonal conflict with the analyst, too, is distinguished by its narcissistic character. It is not to be denied that the conflict is an old one, that it is a repetition, a revival of an emotional attitude that had its original objects and now is re-enacted on a new one. But, while every transference is a repetition, not every repetition is a transference. . . . What the narcissistic 'borderline' patient presents has some elements in common with transference, namely, the element of repetition and the confusion between old and new object. There is however a decisive difference. In transference the id, a repressed drive-element, is seeking satisfaction; in the 'borderline' patient, an injured, narcissistic ego is seeking *reassurance*. . . . [The patient] reacts to the analyst as he reacts to every important person in his present life because the emphasis of all psychological maneuvers is on restoring or keeping up a precarious balance of self-esteem; the attention is narcissistically fastened on himself, his injured ego, and not on the object.
>
> (Kohut 1951, pp. 162–4)

Here Kohut introduces narcissism, the second leg of his triad of interests, into the body of his work. He treats narcissism as an injured ego's restitutive attempt to gain reassurance from an external source, rather than as an offensive force that needs to be civilized. In this early discussion Kohut distinguishes between a transference that expresses a defense and a transference-like experience that expresses a need, an idea he was to expand as his work progressed.

KOHUT'S METHOD OF INVESTIGATION

Scientific attitude

Kohut's grasp of Freud is complemented by a scientific attitude unusual in a North American psychoanalytic community where Freud's theory was generally taken as dogma. This attitude is present in Kohut's discussion, in 1954, of a paper by Iago Galdston (published 1955) concerning Freud's death instinct. Kohut, while repudiating the death instinct, reminds his audience that Freud was fond of creating temporary abstractions that he treated as working hypotheses and which he was prepared to modify when necessary. Kohut quotes Freud as saying, 'For these ideas are not the foundation of science, upon which everything rests: that foundation is observation alone. They are not the bottom but the top of the whole structure, and they can be replaced and discarded without damaging it' (1914, p. 77). This discussion relates to the third leg of Kohut's interests, method of investigation in psychoanalysis.

Empathy as a definer of the field

Written in 1957 and published in 1959, 'Introspection, Empathy, and Psychoanalysis: An Examination of the Relationship between Mode of Observation and Theory' (1959) continues Kohut's discussion of method in psychoanalysis. In this classic paper, Kohut defines what he considers to be the legitimate field of psychological investigation, asserting that the psychological field is limited to data available *only* through empathy and introspection.

Scientists study the physical world by means of the sensory organs and their laboratory extensions, the various scientific instruments. How, asked Kohut, do we investigate the inner world? He noted that whereas thoughts, wishes, feelings and fantasies are the data we seek, they do not occupy space and may not be observed via sensory organs. Nonetheless, the contents of the inner world are real and may be known to oneself through introspection. Vicarious introspection, Kohut's definition of empathy, is the way one can learn about the inner experiences of another. Empathy is *the* data-gathering tool in psychoanalysis and, Kohut argues, an experience or an act may be considered to be psychological *only* when it is observed via introspection and empathy. Any other mode of observation lies within the physical field.

Kohut warns against intermingling theories that are based upon differing modes of observation. He is particularly concerned about mixing the theories of psychology, based upon information obtained through empathic immersion, with the theories of biology and sociology, based upon observations of the external world.

Anticipating those who might argue that free association defines the psychological field, Kohut points out that free association is an instrument employed in the service of the introspective and empathic mode of observation. Free association and analysis of resistance are the psychoanalytic tools that enable internal data to emerge; they are not the method of observation. Empathy is the tool that gathers psychological information. Kohut adds that the tools of observation in any empirical science determine the contents and limits of what may be studied. In turn, the contents and limits of what can be studied determine the theories available to a given field.

Kohut departs from classical psychoanalytic theory at this point in his paper. He turns his attention to the issue of early mental organization and applies the empathic mode of investigation to the study of early mental states. He warns against using terms such as 'wishes' and 'conflicts' when describing these states, believing that such terms apply to a later psychology. When referring to early mental organization, Kohut suggests speaking of a tension rather than a 'wish' and of a tension decrease rather than 'wish fulfillment.' He warns that as the scope of psychoanalysis widens to include early mental states, analysts face the task of empathizing with primitive mental organizations, a task that differs from Freud's investigation of the psychoneuroses.

Freud's introspective method is directed toward the recognition of unconscious infantile strivings and their balancing counterforces. In Freud's model, the analyst is a 'day residue' and carries unconscious forces across the repression barrier into the Preconscious. Kohut suggests that the new data, obtained through introspection and empathy with narcissistic and borderline states, carry new theoretical and technical implications. The new data suggest that poorly structured psyches struggle, in an effort to remain psychologically intact, either to maintain contact with an archaic object or to preserve a tenuous separation from the object. For these people, Kohut notes, the analyst is not a screen for the projection of transference but a continuation of an earlier reality that was too rejecting or too toxic to be transformed into reliable psychic structure.

Kohut suggests that the narcissistic patient experiences the analyst within the framework of an old relationship. The analyst is experienced as the old object with whom the patient tried to maintain contact and from whom the patient attempted to derive some modicum of internal structure. For this group of patients the archaic relationship occupies a central psychological position that corresponds to the central position of conflict in the psychoneuroses.

To demonstrate how the empathic–introspective method of investigation leads to an understanding of psychopathology that is different from the classical psychoanalytic understanding, Kohut addresses the phenomenon of psychological dependence in patients with deficient psychological structure. He takes the addicted person as an example of one who has acquired neither the capacity for self-soothing nor the ability comfortably to make the transition to a sleeping state. Kohut asserts that the addicted person is unable to transform the early childhood experiences of going to sleep into reliable psychic structure and turns to drugs as substitutes for the missing tension-regulating capacity. In a similar way, the addict turns to the therapist and becomes addicted within the psychotherapeutic situation. Kohut cautions that this dependence should not be confused with transference in the classical sense. This dependency represents the patient's *need* for soothing due to *missing* internal structures rather than the projection of existing structures onto the therapist. It will not be decreased by insight, the classical psychoanalytic approach. Instead, Kohut's view is that the major therapeutic task requires an undoing of the denial of the need and an acknowledgment of the dependence. The patient needs help to replace a set of grandiose fantasies that have been a temporary support. (Here we see the harbinger of the concept of the grandiose self.) Kohut hints at another concept he was eventually to develop when he writes that the patient's clinging dependence 'protects the patient . . . by clinging to the therapist who has become the omnipotently benign carrier of projected narcissistic fantasies' (1959, pp. 223–4). In this thought we find a seed of the idealized parental imago.

A GROWING FOCUS ON PSYCHIC STRUCTURE

Kohut's next paper speaks again of music, but this time he integrated his interest in music with his interest in psychological structure and what he calls the 'precarious mental states.' In 'Observations on the Psychological Functions of Music' (1957b), Kohut addresses the unstable psyche and its relation to music. The nominal topic here is the psychological function of music, yet the paper contains important statements about Kohut's understanding of primitive ego organization. Initially, Kohut describes music in terms of its id, ego and superego components. He departs from this perspective, however, as he discusses the psychological function of music and turns his attention to the problem of patients who have a primitive ego organization. Kohut describes these patients as people who struggle to maintain emotional cohesion but who do not form any clearly defined neurotic or psychotic symptoms. He writes:

> Psychoeconomically [there] is another form of psychopathology in which there is also no psychological elaboration of inner tensions in the sense of neurotic or psychotic symptom formation. In these cases we find that an insufficient ego system is unable to deal with any of a wide variety of tensions.
>
> (Kohut 1957b, p. 245)

In an early departure from the traditional therapeutic approach, Kohut suggests that the treatments designed to address the problems of people with structuralized personalities are not directly helpful for people with primitive ego organization. He asserts that classical treatment for these people can 'help only indirectly, most often by creating the experience of being soothed by closeness, or, of being comforted by a powerful therapist. The content of the verbal contact (explanations for example) is not by itself effective' (1957b, p. 245).

The last clinical paper in this early series is Kohut's discussion, presented at the annual meeting of the American Psychoanalytic Association in 1957, of Louis Linn's essay 'Some Comments on the Origin of the Influencing Machine' (published 1958). In his discussion, Kohut refers to the classic paper on psychosis by Victor Tausk (1919) entitled 'On the Origin of the "Influencing Machine" in Schizophrenia.' He notes that Tausk understands the meaning of a particular paranoid delusion as a symbolic expression of a state of inner deadness rather than as an expression of an oedipal conflict which was the traditional interpretation at that time. Kohut suggests that analysts tend to view psychoses either from the dynamic–structural conflictual perspective or from the psychoeconomic perspective of prestructural psychologic organization. He remarks that while Freud and Tausk use both perspectives, Kohut himself prefers the latter and argues that

> this approach [is] more fruitful and more in accord with Tausk's thesis than laying stress on content, as for example, on conflict over masturbatory impulses.
> ... [I]n a narcissistically regressed psyche, object libidinal fantasies cannot be easily stimulated and I would therefore be inclined to emphasize, not the phallic nature of the 'robot,' the 'mechanical man,' and the 'cigarstore Indian' in the patient's dream equivalent, but rather the lifelessness, lack of human warmth and strangeness of these figures.
> (Kohut 1957d, p. 260)

Here we see evidence that Kohut has already set aside conflict theory as the template through which he views all patients. Instead, he approaches the psychological field with an open-minded attitude, employing empathy as the psychological instrument that will give him the information he needs to formulate his hypotheses. Rather than apply formulaic meanings, Kohut attempts to immerse himself in his patient's affective experience to grasp the meaning of symbolic statements. This approach led to his understanding of the deadness for Tausk's patient.

METHOD IN APPLIED PSYCHOANALYSIS

In 1960 Kohut wrote and published 'Beyond the Bounds of the Basic Rule.' This paper is the counterpart, in applied psychoanalysis, of his clinical paper 'Introspection, Empathy, and Psychoanalysis' (1959). A call for definition of the field of applied psychoanalysis, this paper gives credence to the field's method of data collection as well as to the goals of its explorations. The 'basic rule' refers to Freud's instruction to the analytic patient regarding free association, a requirement that the patient report all that comes to mind without any censorship. In a play on Freud's directive, Kohut advocates venturing 'beyond the basic rule,' as the analyst applies the principles of psychoanalysis to other fields.

The paper defines three problems that face applied analysis. The first, an obvious issue that nevertheless must be articulated, is the requirement that the worker in applied analysis have a solid grounding in both psychoanalysis and the field under study. The second problem deals with the method of investigation in applied psychoanalysis. Kohut feels there are serious difficulties in applying a psychoanalytic understanding to artistic works. He observes that although one might consider the body of work being studied as the equivalent of dreams and free associations, applied analysis is deprived of the confirming interplay that exists in the clinical setting between the analyst's interpretation and the patient's response. Yet another problem inherent in the attempt to understand an artist's work exists in the possibility that the artist might have used the work in the service of a false self. The body of work might be a defensive facade the artist erects to protect the authentic, but vulnerable, core self. Without access to the artist, an analysis of the work might miss this point.

The third major problem deals with the general goals of applied psychoanalysis. Kohut believes that the field being studied is too often used as a foil to demonstrate the importance of psychoanalysis. In these situations, the psychoanalytic inquiry becomes self-serving, adds little to the second field and leaves the inquiry itself open to the critique of reductionism.

To illustrate the dangers of such reductionism, Kohut cites the analytic interpretation of Albert Schweitzer's personality offered by Edward Hitschman in his book, *Great Men: Psychoanalytic Studies* (1956). Hitschman repeatedly cites the vicissitudes of the oedipal complex in his understanding of the men he studied and suggests that Schweitzer's behavior is motivated by reaction formation. In support of this, he quotes Schweitzer as saying, 'It struck me . . . as incomprehensible that I should be allowed to live such a happy life, while I saw so many people around me wrestling with care and suffering.' Hitschman's interpretation, based on this statement, is as follows: 'Since this feeling is not a general one, we assume the existence of an unconscious guilt feeling which originated in early years and was revived by regression.' Kohut responds to Hitschman's interpretation, declaring:

> [T]he underlying assumption here that the deviation from the normal attitude is a reaction formation may be correct, yet it would seem that a keen awareness of the misery existing in the world and the determination to live a life devoted to the suffering are the autonomous attitudes of a mature ego. One might rather posit the question why this man was capable of maintaining his ideals beyond the temporary crisis of his early years and thus, during a period of unparalleled crisis of Western Christian civilization, could become by his very existence the spiritual support of so many.
> (Kohut 1960, p. 289)

Reviewing Kohut's early work, we see the threads of his central interests: metapsychology, narcissism and method of investigation in psychoanalysis. These threads were eventually to unite into Kohut's overriding interest, the formation and maintenance of a stable self. As we follow the evolution of his thinking we will witness his conviction in the self as a central configuration, present here in embryonic form, strengthen with time.

Chapter 4
Toward a psychology of the self

The 1960s was for Kohut a period of synthesis, integration and growing confidence. He sharpened the focus of his overriding triad of interests – metapsychology, narcissism and method of investigation in psychoanalysis – and they became the new lenses through which he viewed old understandings. During the 1960s Kohut wrote three major papers from his newly developing perspective: 'Concepts and Theories of Psychoanalysis' (Kohut and Seitz 1963), 'Forms and Transformations of Narcissism' (Kohut 1966) and 'The Psychoanalytic Treatment of Narcissistic Personality Disorders: Outline for a Systematic Approach' (Kohut 1968). In this chapter I discuss these papers as well as Kohut's introduction to his seminal monograph *Analysis of the Self* (1971), which I include here because it provides a bridge between the three papers and the remainder of *Analysis of the Self* (1971), which I discuss in Chapter 5.

CONCEPTS AND THEORIES OF PSYCHOANALYSIS

Kohut wrote 'Concepts and Theories of Psychoanalysis' (1963) with Phillip Seitz, MD, his co-teacher in the theory course, five years after they began teaching. This paper reports the innovative thoughts about transference, trauma and the tripartite model that Kohut first expressed in that course.

Transference: Freud's original definition

In relation to transference, Kohut feels that Freud became imprecise when he strayed from his original definition. Remember that Freud originally defined transference as the intrusion of the Unconscious into the Preconscious. For Kohut, this definition emphasizes transference as an endopsychic rather than an interpersonal process. Accordingly, transference is not related to the analyst's personality, nor is it an outgrowth of the relationship with the analyst. Freud's concept of transference as the revival of unconscious feelings from childhood, projected onto the analyst, came later. Kohut calls this 'clinical transference' and distinguishes it from Freud's original definition. Kohut's conceptual precision is important because it enables him to differentiate between transferences that are intrusions of the Unconscious into the Preconscious and other 'transference-like' experiences. Kohut calls them transference-like because they do not adhere to Freud's original definition but they do, however, express something from within the patient that is experienced with the analyst. With this important distinction Kohut is eventually able to conceptualize the 'narcissistic transferences' (1968), which he later calls the 'selfobject transferences' (1971).

Kohut and Seitz describe trauma as central to the development of psychopathology. Trauma, in childhood, is an emotional event that the child's psyche cannot integrate into the differentiated Preconscious because the intensity of the demand is too great, the structures are too immature or the psyche is transiently sensitive at the time. For Kohut, trauma is a psychoeconomic concept that refers to the intensity of affect, not to the content of the trauma. Trauma is overstimulation. Timing of the trauma is a critical factor. Although a child is always sensitive to trauma, his or her sensitivity is greatest when a new balance has been established following a growth spurt.

Frustrations are traumatic when the tolerance of the infantile psyche is exceeded or when gratifications are unpredictable. In traumatic frustrations, infantile drives and associated memories are walled off in the Unconscious because of the anxiety and despair associated with them. The drives and memories cannot be influenced by new experiences and therefore are incapable of change. They follow the laws of primary process and push for immediate gratification.

Kohut holds that childhood frustrations can be reworked, in manageable increments, when they are mobilized in a therapeutic setting. Change through structure-building is possible through the gradual metabolism of manageable frustrations. The ultimate goal of psychoanalysis is the therapeutic revival and recovery of the unconscious memories of traumatic experiences.

Structural theory and the tripartite model of the mind

In the core of this paper Kohut and Seitz propose an addition to psychoanalytic theory which they describe as follows:

[W]e would like to focus especially on the fact that, as alluded to by Freud in his diagrammatic rendition of the structural model of the psyche (1923 p. 24) but not sufficiently elaborated conceptually by him, the barrier of defenses separates only a small part of the infantile psychological depth from the area of the mature psychic functioning, while the deep, unconscious activities in the remainder of the diagram are in broad uninterrupted contact with the preconscious layers of the surface.

(Kohut and Seitz 1963, pp. 367–8)

Remember that Kohut first commented about this uninterrupted sector in his theory course and called it the 'area of progressive neutralization' (see Figure 4.1), which he distinguishes from the transference inducing area under the repression barrier and describes in the following:

The right side of the diagram represents the area of transferences where the infantile impulses that have met with frustration of traumatic intensity exert their transference influence across the barrier of defenses and produce compromise formations (between primary and secondary processes) with the preconscious contents of the ego. The left side of the diagram represents the area of progressive neutralization, where the infantile impulses that have encountered optimal frustration are transformed gradually into neutralized mental activities.

(Kohut and Seitz 1963, pp. 368–9)

The area of progressive neutralization forms through the process of

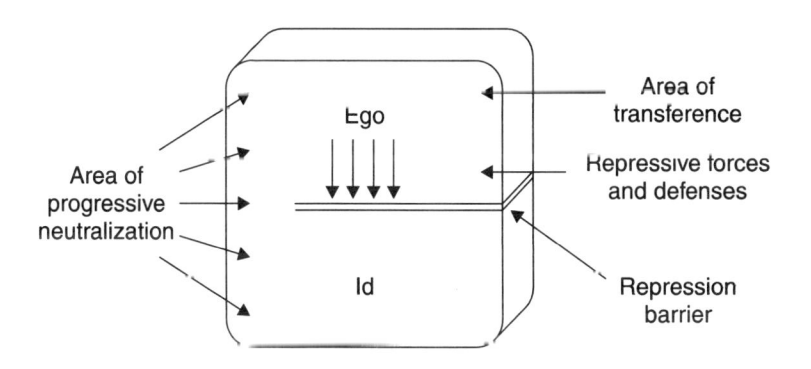

Figure 4.1 The 'area of progressive neutralization'

internalization, under conditions of optimal frustration, and the barrier of defenses forms as a result of traumatically frustrating experiences and prohibitions. Freud treated the environment as though it had little effect upon the child's psyche. Kohut and Seitz, however, suggest that the environment does have a significant influence upon the developing psyche, and address the impact of the environment, mediated through parents' personalities, when they write:

> The differences between childhood experiences of traumatic and of optimal frustration are differences in degree. It is the difference between one mother's harsh 'N-O!' and another's kindly 'no.' It is the difference between a frightening kind of prohibition, on the one hand, and an educational experience, on the other. It is the difference between one father's handling a child's temper tantrum by an equally hostile counter-tantrum and another father's picking up the child and calming him – firm but nonaggressive, and loving but not seductive. It is the difference between an uncompromising prohibition, which stresses only what the child must not have or cannot do, and the offering of acceptable substitutes for the forbidden object or activity.
> (Kohut and Seitz 1963, pp. 369–70)

The child establishes internal replicas of the parent's drive-restraining attitudes. If these attitudes are non-traumatic the child is able to meet its drives with a loving soothing attitude rather than with counter-aggression. These non-traumatic experiences contribute to the portion of the psyche that is not under the barrier of defensive mechanisms. Kohut and Seitz write of these experiences:

> Optimally frustrating experiences lead, therefore, to the formation of a drive restraining (neutralizing) structure which itself is composed of neutralized memory traces and works with the aid of neutralized endopsychic forces . . .
>
> The most important source of a well functioning psychological structure, however, is the personality of the parents, specifically their ability to respond to the child's drive demands with non-hostile firmness and non-seductive affection. . . . If a child is exposed chronically to immature, hostile, or seductive parental reactions toward his demands, then the resulting intense anxiety or over-stimulation leads to an impoverishment of the growing psyche, since too much of his drive equipment is repressed and thus cannot participate in psychic development.
> (Kohut and Seitz 1963, pp. 370–1)

FORMS AND TRANSFORMATIONS OF NARCISSISM

In the second paper of this important series, 'Forms and Transformations of Narcissism' (1966), Kohut turns to the subject of narcissism and articulates the concepts about narcissism that we have seen brewing in his earlier thoughts. He asserts that narcissism has its own developmental line, with unique configurations and developmental endpoints, and differs with Freud's concept of object love as the endpoint in the maturation of narcissism.

Kohut's idea is momentous, for it suggests that narcissism is neither obnoxious nor pathological. Renunciation of narcissism in favor of object love was a goal of Freud's treatment, but Kohut's ideas carry new therapeutic implications. They suggest that narcissistic structures, in disordered states, need to be reordered and integrated into the personality. Figure 4.2 describes Kohut's developmental line for narcissism.

Kohut suggests that narcissism, which he defines as the libidinal investment in the self, holds a checkered position within the psychoanalytic world: when discussed theoretically, narcissism is treated with neutrality, but when discussed informally it is treated with derision. Kohut contends that this judgmental attitude reflects the encroachment of Western values into psychoanalysis. He asserts that the attempt to replace narcissism with object love diminishes the field

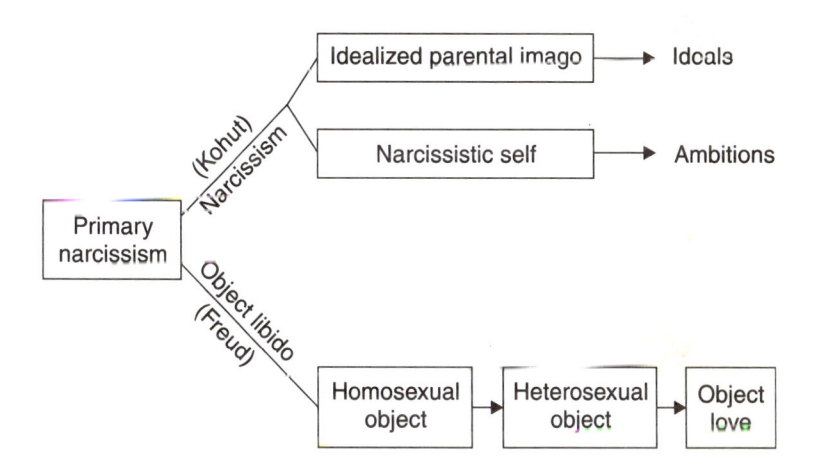

Figure 4.2 Kohut's addition to Freud's developmental line

since it establishes psychoanalysis as an agent for society rather than for the patient. It has been said that Kohut did for narcissism what Dickens did for poverty: he legitimized it.

Forms of narcissism

In the first section of 'Forms and Transformations of Narcissism' (1966) Kohut presents his ideas about the maturation of narcissism and its developmental forms. He postulates that the narcissistic experience begins with the infant's blissful state, which is inevitably upset by the expectable failure of its mother's ministrations. The infant attempts to restore the disrupted bliss by creating two new systems of narcissistic perfection. One system attempts to create a perfect self, a developmental stage where everything good, pleasant and perfect is experienced as belonging to the inside and everything bad as belonging to the outside. Freud called this the 'purified pleasure ego' (1915, p. 135). Kohut calls it the configuration of the 'narcissistic self.'

The second system attempts to restore the lost blissful state by imbuing an outside 'other' with absolute power and perfection. Attachment to the perfect 'other' restores the child's sense of wholeness and bliss. Kohut calls this narcissistic configuration the 'idealized parent imago.' These two forms of narcissism, the idealized parent imago and the narcissistic self, both evolve from the disrupted primary narcissism. Each of these systems follows its own developmental line.

The idealization of the idealized parental imago is created through the projection of a portion of the baby's original bliss, power and perfection onto the parents. The idealization is not an end in itself, however, since it must ultimately be taken back or internalized. To understand this process, Kohut discusses the concept of internalization, a concept central to his theory of development.

According to Kohut, the process of internalization is related to the experience of object loss, as Freud explained in 'Mourning and Melancholia' (1917). In that paper, Freud suggested that the psyche is not resigned to the loss when deprived of an object. Instead, the lost object is 'taken inside' as a memory and becomes a piece of psychic structure that assumes the functions previously performed by the object.

Kohut suggests that, for the child, losses range from the massive actual loss of an object to the minute and manageable losses that occur as the result of unavoidable disappointments in circumscribed aspects of the object. For example, a small quantity of the omniscience assigned to the idealized parental imago is lost when the child's lie goes undetected by the presumed-to-be all-knowing parent. Every parental shortcoming leads to an attempt, on the part of the child's psyche, to preserve the lost parental quality. Following a non-traumatic disappointment, such as the undetected lie, the idealization that was once projected onto the parent is recovered and, through the process of internalization, becomes part of the ego ideal portion of the superego. The esteemed position of our ideals, then, is due to narcissism's maturational path rather than to the content of the values themselves.

The second attempt to restore the original blissful state occurs through the creation of a perfect self, 'the narcissistic self,' a term Kohut later changed to 'the grandiose self' (1968). Kohut speculates that for the narcissistic self, the narcissism is not invested in an 'other' but is retained for investment in the self. Just as the overvaluation of the 'other' is a phase-appropriate step in the maturation of narcissism, so too is the overvaluation of the self. Whereas the idealized parental imago gazes in awe at the object of its idealization, the narcissistic self wishes to be *viewed* with awe and admiration. While the idealized parental imago contributes to the formation of the ego ideal, the narcissistic self is closely related to the drives and their tensions. The idealized parental imago contributes to our ideals; the narcissistic self contributes to our ambitions. Kohut suggests that experientially, an individual is led by ideals and pushed by ambitions. This work marks the beginning of what Kohut was later to describe as the 'bipolar self' (1977).

Ambitions, for Kohut, derive from a childhood system of grandiose fantasies that always seeks witness for the grandeur and perfection of the self by an important 'other.' The 'other' has meaning only insofar as it participates in the child's grandeur and perfection; it has no meaning in and of itself. Its meaning is in terms of the function it serves as witness to the child's exhibitionistic needs. Kohut describes this developmental need in his well-known statement that 'the child needs the gleam in the mother's eye in order to maintain the narcissistic libidinal suffusion which now concerns . . . the functions and activities of the various maturational phases' (1966, p. 252).

Exhibitionism is the normal felt experience of the child's narcissistic self. The child yearns to be admired. The ideational content of the narcissistic self, however, is the grandiose fantasy. According to Kohut, the contribution of the grandiose fantasy to health or disease depends upon how it has been integrated into the realistic purposes of the ego. If the 'early narcissistic fantasies of power and greatness are not opposed by sudden premature experiences of traumatic disappointment but gradually integrated into the ego's reality-oriented organization' (1966, p. 253), then the ego will be able to make adaptive use of the sense of power. The grandiosity eventually becomes integrated into the ego as the healthy enjoyment of activities and successes, accompanied by a feeling of confidence.

Transformations of narcissism

The second section of Kohut's 1966 paper examines the transformations of narcissism into the qualities of creativity, transience, empathy, humor, and wisdom – all transformations that occur as the original narcissism matures. I will describe each in some detail as follows:

1 *Creativity*: The creative individual has the child-like capacity to play imaginatively with that individual's surroundings, because such a person tends to be less psychologically separate from the surroundings. The creative work becomes part of the self. Just as a mother idealizes her unborn fetus, so the creative person, in a transformation of narcissism, extends an idealization to his or her work.
2 *Empathy*: The first perception of the feelings of others comes from the view that the world is an extension of the self. This prepares the self for the recognition that the inner experience of others is similar to one's own. Empathy, the recognition of experiences similar to one's own, is the way in which people gather psychological information about each other. Kohut considers empathy's origin to be the encoding of the mother's feelings and behavior in the experience of the developing self.
3 *Transience*: Kohut believes that the greatest psychological achievement is the acceptance of one's mortality. This accomplishment requires that one abandon the insistence upon omnipotence and accept one's impermanence. This achievement is often accompanied by a higher form of narcissism that contains a quiet pride, even superiority, in having a knowledge unshared with the majority.
4 *Humor*: Kohut suggests that humor, as a transformation of narcissism and not merely an expression of denial, can be used in the acceptance of transience. When present, humor contains a sense of quiet inner triumph, mixed with an undeniable melancholy that differs from the picture of fragmentary or defensive grandiosity and elation.
5 *Wisdom*: For Kohut, the essence of wisdom is the letting go of narcissistic delusions and the acceptance of the inevitability of death. An attribute of later life, wisdom is an amalgam that includes

a stable attitude of the self toward life and the world. It is the result of a movement through life that includes the ideals cathected in youth, the humor cathected in maturity and the acceptance of transience established in older age. It involves the understanding that ultimately one's powers decline and all comes to an end.

Kohut closes this historic paper with the following statement:

> I would like to say that I have become increasingly convinced of the value of these conceptualizations for psychoanalytic therapy . . . In many instances, the reshaping of the narcissistic structures and their integration into the personality – the strengthening of ideals, and the achievement, even to a modest degree, of such wholesome transformations of narcissism as humor, creativity, empathy, and wisdom – must be rated as a more genuine and valid result of therapy than the patient's precarious compliance with demands for a change of his narcissism into object love.
> (Kohut 1966, p. 270)

PSYCHOANALYTIC TREATMENT OF NARCISSISTIC PERSONALITY DISORDERS

The last paper in this series is 'The Psychoanalytic Treatment of Narcissistic Personality Disorders: Outline of a Systematic Approach' (1968), in which Kohut elaborates the therapeutic implications that flow from his new understanding of narcissism. He contends that the transference-like structures of the narcissistic self and the idealized parental imago are mobilized during the analysis of people with narcissistic personality disorders. He refers to these mobilizations as transference-like to distinguish them from Freud's original definition of transference. In this paper, Kohut changed the term 'narcissistic self' to 'grandiose self.' He did so following discussions with Anna Freud (Cocks 1994). Unfortunately, however, the word 'grandiose,' in everyday usage, bears a negative implication. As a consequence, the terms 'grandiose self' and 'grandiose fantasy' are frequently misunderstood.

Kohut repeats his earlier speculations (1966) concerning the developmental course of the grandiose self and the idealized parental imago. He emphasizes here that under the impact of severe trauma, neither of these two structures is integrated into the personality, resulting both in the perpetuation of the grandiose self's archaic demands and in the idealized parental imago's search for an idealized tension-regulating object. These narcissistic configurations, stunted as a result of trauma, are relatively stable and can be revived within a therapeutic relationship in the transference-like experiences specific for each one. Kohut calls the clinical revivals of the narcissistic configurations the 'narcissistic transferences.' He invents the term 'mirror transference' for the mobilization of the grandiose self and the term 'idealizing transference' for the activation of the idealized parental imago. He considered this paper a 'summarizing preview of a broader study' (1968, p. 508) which he presented in *Analysis of the Self* (1971).

ANALYSIS OF THE SELF: INTRODUCTION

Twenty-three years had elapsed between Kohut's initial interest in narcissistic vulnerability, expressed in his sensitivity to Aschenbach's fragmentation in Mann's *Death in Venice*, and the publication of his pivotal monograph, *Analysis of the Self* (1971). His journey in psychoanalysis began with the foundations of classical theory, evolved to a cluster of interests that included method of investigation in psychoanalysis, metapsychology and narcissism, and culminated in his development of a psychology of the self. Kohut developed his ideas during this twenty-three-year period in his papers, discussions and theory course. *Analysis of the Self* represents the harvest of this era; it is a treatise ripe with ideas challenging the prevailing value-laden analytic thinking about narcissism.

To Kohut, psychoanalytic theory was an evolving, rather than static, body of knowledge. As such, he presented his thinking in the spirit of extending Freud's ideas rather than displacing them. A past president of the American Psychoanalytic Association, he understood the rigidity of the psychoanalytic establishment and was careful to present his new ideas within the context and language of the prevailing classical psychoanalytic theories. To do this, he repeatedly compares and contrasts libidinal objects and their unconscious representations with his understanding of the newly formulated narcissistic objects and their unconscious representations. He does this so well that *Analysis of the Self* is an excellent aid for anyone interested in studying libidinal objects and drive–defense psychology.

Overview

Kohut adopts Hartmann's definition of narcissism, namely that narcissism is a 'cathexis of the self' (1971, p. xiii). Like Hartmann, he suggests that the self is separate from the ego and should not be conceived of as an agency of the mind like the ego, id or superego. Instead, the self is a structure within the mind, similar to an object representation, containing differing and even contradictory qualities.

It is important to Kohut to define the narcissistic disorders clearly and to differentiate them from the psychoses and borderline states so that his theories will not be misapplied. He emphasizes the differential diagnoses of these conditions, noting that in the analysis of people with narcissistic personality disturbances, there are, at times, regressive swings with symptoms resembling those found in psychoses or borderline personality disorders. Kohut outlines the psychological assets that set patients with narcissistic personality disturbances apart from psychotic and so-called borderline patients. These assets are the stable, though developmentally arrested, internal objects responsible for a cohesive, albeit shaky, self. The stability of these arrested internal objects makes possible their revival and expression in the form of specific, stable narcissistic transferences without the danger of serious fragmentation. Kohut asserts that the spontaneous establishment of one of the narcissistic transferences is a reliable diagnostic sign, differentiating a person with a narcissistic personality from one who is psychotic or in a borderline state.

In his differential diagnostic considerations, Kohut compares the narcissistic disturbances to the classical transference neuroses where objects are well differentiated and pathology does not reside in the relatively cohesive self. The pathology of the transference neuroses is experienced in terms of conflicts over incestuous strivings toward a childhood object. The ensuing anxiety is related to the threat of punishment or physical abandonment.

For the person with a narcissistic disorder, in contrast, anxiety is related to the self's awareness of its vulnerability and propensity to fragmentation. The central pathology resides in the developmental arrest of the narcissistic configurations which deprives the self of reliable, cohesive sources of narcissism and creates an inability to maintain and regulate self-esteem at normal levels.

The developmental line of narcissism

The introduction to *Analysis of the Self* presents Kohut's hypothesis about the development of narcissism and describes the unconscious narcissistic configurations of the grandiose self and the idealized parental imago. At this point, however, I believe it is useful to digress from Kohut's work and briefly discuss the concept of unconscious configurations.

An unconscious configuration is a cluster of needs, wishes, feelings, fantasies and memories within the Unconscious. The childhood oedipal story is one such configuration. The oedipal configuration represents a collection of wishes, feelings, fears, and fantasies that is contained in the Unconscious and motivates internal life and its expression in the external world. It is, of course, conceptually possible to have other configurations, and Kohut asserts that the grandiose self and the idealized parental imago are similarly configurations within the Unconscious. For Kohut, these configurations constitute the core of the narcissistic sector of the personality. They are central structures within the psyche. The terms 'structure' and 'configuration' are synonymous for Kohut, and he uses them interchangeably.

It is essential to grasp the qualities and nature of the narcissistic configurations since they are central to Kohut's understanding of psychic functioning. The configuration of the grandiose self arises from the fantasy of a perfect self. As I mentioned earlier, I believe that 'grandiose self' is an unfortunate name for this configuration because of its somewhat pejorative cast; 'expansive self' might have been a better term to describe the exhibitionistic narcissism of the grandiose self. Nevertheless, the grandiose fantasy is the ideational content of the grandiose self, containing elements of omnipotence and omniscience. As an example, we might think of the super-qualities of comic strip super-heroes. The exaggerated superpowers of these heroes convey the powers of the grandiose self. The popularity of these figures, for whom anything is possible, is rooted in the appeal, for children and even for adults, of the fantasies that constitute the grandiose self. There are no limits. Anything can be accomplished. These figures can leap tall buildings in a single bound, move mountains and read minds. Flying fantasies abound as well as fantasies of unlimited physical and intellectual prowess. An endless sense of expansiveness is part of the fantasy. The exhibitionistic wish to be seen, adored and admired for unlimited abilities and for nothing other than mere existence is a feeling quality of the grandiose self. We see the raw expression of this unconscious configuration in the two-year-old who acts out the daring, try anything, know everything, 'look at me' feeling of the grandiose self.

Just as the childhood oedipal story is a collection of unconscious wishes, fears and memories that affects feelings and behavior in the external world, so too is the grandiose self, with its story of unlimited abilities and its exhibitionistic wish. Conceptually, it resides within the Unconscious and influences the regulation of behavior, self-esteem and, eventually, ambition.

The other narcissistic configuration, the idealized parental imago, contains the fantasy of a perfect other with whom union is sought. Union with this omniscient being brings contentment, strength and wholeness. The story of the idealized parental imago is the story of a wish to merge with the perfect other who possesses wisdom, kindness, vast knowledge, unending strength and a capacity to sooth, settle and help maintain emotional balance. Union brings wholeness; separation in any form brings fracture. The idealized parental imago is a collection of unconscious wishes, fears and memories that affects the regulation of tensions and ultimately becomes part of one's cherished ideals.

Kohut refers to the grandiose self and the idealized parental imago as the 'archaic narcissistic configurations' since they arise from the early unconscious attempt to preserve the original perfection. Their central mechanisms may be stated as: 'I am perfect' = grandiose self; 'You are perfect, but I am part of you' = idealized parental imago.

Kohut asserts that these two configurations coexist, are present from the beginning and have separate lines of development. The archaic grandiose self eventually becomes tamed and integrated into the adult personality, supplying 'fuel for our ego-syntonic ambitions and purposes, for the enjoyment of our activities, and for important aspects of our self-esteem' (1971, p. 27). Figure 4.3 expands Kohut's developmental line for narcissism and shows the maturation of exhibitionistic narcissism, originating in the grandiose self and culminating in the formation of ambitions. The idealized parental imago also becomes a component of psychic organization, exerting influence through the internal leadership of its ideals (Kohut 1971, p. 28). The maturation of idealizing narcissism, originating in the idealized parental imago, culminating in the formation of ideals, is similarly shown in Figure 4.3.

Arrests in the development of narcissism

Kohut briefly describes the effect of trauma on the developing narcissistic configurations, which he expands later in the monograph. Concerning the grandiose self he writes, 'If the child, however, suffers severe narcissistic traumas, then the grandiose self does not merge into the relevant ego content but is retained in its unaltered form and strives for the fulfillment of its archaic aims' (1971, p. 28). Figure 4.4 shows how trauma deprives

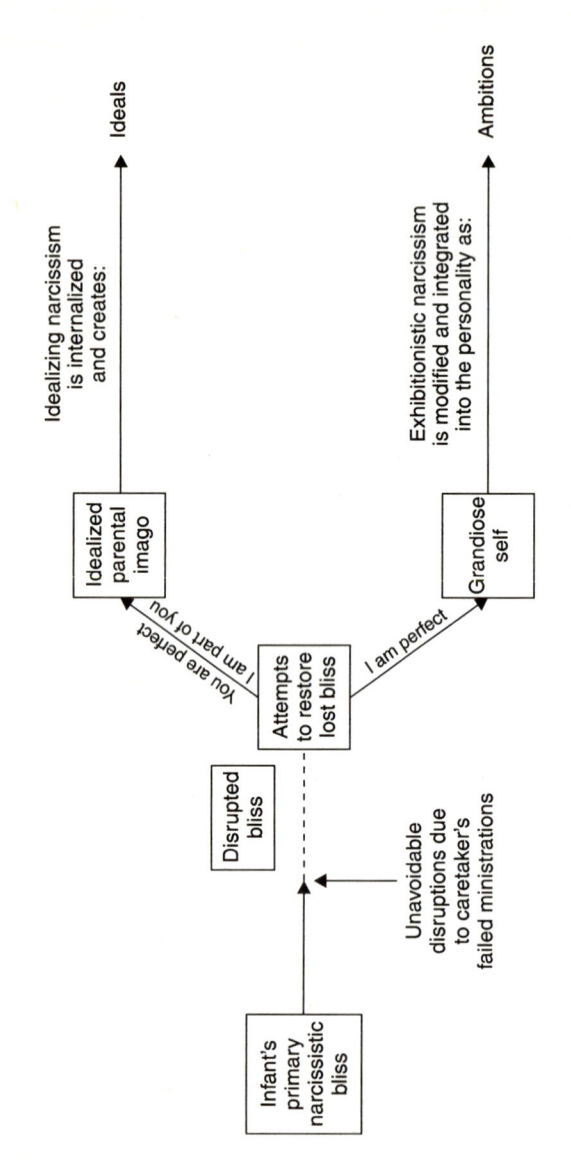

Figure 4.3 Developmental line of narcissism

the grandiose self of the opportunity to complete its development, while Figure 4.5 shows the traumatic situation in the development of the idealized parental imago, about which Kohut writes:

> And if the child experiences traumatic disappointments in the admired adult, then the idealized parent imago, too, is retained in its unaltered form, is not transformed into tension regulating psychic structure, does not attain the status of an accessible introject, but remains an archaic, transitional self-object that is required for the maintenance of narcissistic homeostasis.
>
> (Kohut 1971, p. 28)

```
┌──────────┐  Grandiose and exhibitionistic                    ┌──────────────┐
│Grandiose │  narcissism are not modified      ──────────────▶ │Ego deprived  │
│  self    │  via experience with object                       │of self-esteem│
└──────────┘                                                   └──────────────┘
              They are reinvested unaltered
                 in the grandiose self       Severe trauma
                                             in relation
                                             to object
```

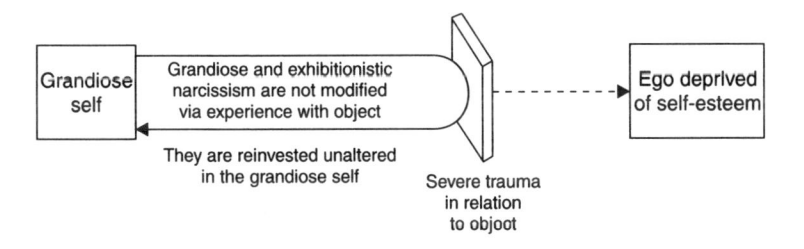

Figure 4.4 Trauma in the development of the grandiose self

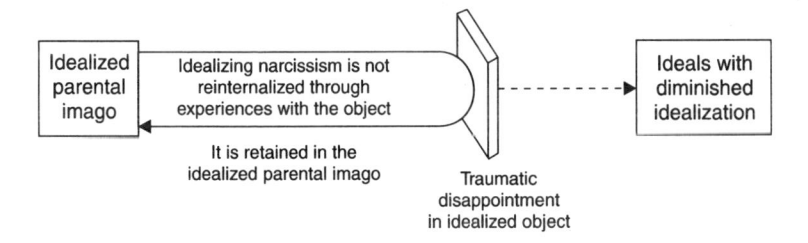

```
┌──────────┐  Idealizing narcissism is not                     ┌──────────────┐
│Idealized │  reinternalized through          ──────────────▶  │Ideals with   │
│parental  │  experiences with the object                      │diminished    │
│imago     │                                                   │idealization  │
└──────────┘                                                   └──────────────┘
              It is retained in the
              idealized parental imago       Traumatic
                                             disappointment
                                             in idealized object
```

Figure 4.5 Trauma in the development of the idealized parental imago

The above are sketchy overviews of arrests in the development of the narcissistic configurations. Kohut asserts that just as the oedipal configurations are expressed in specific transferences, so too are the narcissistic configurations expressed in specific transferences. *Analysis of the Self* (1971), which I will continue to discuss in Chapters 5 and 6, is Kohut's in-depth study of the developmental, transferential and technical issues related to the vicissitudes of narcissism.

Chapter 5

Analysis of the Self: Part I
The idealized parental imago

The next two chapters deal with Kohut's conceptualization of the idealized parental imago and the grandiose self, and the clinical transferences that form as these configurations come to life within the treatment setting. In addition, I will provide case material to demonstrate how one might apply these conceptualizations to the conduct of psychoanalytic psychotherapy.

Reconstruction of early mental states, gleaned from the analyses of adult patients, provides the data from which Kohut formulated the narcissistic configurations. He warned, however, of the difficulty in formulating such early experiences based upon the empathic immersion into the affective life of adults:

> The psychoanalytic formulation of early experience is difficult and fraught with danger. The reliability of our empathy, a major instrument of psychoanalytic observation, declines the more dissimilar the observed is to the observer, and the early stages of mental development are thus, in particular, a challenge to our ability to empathize with ourselves.
>
> (Kohut 1971, p. 38)

IDEALIZED PARENTAL IMAGO

With this caveat Kohut describes the idealizing component of the narcissistic configurations as the 'revival during psychoanalysis of one of the two aspects of an early phase of psychic development' (1971, p. 37). The second aspect is the grandiose self. The two configurations evolve simultaneously in early development and are the infant's attempts at restoring a disrupted state of blissful perfection. In the aspect related to the idealized parental imago, the psyche assigns perfection to 'an archaic, rudimentary (transitional) self-object' (Kohut 1971, p. 37).

All power resides in the idealized object with whom the child seeks constant union in an effort to feel whole and alive. The child eventually must reclaim the idealization, however, or it will forever require an attachment to an idealized figure to feel intact. Kohut theorizes that permanent psychic structures are built during the re-internalization of the idealizing narcissism, which occurs through several processes. In one process, the idealization is gradually modified through the child's experience with the reality of the parents' actual limitations. Kohut calls this process, first described in 1963, 'passage through the object.' In addition to diminishing the idealization, passage through the object allows the child to internalize specific qualities of the parents' emotional attitudes and responses.

'Transmuting internalization,' another structure-building process, is similar to the mourning process Freud described in 1917. According to Freud, psychic structure develops after a loss, when the libido invested in the lost object is withdrawn and internalized in the form of an unconscious memory. The lost object is retained in memory and qualities of the lost object become part of the personality.

For Kohut, psychic structure develops when idealizations are gradually withdrawn from the child's caretakers. These internalizations create new structures that assume the psychological functions previously performed by the idealized object, devoid of the personal qualities of the object. Fractionated withdrawal of idealization occurs when the child's disappointments are gradual and of manageable degree. Kohut calls this gradual disillusionment 'optimal frustration.' In situations of sudden massive disillusionment, the frustration is not optimal, the child is unable to fractionate the overwhelming loss, and transmuting internalization does not occur.

Types of object: self-objects, true objects and psychological structures

Kohut emphasizes that the key to understanding the narcissistic disorders inheres in the idea that the objects that perform psychological functions for the child are experienced in terms of the functions they perform and not in terms of their particular personal qualities. They are experienced by the child as part of the self. When they fulfill their functions they are taken for granted, as is a limb or any other body part. Only when an object fails in its functions does it draw notice. Kohut names the objects experienced as part of the self 'self-objects.' They exist as psychological functions and are not experienced as true distinct objects. In 1978 Kohut removed the hyphen from the term 'selfobject' to provide the idea that the function-providing object is not experienced as separate from the self. Kohut contemplated this change throughout the preceding year and celebrated its finalization on 29 October 1978 at the home of Ernest and Ira Wolf (Wolf 1996). The non-hyphenated 'selfobject' first appeared in a joint publication later that same year (Kohut and Wolf 1978).

In contrast to a self-object, a true object is psychologically separate and distinct from the self. It can be 'loved and hated by a psyche that has separated itself from the archaic objects, has acquired autonomous structures, has accepted the independent motivations and responses of others, and has grasped the notion of mutuality' (1971, p. 51).

Psychological structures, on the other hand, are internalizations of the soothing, tension-regulating and adaptive functions that have previously been performed by the self-objects. They develop as a result of the gradual withdrawal of the narcissism invested in the old idealized objects and they continue to perform their psychological functions even in the absence of the self-object.

Idealizing transference

Kohut notes that optimal internalization cannot occur when a child suffers the traumatic loss of an idealized parent (see Figure 4.5). The necessary psychological structures do not develop through gradual, bit-by-bit internalizations, and the child is left dependent upon transference relationships with self-objects to fill in for the missing psychic structure. The child, according to Kohut,

> does not acquire the needed internal structure and his/her psyche will be fixated upon an archaic self-object in what appears to be an intense form of object hunger. The intensity of the search for and of the dependency on these objects is due to the fact that they are striven for as a substitute for the missing segments of the psychic structure. They are not objects (in the psychological sense of the term) since they are not loved or admired for attributes, and the actual features of their personalities, and their actions, are only dimly recognized. They are not longed for but are needed in order to replace the functions of a segment of the mental apparatus which had not been established during childhood.
>
> (Kohut 1971, pp. 45–6)

Kohut divides the types of disturbances in the idealized parental imago into three groups, the nature of each disturbance being dependent upon the timing of trauma, as illustrated in Figure 5.1. The first group concerns trauma during the early pre-oedipal period which interferes with the development of the basic capacity of the psyche to maintain or re-establish narcissistic balance on its own. This early trauma is severe and usually the result of a caretaker's unempathic personality. The early lack of attunement to the child's emotional needs deprives the child of maternal functions such as stimulus barrier, tension regulation and optimal stimulation. Often, people who suffer this trauma become addicts who turn to the addictive substance to replace the tension-regulating and self-soothing functions of the missing internal structures.

The second group of disturbances consists of later pre-oedipal trauma, which interferes with what Kohut calls the drive-controlling and drive-neutralizing 'basic fabric of the ego.' Trauma during this period creates a tendency to sexualize narcissistic needs which, in the adult, is expressed in the form of sexualized behaviors. Kohut understands these sexualizations as attempts to soothe and settle a narcissistically disrupted self.

The third group of disturbances occurs as the result of trauma in the oedipal or even early latency period when the superego is not yet complete. The adult who experiences trauma during the late oedipal and early latency years will have a superego that contains values and standards, yet he 'will forever search for external idealizable objects from whom he needs to obtain the approval and leadership which his insufficiently idealized superego cannot provide' (Kohut 1971, p. 49).

Kohut asserts that the various idealizing transferences, which express the specific arrested needs of the idealized parental imago, are pathognomonic of narcissistic personality disturbances and become established during the course of an analysis with these people.

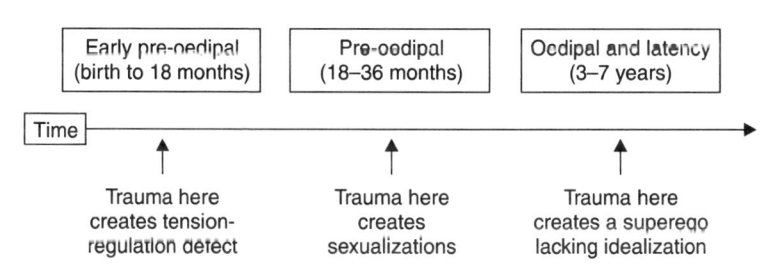

Figure 5.1 Consequences of trauma in the developmental sequence

Clinical illustration

To demonstrate the clinical issues surrounding the idealized parental imago and its corresponding transference, Kohut presents Mr. A, a man in his twenties who came for treatment complaining of a vague depression, homosexual fantasies, decreased zest and diminished creativity in his work. Mr. A's symptoms surfaced whenever he felt a lack of interest on the part of older men who were important to him. Evidence of their disapproval brought a depressed, deadened feeling, followed by an enraged, cold, haughty isolation and a decreased creativity. Mr. A's zest for life returned when, once again, he felt accepted by these men.

Mr. A's sensitivity to the approval of older men grew out of his experience with his father, a successful European businessman. As a latency-age boy, Mr. A idealized his father who had a thriving business which he lost during the German occupation. The family moved to a new country where the father resiliently re-established himself. Triumph turned to depression, however, when the Germans invaded the new country and his father lost his business again. His father's depression was a trauma for Mr. A, who previously had seen him as invulnerable, even in the face of the German army. Kohut explains Mr. A's later vulnerability as the result of a disruption in the process of transmuting internalization, precipitated by the massive de-idealization that occurred when Mr. A's father became depressed and ineffective. The disruption left Mr. A with an insufficiently idealized superego. Having internalized his father's values, his superego functioned in terms of its moral imperatives. Yet, because Mr. A had been deprived of the necessary gradual internalizations, his superego lacked its exalted status and was unable to raise Mr. A's self-esteem when he had, in fact, met its standards. Mr. A's self-esteem was sustained only when an external source, in the form of an older man, provided praise for him and his work.

Kohut describes three major components of Mr. A's narcissistic disturbance:

1 A diffuse vulnerability in managing tensions and in soothing himself when upset.

Although the overtly traumatic events in Mr. A's life occurred during latency, the seeds of the vulnerability were sown during his early pre-oedipal years when Mr. A's unattuned mother was unable to respond empathically to his needs. There was no single traumatic event early in

Mr. A's life. The trauma was the mother's personality. In this regard, Kohut maintains that a mother's appropriate empathy, in the earliest years, promotes the internalization of her soothing, tension-regulating qualities. With an empathic mother, the child builds regulating psychological structures through the multiple minute internalizations of the mother's calming, regulating functions. Structure-building internalizations do not occur when a mother is overempathic or unempathic, which leaves the child dependent on outside sources for soothing and tension regulation.

In situations like Mr. A's, where the mother is empathically out of tune, the child frequently turns, in a compensatory way, toward the father. Important structures can still be formed if the father is able to allow himself to be idealized and then de-idealized in gradual, psychically manageable amounts. When the de-idealization of the compensatory parent is massive, as was the case for Mr. A, then the second chance at structure-building is lost and the child is left with a broad vulnerability.

2 The sexualization of self-soothing and tension-regulating capacities.

When plunged into a depression following the loss of an idealized man's affirmation, Mr. A had fantasies of subduing and masturbating physically powerful men. Through analytic work, Kohut learned that these fantasies, which Mr. A did not enact, expressed his wish, in a sexualized form, to obtain the strength of an idealized man. They were restorative attempts to regain a lost vitality.

3 The mobilization of a reactive grandiose self in response to narcissistic injuries.

I will expand upon this point when discussing Kohut's view of the grandiose self and the mirror transferences. For now, the reactive grandiose self can best be understood as a defensive grandiosity that emerges in reaction to a hurt, best exemplified in the retort, 'You can't fire me, I quit!' Reactive grandiosity was responsible for Mr. A's haughty, cold, isolated demeanor after he had been hurt.

Clinical and therapeutic aspects of the idealizing transference

Kohut distinguishes the idealizing transference of narcissistic origin from other forms of idealization. In the idealization of the oedipal object, for example, the object is experienced as a separate entity, as differentiated from the self, and as having its own independent initiatives. A relationship with an oedipal object contains elements of mutuality. This differs from the idealization of the selfobject, where the object is not experienced as a separate entity and mutuality is not possible.

Another idealization, the idealization of the analyst's analytic function, is part of the positive transference. It is present in all psychotherapies and is responsible for making analytic work possible. Although the idealization of the analytic function is essential for analytic work to proceed, Kohut feels it is an auxiliary transference and is not central to the content of the analytic work. In contrast, the idealizing transference set in motion by the therapeutic reactivation of the idealized parental imago sits at the center of the deficient psychological structures and is the essence of the analytic work.

Kohut identifies several types of idealizing transference and notes that timing plays an important role in the form of a specific transference. People who experience early trauma tend to suffer a broad, diffuse vulnerability to narcissistic injury. They have difficulty restoring balance when their self-esteem is upset and look to the idealized analyst to provide the soothing and tension-regulating functions they lack. Kohut feels that these idealizing transferences reflect a defect in the ability of the child's early caretaker to protect the child from over- or understimulation, to help it settle down when upset and to provide the function of tension regulation.

The idealizing transferences that arise from later trauma are easier to recognize. As with Mr. A, they grow out of sudden massive de-idealization due to the loss, illness, etc. of the idealized object. In these situations, the yearning for attachment to an omnipotent object, an expression of the idealized parental imago, remains hidden and is either repressed beneath the horizontal split (repression barrier) or disavowed in a vertical split of the kind to be discussed in Chapter 6. The opportunity gradually to de-idealize the object is lost, transmuting internalization cannot occur and the superego is deprived of its idealizations. This creates an endless search for idealized objects with whom to unite.

Kohut addressed some of the technical considerations necessary to initiate and maintain an analytic process for people with narcissistic disturbances. He also presented what he considered, in 1971, to be the essence of the curative process. Thirteen years later he would expand his ideas about the curative process in *How Does Analysis Cure?* (1984).

In a similar way to analytic work with the classical transference neuroses, clinical work with the narcissistic disorders can be divided, according to Kohut, into the period when the transference is being established and the period of working through after its formation. The first period contains resistances to the mobilization of the idealizing transference, evidenced in dreams and other associations. Fears about the mobilization of the transferences are many, some being due to the cold, unreliable and unpredictable personalities of the early idealized objects and the fear of re-exposure to that traumatic experience. Another resistance-inducing fear is the anxiety of losing one's personality as the wish to merge with the idealized object emerges.

In a technical recommendation Kohut suggests:

> The analyst should acknowledge the presence of all these resistances and define them to the patient with friendly understanding, but in general he need do nothing further to provide reassurance. He can, on the whole, expect that the pathognomonic regression will establish itself spontaneously if he does not interfere by premature transference interpretations . . . or other deleterious moves. The description of the analyst's proper attitude as given by Freud for the analysis of the transference neuroses also applies in general to the analysis of narcissistic personality disturbances . . .
>
> At this time I wish to emphasize only that an unusually friendly behavior from the side of the analyst, at times justified by the need to create a therapeutic alliance, is no more advisable in the analysis of narcissistic personality disturbances than it is in the analysis of transference neuroses. In the latter case it is experienced as seductive and is likely to produce transference artifacts; in the case of the narcissistic personality disturbances it is in general reacted to by the sensitive patient as a patronizing attitude which hurts the analysand's pride, increases his isolation and suspiciousness (i.e. his propensity to retreat toward an archaic form of the grandiose self), and thus interferes with the spontaneous establishment of the patient's specific pathognomonic regression.
>
> (Kohut 1971, pp. 130f, and 88–9)

Kohut has frequently been attacked by his traditional critics, who warn against gratifying the unconscious wish, for establishing too friendly an attitude toward his patients. This criticism, which confuses the analyst's human responsiveness with the gratification of an unconscious libidinal wish, is based on a misunderstanding of Kohut's technical recommendations. As can be seen, Kohut's recommendations are basically the same for both the transference neuroses and the narcissistic disorders.

Kohut describes how, in narcissistic disorders, the process of working through begins only after the pathognomonic narcissistic transference has been established and a narcissistic equilibrium, based upon union with the idealized selfobject, has been achieved. When the bond with the idealized selfobject analyst is intact, the analysand feels whole, well, attractive and creative. Working through is set in motion when the bond is disrupted. In these disorders the disruption is due to a disturbing event between analyst and patient rather than to an unconscious response to an offending wish aimed at the analyst, as is the case for the transference neuroses.

When a disruption of the narcissistic bond occurs, the patient often becomes despondent, rageful, cold and aloof. The despondency associated with the disruption is similar to the despondency experienced in losing control of one's body because of illness or accident. Before the disruption the patient believes that they have the same total control over the selfobject analyst as they have over their own body. The ruptured bond brings home the realization that the selfobject analyst cannot be controlled. In the pathognomonic regression of the idealizing transference, the analyst is not experienced as a separate and independent person. Any experience of separateness, such as the analyst's decision to take a vacation, signs of coolness on the part of the analyst, lack of immediate understanding, schedule changes, weekend separations, tardiness or even schedule changes to benefit the patient, precipitate a reaction of despondency and rage.

If the therapist is able to understand the developmental nature of the transference, then it is possible to comprehend the patient's complaints about these disruptions, however minute they might seem to an outside observer. The archaic nature of the transference accounts for the patient's experience of the disruption. To treat the narcissistic disturbance effectively, the therapist needs to adjust his or her empathy to the level of the patient's narcissistic attachment.

Patients' reactions to disruptions occupy a central position in Kohut's treatment. His technical recommendation regarding the disruption is to scrutinize the precipitating external events as accurately as possible, looking for the psychological meanings of the specific interactions that have set the disturbance in motion. Kohut presents a vignette from the analysis of Mr. G, to demonstrate a patient's sensitivity to narcissistic injury and the level of empathy required to understand it. During one session, Kohut announced that he would be away for one week, and Mr. G responded angrily, in a cold, aloof manner. Attempting to understand Mr. G's response, Kohut focused on the coming separation, but his explorations and interpretations were of no avail. Eventually, Kohut stumbled upon what seemed to be a correct understanding of the rupture. On the basis of previous experiences, Kohut had anticipated an intense reaction, with frequent phone calls, when he told Mr. G of the impending separation. Kohut steeled himself against the anticipated reaction when he made his announcement. His voice conveyed an exasperated tone of 'here we go again,' and Mr. G responded to Kohut's tone, feeling that he had lost what he had previously experienced as Kohut's limitless empathy. When they discovered the precise nature of the rupture, Mr. G regained his equilibrium and re-established his attachment to his idealized selfobject.

While the clinical variations are innumerable, Kohut describes the 'few comparatively simple principles' (1971, p. 94) he believes are the essence of the curative process, in the narcissistic disorders:

> In contrast to the conditions which prevail in the analysis of transference neuroses, the major part of the working-through process in the analysis of narcissistic personality disturbances does not concern the overcoming of ego and superego resistances against the undoing of repressions. Although such resistances also occur here . . . the essential part of the working-through process concerns the ego's reaction to the loss of the narcissistically experienced object. . . . The essential working-through process, however, aims at the gradual withdrawal of the narcissistic libido from the narcissistically invested, archaic, object: it leads to the acquisition of new psychological structures and functions as the cathexes shift from the representation of the object, and its activities to the psychic apparatus and its functions.
>
> (Kohut 1971, pp. 94–6)

In 1971, Kohut considered the essence of the analytic cure for narcissistic disorders to be the specific components of the working-through process, which are: manageable disruptions in the bond with the analyst, followed by the withdrawal of narcissistic investments in the idealized selfobject, resulting in the buildup of psychic structure through the process of transmuting internalization.

The therapeutic response that facilitates the working-through process is the careful scrutiny of the interactions between analyst and patient whenever the bond with the idealized analyst is disrupted. When the exact nature of the rupture is correctly understood, as was the case for Mr. G, the idealizing transference will be re-established and the patient will usually respond with memories that shed light upon the dynamics of the current disruption. Working through will lead to the accretion of structure and an increased tolerance for the tension associated with the analyst's absence. With time, as the idealized selfobject is gradually relinquished, the idealization will not be withdrawn so quickly and the process that leads to transmuting internalization will be enhanced.

Kohut warns of countertransference responses to the idealizing transference. He writes: 'If the analyst has not come to terms with his own grandiose self, he may respond to the idealization with an intense stimulation of his unconscious grandiose fantasies' (1971, p. 267). This will evoke feelings of embarrassment, shame and self-consciousness in the therapist, who might then respond defensively to the patient's idealization. In an effort to ward off the disrupting idealization, the therapist might prematurely interpret the transference, deflect attention to idealized figures of the past, and/or interpret the idealization as a defense against hostility. These defensive responses on the part of the therapist have significant consequences since they fend off the idealization, abort the mobilization of the idealized parental imago and interfere with the unfolding analytic process in the treatment of narcissistic personality disorders.

A countertransference response that Kohut did not describe is the stimulation of the therapist's unmodified grandiosity by the patient's idealization. If the therapist's need for 'the gleam in the mother's eye' has not been accommodated sufficiently during development, the therapist might become pathologically attached to the self-enhancing nature of the idealization. This is a transference response of the therapists which, if not acknowledged, can present significant problems for the therapy.

Clinical demonstration

Exaggerated forms of pathology are useful demonstration tools. A good example is a patient of mine named John, a twenty-three-year-old white man who became enslaved in an idealizing transference to an exploitative man. My goal in presenting him is twofold. Through this case I hope to illuminate further the concept of an arrest in the configuration of the idealized parental imago as well as demonstrate how a self-psychologically informed psychodynamic psychotherapy helped return an injured self to its developmental track.

John sought help for a problem in an important relationship with an older man whom he met during his first year in college, three years before coming for treatment. Prior to this relationship he had been struggling with his adjustment to living at college, away from home. He met a young woman who helped make the transition easier but she abruptly left him. John became distraught and at this point he met Elliot, a charismatic, older man. John, dazed and bewildered after the loss of his girlfriend, felt whole again as he heard Elliot espouse his quasi-religious philosophy of openness and total sharing.

Elliot had been drifting and invited John to join him. John, having found a seeming anchor in Elliot, accepted the invitation and they roamed the country until they eventually established a profitable, but illegal, business in one locale. After a while, Elliot persuaded John to manage the business while Elliot moved to California. John was to send all the earnings to Elliot except for the small amount necessary for life's essentials. John's tie to Elliot was crucial and he devoted himself to the business and to maintaining Elliot's comfort. John, vulnerable to Elliot's ever-present threat of withdrawal for disobedience, was sustained by five to six daily phone calls to Elliot.

When John came for treatment his life was in disarray. Intent upon maintaining his tie to Elliot, his life consisted of his devotion to the business, the multiple life-sustaining phone calls and sleep. There was nothing else. John visited Elliot twice a year and it was during the last of these visits that the 'problems' arose that brought John for help. Exploring the 'problems' closely we found that Elliot's tyrannical demands made John feel irritable and testy. John's feelings, however, held no veracity for him and he had hoped treatment would help him comply with Elliot's demands so that he could maintain this essential relationship.

In my attempt to understand the psychological origins of John's bondage, I turned to the story of his family. John, the third in a sibship of five, initially had little to say about his family. Eventually we learned that his mother, like Mr. A's mother, was empty and unattuned to the emotional lives of her children. Unpredictable in her empathy, she lacked the ability to soothe them when they were upset. John's mother's personality and her lack of attunement left him with a diffuse vulnerability in the management of his internal life.

Children of such a mother turn, in a compensatory way, toward their father. If he is emotionally available, important psychological structures can still form. Needless to say, John's father, who worked as the foreman of a lumber mill, was immensely important in John's life. John was proud of his father and recalled his exhilarating visits to 'Father's mill.' The mill, however, closed when John was a pre-adolescent. His father lost his job and became seriously depressed. John noticed how easily his fragile father's feelings were hurt and John became protective of him. When his father became depressed, John lost the stabilizing idealized selfobject he required. Secretly, however, he yearned for the strong father who had previously made him feel proud and whole. Children lose their second chance at structure-building when the de-idealization of the compensatory parent is sudden and massive. In such a situation the child is left with a broad emotional vulnerability, and such was the case for John. The traumatic loss of his father during pre-adolescence left him with an unsatisfied need for a stabilizing idealized selfobject. John's vulnerability pushed him toward athletic coaches and other idealized men, whom he sought to please in an effort to establish a selfobject bond.

History seemed to repeat itself in John's life when he left home to attend college. He found a woman to help him make the transition and became distraught when she abandoned the psychological function she had performed for him. John, once again, turned to an idealized man to stabilize himself. This time, however, the consequences were disastrous. The intensity of John's need, coupled with the missing veracity of his feelings, resulted in his enslavement to Elliot, the idealized selfobject.

I approached John's treatment with a number of concerns, the first of which was a diagnostic question. The disarray of John's life suggested a chaotic internal world. My diagnostic question focused on whether John suffered from a covert psychosis, often termed borderline personality, or whether his internal structure was stable, but arrested. Stated in the language of metapsychology my question was: were the internal objects insufficiently structured or was the idealized parental imago stable, but frozen in an early developmental form? If the idealized narcissistic configuration was organized but stunted, then growth in the arrested sector could resume through the remobilization of the stable transferences in a therapeutic situation. If, on the other hand, the internal objects were insufficiently structured, then the transferences would not be stable and growth could not resume. In that event the goal of therapy would be to support defenses and prevent overstimulating experiences.

Unclear about the nature of John's internal world and uncertain about his capacities to manage affects, I did not want the treatment to stimulate an intense regression. I regulated the intensity of his experience by seeing him for psychotherapy on a once-weekly basis. Contrary to my concerns, and much to my surprise, the treatment proceeded for nine years in a regular, non-chaotic manner.

In the beginning, our work focused on the real dangers of John's life as well as on the 'problems' he experienced in his relationship with Elliot. In a non-judgmental way I allied myself with John's need to be safe. I did not assume a moralistic position that opposed the illegal nature of his work. In time John's disavowal of the dangers in his life diminished and he came to appreciate the realities of his precarious situation.

Without attacking Elliot we explored the 'problems' in their relationship. I affirmed John's experience that Elliot was a tyrannical person and commented that the 'tension' he felt was a natural reaction to a difficult and demanding person. I suggested that while the 'tension' was healthy and normal for that situation, John's inability to trust his feelings was a problem.

Slowly John realized how Elliot had exploited him. After approximately two years of non-interpretive, non-judgmental, reality-oriented work, John voiced a wish to free himself. He worried that Elliot might harm him in retaliation for leaving but Elliot simply vanished when John stopped calling. My concern about a tumultuous treatment experience proved incorrect. The treatment moved forward smoothly and without any significant disruptions. How do I explain this surprising course?

I believe that over time John established a silent idealizing transference with me which fulfilled his need for a stabilizing attachment and enabled him to let Elliot go. John's ability to form a stable transference answered my original diagnostic question. The structure necessary for the resumption of growth was present, but arrested. At this point, however, no structural change had occurred. John's need for an attachment to an idealized selfobject remained the same; only his choice of object had changed.

With the critical diagnostic question settled and given that I was now confident in John's capacity to tolerate affect, it felt safe actively to engage the idealized transference. Opportunity for this work arose when John thought about obtaining a regular job and about returning to college. I wondered to myself whether some part of these thoughts related to the transference. At an appropriate time I raised the issue of John's need to please in order to maintain his tie with an idealized selfobject. I posed the question of whether his thought of returning to work and school were part of a need to please me.

John acknowledged that that was the case. He assumed that if he took a regular job and returned to school, his efforts would make me like him as a person and make me feel good about myself as a therapist.

He had changed the form of the currency that he assumed he must pay for a selfobject's interest from money to therapeutic ambition. He had substituted what he perceived to be my needs for what he knew to be Elliot's.

Having acknowledged the existence of the idealizing transference we were able slowly and carefully to explore its nature and meaning. Opportunities for this exploration came whenever the transference tie was disrupted. This usually occurred around my vacations or on occasions when I had to cancel or reschedule an appointment. Disruptions also occurred whenever I was distracted by my own thoughts. John withdrew during these disruptions. He became sad, lethargic and quietly angry. In response, I first attempted to help him identify and articulate his glum and dejected mood. Once he was aware that he was in a disrupted state, I then attempted, through close scrutiny of our interactions, to discover what had precipitated the disruption. When we could articulate the disruption and locate its cause, the transference bond was restored. Through this work, repeated many times, John came to know that he required an attachment to an important person to feel whole and alive. Concomitantly, he realized that he felt dead when he lost the vitalizing tie. At first this realization frightened him. Eventually, though, he understood how the intensity of his need made him vulnerable and drove him to surrender important parts of himself. We worked extensively with the idealized sector of John's personality. Over time, through the processes of internalization which Kohut describes but which space does not allow me to elaborate, John slowly internalized psychological functions I had provided.

Eventually John applied to and was accepted by a local university. He worked diligently, graduated and found a rewarding job. His old interest in athletics returned. This was a pursuit that clearly belonged to John since he assumed I was the 'intellectual type,' not interested in physical activity. He had fantasies of fighting with me as his assertive, physical self emerged. He remembered his need to protect his fragile father from his assertiveness and appreciated the fact that his strength did not threaten me. As John became free to express his assertiveness in our work, he also became more assertive in the world. He graduated college and actively pursued and won a job with opportunities for significant growth.

Aware of his vulnerability in relationships, John had decided, early in our work, to avoid them until he was psychologically stronger. After many years, he felt less vulnerable and he began to date. He eventually met a woman and their relationship became serious. He felt ready for marriage but the woman became frightened and fled. This loss tested John's gains, for, as you will remember, his initial regression had been precipitated by a woman's rejection of him. John was terribly upset, worked through the loss and overcame the hurt without a serious regression.

John soon felt ready to leave treatment. I concurred with his thought that he was ready, but my accepting response upset him. It made him feel that I did not care about him and reminded him of how easily his father let him run off with Elliot. He had wished his father would have stopped him then, as he wished I would stop him now. Yet, John asserted, if I did try to stop him it would be for my needs, not his, as he wanted to live his life for himself now.

John worked through a successful termination and left without unusual difficulty. He has returned to see me at various times over the years. He is doing quite well and navigates life's waters with remarkable skill. The psychotherapy, conducted once a week over a period of nine years, effected a repair in the idealized sector of John's personality.

Chapter 6

Analysis of the Self: Part II
The grandiose self

Just as Kohut identifies the idealized parental imago, so he identifies the grandiose self as the second unconscious structure that is reactivated in the treatment of narcissistic personality disorders. Remember that in Kohut's schema, the grandiose self is the result of the child's second attempt to regain the lost blissful state by creating a sense of perfection within the self. In this effort, all imperfection is assigned to the world outside. These two configurations, the idealized parental imago and the grandiose self, are part of two equally weighted, simultaneously occurring, streams of maturing narcissism. The tendency to think of the omnipotence and exhibitionism of the grandiose self as the more primitive of the two bespeaks another value-laden prejudice. In a given person, however, there is often a weighting of one stream over the other, depending upon the nature and the timing of the traumatic events in early life.

Omnipotence, grandiosity and exhibitionistic narcissism are the features of the grandiose self. These features undergo transformation when the child's grandiosity is accepted and even enjoyed by the parents. When the demand for an echo to its feelings of expansiveness and unlimited power are responded to in a favorable way, the child eventually relinquishes its crude exhibitionistic demands and grandiose fantasies and accepts its real limitations. The noisy demands of the grandiose self become replaced with pleasure in realistic functioning and realistic self-esteem.

The personalities of the child's caretakers are essential in the formation of the child's psychological structures and make their imprint on the child's grandiosity through the process of 'passage through the object.' The grandiose self cannot be integrated into the fabric of the personality when its optimal development is interfered with, either through the unempathic personality of the child's caretaker or through trauma. In either situation, the grandiose self will persist in its archaic form, repressed or split off from the reality ego, uninfluenced by the world outside (see Figure 4.4).

To illustrate the 'just right' participation of a healthy parent in his child's normal grandiosity I tell of a game I witnessed between a father and his two-year-old son in which the boy attempted to stand upright on the palm of his father's outstretched hand. The little boy climbed onto the outstretched palm and, after a short struggle to find his balance, stood straight and tall. The father proudly proclaim, 'Champion of the World!!!' and the boy thrust his arms triumphantly above his head, beaming from ear to ear. Statue-like, they stood united until the boy, knowing just the right moment, turned and jumped into his father's arms as they embraced in a cuddle of delight.

The game is a lovely example of a father's participation in and literal support of his son's exhibitionistic narcissism. The father's comfortable acceptance of his son's grandiosity fosters the smooth integration of the boy's exhibitionism into the self. The father provides the psychological function of a mirror that validates, accepts and calmly reflects the boy's grandiosity. The father's participation in the game and his clear joy over his son's expansiveness help modulate the intensity of the grandiose exuberance. The father creates a safe playground in which the boy's narcissism can exist unencumbered by shame, guilt, embarrassment or overstimulation.

Another experience with this same pair poignantly demonstrates a different sort of mirror experience. Father and son visited me when I was doing military service. We toured an airbase and were permitted to enter a large hangar. As we walked through the massive building a jet turned onto the runway directly in front of us. The noise was deafening. The ground shook and the air distorted as waves of heat rose from the roaring engines. It was a frightening experience for us all. In a matter of seconds 'Champion of the World' had melted into a puddle of terrified tears and the same hand that supported his mighty exhibitionism now scooped him up and held him in a different sort of embrace. No cuddle of delight, this embrace recognized and accepted 'Champ's' terror and supported 'Champ's' vulnerability with the same strength that had earlier supported his expansiveness. It had the effect of validating the boy's terror without subjecting him to shame or humiliation.

TYPES OF MIRROR TRANSFERENCE

In the treatment setting, the grandiose self is reactivated and experienced in the form of a transference that Kohut calls a mirror transference. The addition of the idealized parental imago and the grandiose self to the concept of the unconscious configurations creates a total of three possible broad transference configurations as shown in Figure 6.1: the transference neuroses, the idealizing transferences and the mirror transferences.

```
                    Kohut    ┌─────────────────────────┐
                      ╱      │ Idealized parental imago│──▶ Idealizing transference
                     ╱       └─────────────────────────┘
                    ╱        ┌─────────────────────────┐
┌──────────┐       ╱         │ Grandiose self          │──▶ Mirror transferences
│ Primary  │──────            └─────────────────────────┘
│narcissism│
└──────────┘       ╲
                    ╲   Freud
                     ╲       ┌─────────────────────────┐
                      ╲      │ Object love             │──▶ Transference neurosis
                             └─────────────────────────┘
```

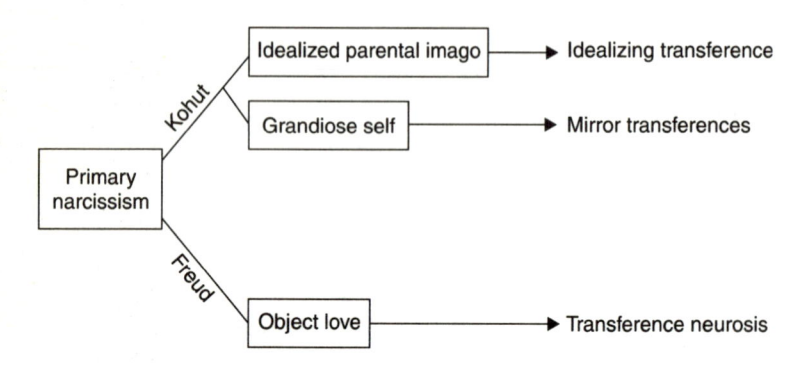

Figure 6.1 Types of transference

Developmental considerations

The mirror transference is an expression of the grandiose self. Kohut describes three types of mirror transference, each with a different form depending upon the timing of trauma during development.

1 *The merger through the extension of the grandiose self.* This form of mirror transference develops when trauma occurs early in a child's development. Clinically, the grandiose self extends to include the analyst, who exists only as the carrier and echo of the child's grandiosity and exhibitionism. In this experience, the patient expects unquestioned control and dominance over the therapist, just as the young child expects the same over its parent. The therapist, experienced as part of the self, often finds this transference oppressive and tends to rebel against its tyranny.
2 *The alter ego or twinship transference.* Developmentally more mature, the trauma occurs later in this form of the mirror transference and the grandiose self has some degree of separateness from the object. Clinically, the therapist is experienced as being similar to or like the grandiose self and the patient assumes that the therapist is very much like him or her. In *How Does Analysis Cure?*

(1984), Kohut amended his thinking and considered the *alter ego* transference to be another category of transference separate from the mirror transference.

3 *The mirror transference in the narrower sense.* This is the most mature form of the mirror transference. The offending trauma occurs late and the therapist is experienced as a separate person, but one who is important only within the framework of the needs of the reactivated grandiose self. Describing this form of the mirror transference, Kohut writes:

> [T]he therapeutic reinstatement of that normal phase of the development of the grandiose self in which the gleam in the mother's eye, which mirrors the child's exhibitionistic display . . . confirm[s] the child's self-esteem and, by a gradually increasing selectivity of these responses, begin[s] to channel it into realistic directions. As was the mother during that stage of development, so is now the analyst an object which is important only insofar as it is invited to participate in the child's narcissistic pleasure and thus to confirm it.
>
> (Kohut 1971, p. 116)

Kohut understands the import of the visual realm between mother and child. Being looked at by the mother and looking at her are critically important. The child needs the mother to watch and participate happily in its exhibitionism. Her participation in the child's body-self is essential to the child's knitting together a sense of body-wholeness, as Kohut describes:

> We may thus conclude that the mother's exultant response to the total child . . . supports, at the appropriate phase, the development from autoerotism to narcissism – from the stage of the fragmented self (the stage of self nuclei) to the stage of the cohesive self . . .
>
> Yet we know that children also enjoy games in which body parts are again isolated – counting toes, for example: 'This little piggy went to market, this little piggy stayed home . . .' Such games seem to rest on the setting up of slight fragmentation fears at a period when the cohesiveness of the self has not yet become totally entrenched. The tension, however, is kept in bounds (like the separation anxiety in the peek-a-boo game (Kleeman, 1967)), and when the last toe is reached, empathic mother and child undo the fragmentation by uniting in laughter and embrace.
>
> (Kohut 1971, pp. 118–19)

A healthy supply of exhibitionistic narcissism creates a feeling of wholeness and well-being, strengthens ego functions and increases the capacity for work. Kohut notes parenthetically, however, that excessive work is one of the many frantic activities used to counter the deadness of a self that has been deprived of the nourishment of its narcissistic exhibitionism. Excessive work is so commonly associated with fragmented states that people usually confuse cause and effect. They see overwork as the precipitant for a fragmentation when, in truth, the fragmentation has quietly been in progress for a while and the increase in work is the attempt to ward off the growing sense of deadness.

In the mirror transferences, the analyst becomes the figure around whom constancy, in the narcissistic realm, is established. The listening, echoing presence of the analyst reinforces the psychological forces that maintain the cohesiveness of the self. Disruptions in the mirror transference lead to fragmentation of the body–mind–self and focus on isolated body–mind functions and actions. These disruptions are therapeutic opportunities, similar to the insight-producing disruptions that occur with the idealizing transferences, and are part of the working through of the unconscious grandiose fantasies. Although Kohut has identified three forms of the mirror transference, the clinical effect is similar for all three and therefore he refers to them collectively as the mirror transference.

Genetic–dynamic considerations

Kohut describes another classification of the mirror transferences based upon genetic–dynamic considerations. Here too he identifies three types of mirror transference. The first he calls the 'primary mirror transference,' which is the transference that develops as the grandiose self is mobilized during the treatment. The second is the 'reactive mobilization of the grandiose self,' a regression in response to the disruption of an idealizing transference, demonstrated by Mr. A. Here the wholeness achieved through merger with a perfect other is shattered and a retreat to the lonely self as the only source of perfection and safety ensues. Righteous indignation, marked by an air of hostility, cold aloofness, arrogance, sarcasm and silence, surrounds this position. These regressive swings are neither avoidable, since the therapist's empathy, like the mother's, cannot be perfect, nor are they undesirable. They are therapeutic opportunities. Instead of exploring the *content* of the regressed state, Kohut pursues the *meaning* of the precipitating event:

The analytic work, however, does not focus on the regressive position itself which constitutes a retreat from a workable narcissistic transference; and the *isolated* interpretation of the content of the manifestations of the archaic grandiose self or of the patient's hypochondriacal worries and shame experiences would thus be fruitless and a technical error. Once the dynamic context of the current transference swing has been clarified, there is no need to avoid the empathic reconstruction of the childhood feelings which correspond to those which accompany the temporary regressive position in the analysis. Thus an analogy between the patient's present hypochondriacal concerns and the vague health worries of a lonely child who feels unprotected and threatened can be drawn, facilitating the patient's grasp of the deeper meaning of his present condition as well as of its genetic roots. The primary task of the analyst, however, at these junctures, is still the recognition of the total therapeutic movement, and his interpretations must focus primarily on the traumatic event that precipitated the retreat.

(Kohut 1971, p. 137)

The 'secondary mirror transference' is the third type of transference in the group based on genetic–dynamic considerations, and it appears after an idealizing transference has formed in treatment. The idealization is the first step backward in the recreation of the life story of the analysand. As the treatment unfolds, an earlier arrest in the development of the grandiose self, expressed through a mirror transference, emerges from under the idealization. The mirror transference that forms after an idealizing transference has formed differs from the reactive mobilization of the grandiose self. It is not a reaction to a disruption but rather a sequential recounting, in transferential form, of early traumas and attempts at restoration.

Clinical illustration

Kohut presents Mr. K to demonstrate the difference between the reactive mobilization of the grandiose self and the secondary mirror transference. Mr. K, a young man, experienced a brief idealization of his analyst, followed by a lengthy period during which a mirror transference was prominent. Through reconstructions, Kohut understands that the brief idealization repeated Mr. K's abortive childhood attempt to idealize his father after the birth of Mr. K's younger brother. The turn to his father became necessary when Mr. K's mother, who could attach to only one child at a time, abruptly withdrew from him to care for the new brother. Her attitude changed from unqualified adoration of his every move to a critical rejection of his need for her to enjoy his company. Mr. K attempted to stabilize himself by attaching to an idealized father, but this move failed because his father was uncomfortable with the idealization. Thwarted in this restitutive attempt, Mr. K again appealed to his mother through the exhibitionistic displays of athleticism that she had previously adored. This childhood story of idealization, followed by revival of the grandiose self, repeated itself in the analysis. This activation of the grandiose self differs from the *reactive* mobilization of the grandiose self induced by an empathic rupture.

THERAPEUTIC PROCESSES IN MIRROR TRANSFERENCES

As is his style, Kohut compares the therapeutic process in the working-through of the grandiose self to the working through process in the transference neuroses. In the transference neuroses, the goal of treatment is to increase the ego's dominance over the unconscious libidinal wishes. This is achieved by interpreting the wishes, and their associated defenses, as they emerge in the transference. Similarly, the crude exhibitionistic demands of the grandiose self remain outside of awareness either through a vertical split, as discussed below, or by the forces of repression. As a consequence, the healthy narcissistic energies that are attached to the grandiose self are unavailable for ego-syntonic activities and realistic successes. Deprived of this source of narcissism, the reality ego suffers a lowered sense of well-being and a diminished self-esteem.

To comprehend Kohut's technical approach, it is essential to understand the concept of the 'vertical split,' which is illustrated in Figure 6.2. The vertical split is a sector of the personality that is split off from the central sector. It is maintained by the defense of disavowal, which makes possible the simultaneous knowing and not knowing of something that is unacceptable. This defense enables a person to hold ideas and engage in acts, such as perversions, that are at variance with values held in the central sector of the personality. The vertical split is responsible for the vast contradictions in thought and action that can exist in one person.

The humiliation, shame and fear of overexcitement that are usually associated with the grandiose self reside in the split-off sector because they are so much at variance with the rest of the personality. Figure 6.3

demonstrates a vertical split in a narcissistic disorder that involves the grandiose self.

	VERTICAL SPLIT	
Split-off sector contains disavowed contents of the personality		REALITY EGO Experience of self
		REPRESSION BARRIER (horizontal split)
		Unconscious contents of the personality

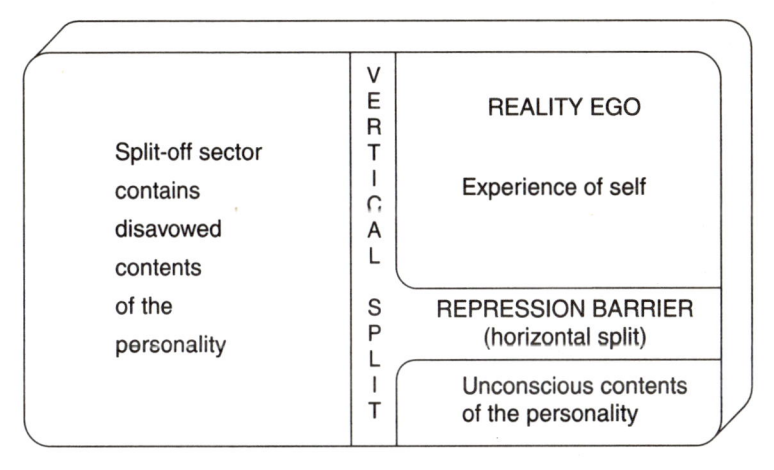

Figure 6.2 The vertical split

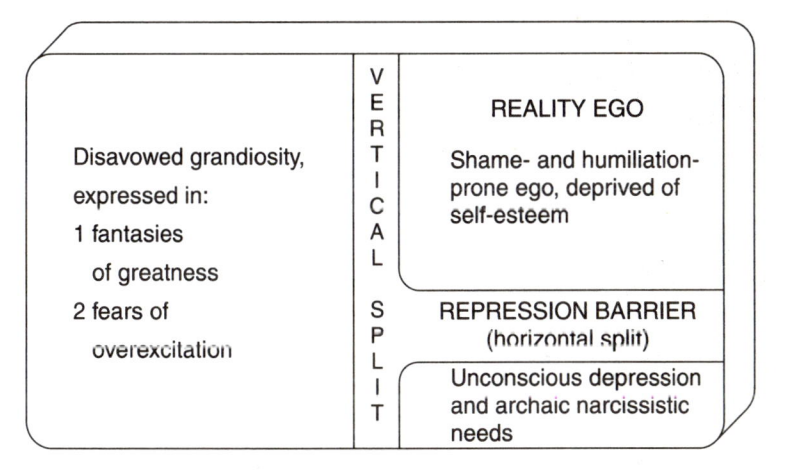

	VERTICAL SPLIT	
Disavowed grandiosity, expressed in: 1 fantasies of greatness 2 fears of overexcitation		REALITY EGO Shame- and humiliation-prone ego, deprived of self-esteem
		REPRESSION BARRIER (horizontal split)
		Unconscious depression and archaic narcissistic needs

Figure 6.3 Vertical split containing disavowed grandiosity

Treatment attempts to heal the split by gradually exposing the disavowed contents of the split-off sector so that they can be integrated into the rest of the personality. During the healing of the vertical split, people come in contact with parts of themselves that had previously been held in abeyance and often remark, with shock and surprise, 'Is this me?' or 'How'd this get into me?' Kohut presents patients C and D to illustrate the revelation of the grandiose self during the course of treatment:

> Patient C . . . had the following dream during a period when he was looking forward to being publicly honored and celebrated: 'The question was raised of finding a successor for me. I thought: How about God?' The dream was partly the result of the not altogether unsuccessful attempt to soften the grandiosity through humor: yet it aroused excitement and anxiety, and led, against renewed resistances, to the frightening recall of childhood fantasies in which he felt that he was God.
>
> In many instances, however, the grandiosity which forms the nucleus of the fantasies revealed by the analysand is only hinted at. Patient D, for example, recalled with intense shame and resistance that as a child he used to imagine that he was running the streetcars through a 'thought control' which emanated from his head, and that his head (apparently disconnected from the rest of his body) was way above the clouds while it exerted its magical influence.
>
> (Kohut 1971, p. 149)

The healing of the split and the revelation of its disavowed contents usually occur during the first part of a treatment. When the split is healed the ego is strengthened since energy is no longer needed to maintain the split. The strengthened ego is better able to engage the archaic elements of the grandiose self that are maintained below the repression barrier, which Kohut calls the 'horizontal split.'

The grandiosity which was hidden by the vertical split and/or walled off beneath the horizontal split becomes mobilized and the grandiose fantasies associated with the mirror transference are exposed. The aim of the treatment is the integration of the grandiose self, with its wish to be known as beautiful, wondrous, admirable and exalted, into the rest of the personality. The humiliating, crude, exhibitionistic narcissism that previously was disavowed modifies and is available to enhance self-esteem. When the grandiose fantasies cannot be clearly articulated they often appear as vague recurrent themes of being special, unique or precious. Figure 6.4 shows a healed vertical split with an integration of the grandiosity into the personality.

The central anxiety in the narcissistic disorders is not castration anxiety but a fear of the intrusion of the intense excitements associated with the narcissistic structures. People fear a loss of the self in the ecstasy of a merger with the idealized selfobject. They fear the permanent isolation that accompanies the experience of isolating grandiosity and they fear the frightening experiences of shame and self-consciousness associated with the intrusion of exhibitionistic wishes.

Kohut's technical recommendations in the treatment of disorders of the grandiose self are clear and merit direct quotation:

> [D]uring the working-through phase of the mirror transference . . . the analysand assigns to [the analyst] the performance of only one function: to reflect and echo his grandiosity and exhibitionism . . . .
>
> If the analyst, however, truly comprehends the phase appropriateness of the demands of the grandiose self and if he grasps the fact that for a long time it is erroneous to emphasize to the patient that his demands are unrealistic but that, on the contrary, he must demonstrate to the patient that they are appropriate within the context of the total early phase that is being revived in the transference and that they have to be expressed, then the patient will gradually reveal the urges and fantasies of the grandiose self and the slow process is thus initiated which leads – by almost imperceptible steps, and often without any specific explanations from the side of the analyst – to the integration of the grandiose self into the structure of the reality ego and to an adaptively useful transformation of its energies.
>
> (Kohut 1971, pp. 175–6)

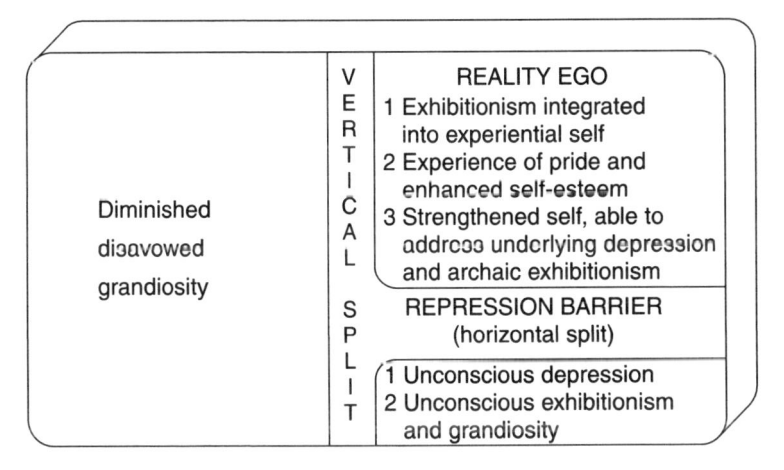

Diminished disavowed grandiosity	VERTICAL SPLIT	REALITY EGO 1 Exhibitionism integrated into experiential self 2 Experience of pride and enhanced self-esteem 3 Strengthened self, able to address underlying depression and archaic exhibitionism
		REPRESSION BARRIER (horizontal split)
		1 Unconscious depression 2 Unconscious exhibitionism and grandiosity

Figure 6.4 Healed vertical split integrating the disavowed grandiosity

THE THERAPIST'S REACTIONS TO THE MIRROR TRANSFERENCE

The therapist's reaction to the mirror transference depends upon the specific form of the transference. Kohut notes that in the mirror transference in the narrower sense, the therapist's existence as a separate object is acknowledged to a limited extent, though he or she is assigned the function of being an approving witness and an admiring echo of the patient's exhibitionism and greatness. In the twinship and merger transferences, which arise from developmentally earlier times, the therapist's existence as an independent being tends to be obliterated. This is a potentially painful experience for the therapist, whose own narcissistic needs are not met. The therapist's task is to accept the grandiosity, interpret the resistances to its revelation and demonstrate its once phase-appropriate nature. In this work, the therapist must deal with the boredom and inattentiveness that grow out of the experience of not being engaged as a separate object. The narcissistic demands of the grandiose self feel like an enslavement for the therapist. Kohut calls this countertransference to inattention and warns against the enactment of forms of impatience such as overt anger, exhortations and forced interpretations about resistances.

Clinical illustration

One of my patients provides an opportunity to study an arrest in the sector of the grandiose self as well as another opportunity to observe a self psychologically informed treatment. I wish to emphasize that although both narcissistic configurations and their respective transferences are always present, one might predominate, as is the case for Vince, a twenty-eight-year-old lawyer.

Vince was referred by his wife's therapist for the treatment of a sexual problem. It quickly became apparent, however, that concern over the problem belonged to his wife alone. Vince understood his sexual disinterest as his response to her frequent uncontrollable intimidating rages. He found her unappealing when she was caught in a tantrum and he withdrew to protect himself. He had no difficulty when she was not enraged and did not think of his disinterest as a sexual problem. Vince added wistfully that his wife was only the most vocal and violent of several frightening people in his world. He volunteered that he was intimidated by his father and by his bosses as well, although none of them had overt rages.

Vince voiced a more troubling complaint of his own. He believed that although he was a gifted person he suffered from a profound sense of ineptitude that made it impossible for him to assert himself comfortably in his career as a lawyer. He felt retarded and ineffective, rather than confident and proud of his talents. He yearned to experience the pleasure inherent in his exciting career rather than the constant dread of being fired for ineptness. Vince thought of himself as like a 'powerful sports car' but he was unable to 'turn on the engine.' He felt that he lived behind a transparent curtain, separated from the rest of the world.

Vince, the second of two children born to an Italian father and an American-born mother, described his relationship with his parents as disappointing. His father was the dominant parent, emotionally unavailable as he devoted himself to his successful academic career during Vince's latency and adolescent years. Vince longed for his famous father's active participation in his life. He poignantly recalled a teacher's suggestion that his father spend more time with him and his father's devastating reply that he would happily do so if only Vince could become involved in *his* interests.

Vince's father placed a high value on intelligence and critiqued the brightness of Vince's friends. Highest praise was reserved for the brightest friends. The others did not seem to matter. In a similar vein, Vince remembered the pain of nightly dinners when his father quizzed the family about world affairs. During these quizzes Vince's father ridiculed his mother, chiding her for stupidity, asserting that her opinions had no foundation. Vince's ability to think seemed to vanish when his father turned his questions toward him. Vince felt flustered, became non-verbal and floated off into a daze, which became a familiar and persistent state.

Vince's dazed state continued when he went to school, where he lived in constant terror of being questioned by his teachers. Despite his brightness he was unable to function well. His teachers repeatedly told him that although he had great potential he was a disappointment because he did not work hard enough. Vince came to believe that he was retarded, lazy and a disappointment. His father arranged for tutors, but remedial help only confirmed Vince's fear that he was stupid.

Within the family, Vince's mother was seen as empty and inept. Her concerns seemed to be about appearances and the decoration of her homes rather than about people. With a touch of black humor Vince recalled his mother's comment as she once cleaned her vacation home following a family visit. 'There,' she said, 'it's perfect. It looks like no one ever lived here.'

Vince believed that his older sister was the brighter, more valued child. Paired with their intelligence-loving father, she flaunted the prize of father's coveted attention. Vince, meanwhile, was condemned to the company of their devalued mother.

Vince and I met for sessions twice weekly in a psychoanalytic psychotherapy. We made little progress during the first year as he spoke endlessly about his dread of being fired. Terrified by his sense of ineptness, he was unable to acknowledge his deep sadness. He also rarely experienced happiness. On the rare occasion when he was happy, he feared the excitement connected to his joy. He said it made him feel crazy.

A self psychologically informed understanding of Vince's problems suggests that he suffered from a developmental arrest in two areas. One area relates to his broad difficulty in experiencing affects due to a failure of the early idealized selfobject to fulfill its function. The source of this difficulty lay in his early experience with his mother. Unable to tolerate her own internal experiences, she was unable to help Vince manage his affects and regulate their tensions. This created the diffuse narcissistic vulnerability in which his feelings were easily hurt.

The other area relates to an arrest in the grandiose self, evidenced by Vince's sense of ineptness and low self-esteem. In an effort to stabilize his weakened self, Vince turned to his idealized father, the valued parent. Vince yearned to strengthen himself by participating in his illustrious father's glory, but his father was emotionally unavailable for the merger and the internalizations Vince required. In addition, Vince yearned to experience his father's pride in him. He needed his father's affirmation to stabilize his self-esteem and eventually modulate his exhibitionistic narcissism. His father, however, failed again, this time as the compensatory selfobject, assigned the function of mirroring the grandiose self.

Vince's issues are multiple. I present him to draw attention to the traumatic effect a failed mirroring selfobject experience has upon the development of the grandiose self. For Vince, the deficient mirroring experience with his compensatory parent left his grandiosity unmodulated, replete with intense archaic demands for perfection and expansiveness. Unable to meet the demands of these unconscious grandiose fantasies, he carried an eternal sense of failure and ineptitude, not mitigated by the reality of his significant talents. In addition, as I learned later, Vince's sense of ineptitude served a protective function. His fear of incompetence kept him from engaging in challenging situations and protected him from the noisy demands of the grandiose self.

This self psychologically informed explanation differs from the classical psychoanalytic formulation that would understand Vince's sense of ineptitude as a defense against anxiety generated by his libidinal and aggressive wishes. In the classical understanding the anxiety flows from the fantasy that his father sought a castrating vengeance for Vince's wishes. In this formulation, Vince's persistent feeling of ineptness conveyed the message, to both Vince and his father, that he was not a danger. He was a bumbling, inept boy instead.

Because no psychological movement occurred over the course of the first year, I felt that a more intense treatment was indicated. I suggested a course of psychoanalysis, and Vince accepted my recommendation on a trial basis. In the analysis his hopelessness deepened. He voiced an unending sense of 'what's the use?' He experienced no enthusiasm about the sessions even though he came regularly. Every discovery was further proof of the depth of his illness. Nothing brought excitement. I responded to Vince's unyielding hopelessness with a feeling of my own ineffectiveness. I questioned whether my formulation was correct; might a classical oedipal conflict be at the heart of Vince's dread? I sought consultation which affirmed my impressions. Such affirmation was an experience sorely lacking in Vince's life. In our work, Vince's difficulty in comfortably experiencing his affects emerged as an early central issue. Neither the experience of sadness nor that of elation felt safe or tolerable. I attempted to explore this area, focusing on Vince's early experience with his mother. The attempt was fruitless, however, as Vince summarily dismissed her as ineffective. He did, however, recount his many disappointed attempts to win his father's pride, and sadness soon emerged.

Vince feared his sadness would overwhelm him. Similarly, when he finally received a good review at work he feared his elation would make him crazy. Lacking a reliable capacity to feel comfortable in the face of his affects, Vince kept himself safe by avoiding emotionally stimulating situations. He avoided intense feelings in the world and he feared their emergence in the analysis. In association, he remembered his father berating him for getting 'too excited' when he and his sister became giggly in their childhood play.

In this early work, I focused on Vince's *fear* of affect rather than upon the source of the affect. He came to experience me as an attuned tension-regulator and gradually developed a sense of affective safety. His ability to voice a troublesome grandiose fantasy grew out of this work. Humiliated by the shame associated with his unmodified grandiosity, Vince revealed the hidden fantasy of how he was to behave at his firm, where the brilliance of his insights was to be dazzling. The breadth of his knowledge was awesome and his ability to integrate disparate themes was stunning. Vince cried with relief as he understood the discrepancy between the demands of the grandiose fantasy and the limits of reality.

Vince reported no dreams during our early work. He focused instead on the repeating nightmare at his firm, where he believed his retardation was constantly exposed. The analysis became another arena where he felt the demands of the archaic exhibitionistic fantasy. He believed he was to talk non-stop, with endless insight. Vince feared I would be bored, irritated and think him a jerk if he were silent. In addition to becoming a playground for the incessant noisy demands of the grandiose self, our sessions replicated the traumatic inquisitional dinners of Vince's boyhood as well as the pain of his classroom experiences. Participation in treatment reminded Vince of his boyhood need for remedial help. Need for treatment was further proof that he was retarded. Rather than being an affirming experience, treatment brought despair by affirming Vince's desultory view of himself. As he said, 'I feel shame when we find that boy inside of me. I haven't been able to grow up and that embarrasses me. It's that simple.' Despite his despair, Vince moved deeper into the analytic experience. His affects became increasingly available and tolerable, though still frightening. The tensions associated with the disavowed grandiosity came steadily into view as he described them metaphorically. A skier of many years, he only skied the smaller, less challenging slopes:

> I ski the blue [easier] runs. I've been skiing a long time. I can do the expert runs but I fear the challenge and I fear falling. Falling is a defeat, so I ski under my ability so that I won't fall. I recently took a lesson though and my instructor pushed me. We went on the blacks [difficult] and actually I felt better, but I don't push myself.

Suffering as he was from the tyrannical demands of the disavowed grandiosity, any imperfection was a humiliating defeat. Vince protected himself against humiliation with a debilitating caution that kept him off the steeper, more challenging slopes of his life as well.

In the analysis, both an early idealizing transference and a mirror transference 'in the narrower sense' formed, but the latter predominated. My non-judgmental acceptance of Vince's unmodified grandiosity enabled him to accept and explore this disavowed sector. My belief in his realistic abilities, implied by my consistently hopeful attitude, affirmed his healthy expansiveness. It had the effect of supporting his wish to attack the 'steeper slopes.'

Vince acknowledged that he had 'played it safe' his entire life but recently he felt he was 'on a mission' to embrace the strength he secretly possessed. These hopeful thoughts expressed the strengthening effect of the mirror transference which Vince expressed in the metaphor of his ski instructor encouraging him onto the steeper slopes. He reported something similar in the following dream:

> My family made a decision that I was to die tomorrow, so we held a funeral party at my parents' home that night. I participated in the decision and in the funeral party because it seemed like the right thing to do. As the evening progressed I began to disagree with the decision. Eventually I decided I that I am young, healthy and not ready to die. I didn't like my family's plan for my death. I didn't want to go through with it and began to complain. I told my mother that I had changed my mind. I said it was a humiliating plan and I didn't want to go through with it. I began to change my mind after I had talked with a British man who was at the party. He was the catalyst for my change.

In his associations to the dream, Vince thought of the many ways he had blindly followed the path his family laid out for him. He then thought about the British man in the dream, who he believed represented me. The man was young, philosophical and seemed to understand him, especially when he agreed that the decision to die was wrong. Vince wondered, though, why death would appear in his dream since death frightened him so.

I replied that death in the dream symbolized the deadly experience of his family's long-standing absent affirmation. Their lack of belief in him felt like a death. Death was also Vince's experience when he lived the life of 'little Vinny,' the boy who didn't matter. I added that the dream suggested that Vince was coming alive and was no longer willing to tolerate life in a deadened state.

Although my understanding of the dream seemed on target, Vince's associative response surprised me. He felt that the analysis was helping him to change, but berated himself for having been childish and unassertive all these years. I gradually understood that this despair, initially puzzling, served a protective function. Like his experience in the world, his accomplishments in our work brought feelings of defeat. Although painful, hopelessness was familiar to him and as such it was more tolerable than the tensions associated with the joy of an accomplishment. For Vince, hopelessness was a way to regulate his affective tensions. It was a modulator of intense feelings.

Vince's response to the hopeful dream suggested that, once again, it was difficult to keep himself on an even emotional keel. I suggested that berating himself for what he had not been able to do in the past was his way of managing his excitement in the present. In an attempt to dampen the tension-filled joy associated with his new-found assertiveness, he was looking at the painful and disappointing years gone by instead of at the hopeful present. I suggested that for Vince, hopelessness functioned as an emotional brake. It was similar in function to his fear of skiing challenging runs. On the steeper slopes one skies exuberantly, on the edge of control. I suggested that Vince slowed himself down, on the slopes and in his life, to prevent the excitement that made him feel crazy.

My affirmation of Vince's wish to be alive, assertive and vital, coupled with the gradual exposure and modification of the hidden grandiosity, slowly enhanced his expansiveness and self-esteem. Evidence of his growing strength emerged when he complained openly and bitterly after I had changed one of our regular session times. Such open expression was unusual for him. He said that my action made him feel inconsequential. It reminded him of how he felt like a non-being, whose existence was denied, when his family took him for granted. Shortly after this episode, Vince bought a new car. He described both his joy and his fright as he openly expressed himself in the selection of his new highly charged purchase:

> I feel in control of the road. The engine has the roar of a sports car. I love that sound. I like the power. It has a great stereo system. I turned up the radio – very powerful. I got into it – but not completely. A fear was there. It got in the way. It felt dark and scary. I felt a tinge of apprehension venturing out onto the road on my own, not knowing where I was going. At first I was going to take the expressway since it was more familiar and felt safer but then I decided to take the other route. It was more interesting even if it was unknown.

Vince soon voiced a wish to leave his firm and establish a firm of his own, a move he had yearned for but had not been able to effect. Concomitantly, he reported that he had stood his ground during one of his wife's tantrums and, in fact, had helped her calm down and regain control. He became assertive with me in another way. He declared one day that he felt like being quiet during the session. After lying quietly Vince said that it was an accomplishment to feel safe in saying nothing. It was one of the rare moments in his life that he felt relaxed, and he jokingly thanked me for the rest when he left.

Feeling stronger, Vince said that he wanted to take control of his treatment. He no longer felt the need for 'remedial help' and asserted that he wanted to return to our twice-weekly sessions. Carefully, I posed the question of whether this wish represented a retreat from the expansiveness he had been experiencing. I did not want to diminish the possible healthy expansiveness expressed in Vince's 'takeover,' but I was concerned about whether this request was an attempt to slow himself down in order to feel safe. We explored the question and this did seem to be a healthy assertion rather than a regression. We decided to make the change on a trial basis.

Evidence that Vince was not retreating came quickly, as he acted upon his wish to form a firm of his own. The transition was smooth and successful, and occurred without the internal disruption he had feared. My efforts at helping Vince regulate his tensions, coupled with the work in the sector of his disavowed grandiosity, helped him move to a normal developmental track.

Vince became more comfortable with his narcissistic tensions, which simultaneously had lessened. His enhanced ability to experience his affects, along with our work in the grandiose sector, enabled him to modulate the grandiose fantasy and safely embrace his expansiveness and healthy exhibitionism. The psychotherapeutic work enhanced Vince's self-esteem and removed his deadly sense of ineptness.

Chapter 7

The Restoration of the Self: Part I
Innovations in theory

THE SELF AS THE CENTRAL PSYCHOLOGICAL CONFIGURATION

Historical note

Kohut's 1971 publication of *Analysis of the Self* opened a window of fresh debate in the psychoanalytic atmosphere. His new ideas met with great enthusiasm in some quarters and elicited a vehement response in others. His suggestion that narcissism has a separate line of development carried new clinical implications while simultaneously challenging the centrality of the oedipal complex.

Kohut realized he was treading on sacred ground and asserted repeatedly that his ideas were part of the evolving body of psychoanalytic knowledge. He insisted he was adding to Freud's theories, not replacing them. Although he had anticipated opposition and debate in response to his new ideas, he was not prepared for the ferocious intellectual and personal response he encountered. He was stunned when some of his friends and colleagues within the psychoanalytic establishment shunned and snubbed him for what he had written.

In addition to the mixture of intense and differing responses to his monograph, Kohut received devastating medical news in the fall of 1971, the same year *Analysis of the Self* was published. He learned that he had developed leukemia. Ironically, at the age of fifty-seven, upon publication of his groundbreaking contribution, Kohut was confronted with the very transience he had described earlier (1966). Devastated, he kept his illness secret even from his closest friends and colleagues. No one outside his family knew the true diagnosis. In a move that was mysterious to the unknowing world, Kohut reduced his teaching and clinical activities in order to use the unknown amount of time he had left to write.

I believe that Kohut, faced with an early death, gained courage and was moved to distinguish clearly between his ideas and the prevailing theory more quickly than he might otherwise have done. Kohut made his break with what he calls the classical 'mental apparatus' psychology in *The Restoration of the Self* (1977) where he contended that while he had not abandoned classical theory he nevertheless had come, in his words,

> to recognize the limits of the applicability of some of the basic analytic formulations. And with regard to the classical psychoanalytic conceptualization of the nature of man too – however powerful and beautiful it might be – I have become convinced that it does not do justice to a broad band in the spectrum of human psychopathology and to a great number of other psychological phenomena we encounter outside the clinical situation. . . . And I know that the suggestion that it is inadequate, or even that in certain respects it leads to an erroneous outlook on man, is bound to arouse opposition.
> (Kohut 1977, p. xviii)

Experience-near theory versus classical theory

The Restoration of the Self (1977) is Kohut's argument for a new psychology that derives from data obtained through the empathic–introspective mode of observation alone. The structure of Kohut's argument is interesting in that it begins with a discussion of the termination of an analysis. The issue of termination calls the conceptualization of mental health into question, for in evaluating the readiness for termination one measures the gains of an analysis against one's understanding of health and illness. One takes this measure to determine whether the analytic tasks necessary for mental health have been accomplished.

From 1959 on, Kohut emphasized that psychoanalysis is the science that studies humankind's inner world via the instruments of introspection and empathy, the psychologist's data-gathering tools. These psychological tools define the psychologist's field of study just as the microscope defines the histologist's field. Kohut calls theory developed via empathy and introspection 'experience-near' theory since it derives from the study of patients' actual felt experiences. He differentiates 'experience-near' theory from what he calls 'experience-distant' theory, which is theory that derives from abstract speculations rather than from observations in the clinical field.

Kohut argues that experience-distant theory is subject to the intrusion of many biases and criticizes Freud for unknowingly building a theory that allowed biological principles and Western morality to intrude. Although no theory is completely bias-free, Kohut challenges the intrusion of cultural bias and speculations from other sciences into the theory of psychology. Freud's need to legitimize his new science, Kohut suggests, led to Freud's attempt to unite psychoanalysis with Darwin's established and well-respected biology. Instinct-based drive psychology was Freud's attempt to unite biology and psychology. In this effort, Freud suggested that the instincts that preserve the species and the individual are expressed in the biologically based sexual and aggressive drives. For Freud, the drives are the primary motivators in human experience, hence the core of Freud's theory derives from biological speculation rather than from observations in the field that is defined by empathy and introspection.

Western morality introduces another bias into the tenets of classical theory. Western morality has influenced the goals of classical psychoanalysis by defining mental health as the harnessing and channeling of the primitive drive energies into productive outlets. The therapeutic aim seeks to tame the drives that threaten civilization.

The regard for altruism and selflessness, another set of Western values, is expressed in the classical psychoanalytic position that conceives of normal development as a progression from the narcissistic position to the eventual love of another. According to this perspective, health requires the relinquishment of self-interest and a move toward selflessness. Narcissism, while discussed dispassionately by analysts and therapists in scientific discourse, often carries the covert onus of being obnoxious.

Independence and self-sufficiency constitute yet another set of Western values embedded in classical theory. The Western valuing of independence informs the theoretical position that emphasizes separation from its objects as the child's ultimate developmental task. The Western valuing of self-sufficiency finds its way into clinical theory when 'separation, autonomy and independence' are the goals of successful treatment. Kohut contends that the classical psychoanalytic view integrates all these biases in the form of the oedipal configuration, which it regards as the central motivating force in human life.

New view of health; new criteria for termination

Kohut's view of the human condition, on the other hand, is quite different. He understands narcissism as a normal part of life, present from birth to death, not to be relinquished in favor of object love. For Kohut, narcissism has a natural course of development that eventuates in a whole and functioning self. Kohut proposes the configuration of a self that evolves from the narcissistic structures he describes in *Analysis of the Self*. He asserts that narcissistic disorders are the result of defects in the narcissistic structures of the self rather than the result of a conflict between intact structures of a mental apparatus. For Kohut, then, the correct assessment of a completed analysis requires an evaluation of the narcissistic structures and an assessment of their rehabilitation when they have been defective.

In evaluating the defective narcissistic structures, Kohut considers both the primary defect established during childhood and what he terms 'secondary structures,' which, in turn, are of two types. The first type he calls 'defensive structures,' the second he calls 'compensatory structures.' Defensive structures cover over and hide the primary defect in the self whereas compensatory structures effectively compensate for, rather than simply cover over, the defect. Kohut maintains that a termination phase is reached when either the primary defect in the self has been exposed and structuralized via working through and transmuting internalization, or when the compensatory structures become stable and functionally reliable.

Kohut does not insist upon the complete structuralization of a defect. This is a departure from the classical attitude that emphasizes the completeness of an analytic task. It is a position that invites that most severe of all psychoanalytic criticisms, namely the charge that the analytic work being done is not analytic. The classical position considers an analysis complete only when an issue, such as the oedipal conflict, is 'fully resolved.' Kohut, however, suggests that an analysis can be considered successful even if a defect continues to exist, provided that the defect is adequately compensated for by skills and talents that have become more reliably strengthened. Kohut is concerned with the functional reliability of newly rehabilitated structures. His emphasis on the *functional* intactness of the self introduces a new approach to the consideration of an analysand's readiness for termination.

Clinical illustration

Kohut presented the case of Mr. M, to illustrate the role of compensatory structures in an analysis and to make his point about the readiness for termination despite the continuation of a defect in the self. Mr. M, a young writer, came for treatment complaining of a writer's block, low self-esteem and a feeling of empty lifelessness. He also reported sexual fantasies, which he sometimes enacted, in which he exerted sadistic control over women by binding them.

Kohut considered the writer's block to be a critical symptom since writing was an important potential source of self-esteem for Mr. M. Kohut's understanding of the block was complicated and considered several components of Mr. M's personality, one central component being his inability to contain the excitement he felt as his imagination was stimulated in the process of writing. Unable to manage his excitement, Mr. M either suppressed his imagination or stopped his work altogether in an effort to protect himself from overstimulation. Kohut believed that this unmanageable excitement was associated with Mr. M's exhibitionistic narcissism. Through the recovery of memories during the analysis, Kohut learned that Mr. M had experienced his mother's early responses, in the grandiose–exhibitionistic sector of his personality, as faulty. Kohut surmised that Mr. M's mother's inability to function as an appropriate mirror and container for her son's healthy childhood exhibitionism was responsible for a primary structural defect. In this defect, the psychological structures were unable to manage the stimulation and excitement associated with Mr. M's exhibitionism. Had his mother been able to respond appropriately to his childhood exhibitionism, Mr. M gradually would have developed structures capable of managing his excitement. Instead, he was fixated upon brittle 'either–or' defenses to help him manage. Either he suppressed his exhibitionism and inhibited his writing, which deprived him of the healthy self-esteem his writing offered, or the exhibitionism broke through in the enactment of sexualized fantasies where an admiring, mirroring woman was his slave, under his complete control, complying with his every wish.

A second component of Mr. M's writing block was a defect in what Kohut calls a compensatory structure. Remember that Kohut defines a compensatory structure as a talent, skill or even a relationship that is reliable and may function, as in this case, as a source of healthy self-esteem. It is not a defense. For Mr. M, writing was an unreliable compensatory structure. It had not failed him completely, since he still functioned as a writer, yet because of his defect his craft did not provide him with a stable, sustainable source of enhancing narcissism. For Kohut, the development of stable compensatory structures constitutes an important aspect of the analytic cure and is a measure of progress in an analysis. The establishment of reliable structures that compensate for a primary defect in self-esteem is an appropriate aim and outcome of an analysis. This is especially so when the in-depth pursuit of the primary defect threatens the wholeness and safety of the self. Kohut believes that some primary defects in people with self disturbances are best left alone and cautions against being an analytic bull in the internal china shop.

The story of Mr. M's writing is quite interesting, for it evolved partly from his innate talent, partly from his relationship with his language-loving, wordsmith father. Throughout his adolescence, Mr. M emulated his idealized father and expressed his exhibitionism through the written word. Tragically, however, Mr. M's father was uncomfortable with his son's idealization. He withdrew from the boy, leaving Mr. M disappointed in his second attempt at finding a selfobject who could help him experience his exhibitionism with safety. Kohut postulates that in a healthy childhood Mr. M would have experienced a successful merger with an idealized father. The inevitable minute disappointments would have occurred and buffering psychological structures would have accrued through transmuting internalizations. Mr. M's self-esteem would have been enhanced through the merger, and internal structures might have developed to offset the damage of his mother's earlier insufficient mirroring.

Mr. M's difficulty containing the excitement associated with his fantasies prevented him from putting his thoughts into words. This difficulty created the writer's block which, in turn, weakened a potentially important compensatory structure. The analytic work proceeded in the grandiose sector of Mr. M's personality and some structuralization of the primary narcissistic defect occurred. At termination, however, Kohut felt that the work in the sector of the grandiose self was incomplete. He believed that the analytic work most responsible for Mr. M's vastly improved psychological state had occurred in the area of the rehabilitated compensatory structure, and took two routes. One route was via the working through of the insufficient mirroring responses of the mother, which helped integrate Mr. M's exhibitionism with the rest of his personality. The other route was via the working through of his father's withdrawal when Mr. M attempted to merge with his idealized father, especially in the realm of words. Kohut summarizes the core issues in Mr. M's analysis and states general principles concerning the effect of rehabilitated compensatory structures in the following way:

The fact, it may be added, that in Mr. M's case the decisive improvement took place in the compensatory structures, and not in the area of the grandiose–exhibitionistic self, establishes a principle that the valid termination of an analysis may be reached in this way. . .

Translating this summary into a general statement, we can say, then, that the psychoanalytic treatment of a case of narcissistic personality disorder has progressed to the point of its intrinsically determined termination (has brought about the cure of the disorder) when it has been able to establish one sector within the realm of the self through which an uninterrupted flow of the narcissistic strivings can proceed toward creative expression.

(Kohut 1977, pp. 53–4)

The incomplete nature of Mr. M's analysis provides Kohut with an opportunity to discuss his view of emotional health, which is not a matter of resolving a conflict between two agencies of the mental apparatus. Health, an appropriate goal for an analysis, is the establishment of a functional self in which there is an unbroken continuum of ambitions, talents and ideals. For Kohut, the healthy self is a self in which the ambitious push of exhibitionistic tensions is experienced in comfort and is guided by reliable ideals that make the realization of skills and talents possible. This unbroken continuum within the self gives life a joyful and creative sense. This functional view makes it entirely possible for one sector, such as the sector of compensatory structures, to make up for defects that cannot be corrected in another sector because of the depth or severity of developmental trauma.

DOES PSYCHOANALYSIS BENEFIT FROM THE CONCEPT OF THE SELF?

Kohut poses the rhetorical question, 'Does psychoanalysis need a psychology of the self?' In his affirmative answer he demonstrates the explanatory power of self psychology and accentuates the differences between classical theory and his new psychology of the self.

He first considers some of the forces that influenced the original psychoanalytic theoretician. Although a physician, Freud was not a healer. His primary interest was not the establishment of health. Freud valued knowing the truth and courageously facing reality. This translated into a treatment process that emphasized cognition and expansion of knowledge. Making the unconscious conscious was a major goal of Freud's treatment. Another goal was the increase of the reality ego over the forces of the unconscious drives.

Kohut notes that Freud was a proponent of 'scientific objectivity,' a stance that conceives of the observer as entirely separate from the observed. This view, however, fails to consider the impact the observer has upon the observed. The notion that a distinct separation exists between observer and observed is a mistaken idea that has profoundly affected theory formation in psychoanalysis. Freud's belief in 'scientific objectivity' limited his work since it prevented him from considering the impact of the analyst's presence and actions upon the analysand. Kohut does acknowledge the significant explanatory power of Freud's theory in describing disturbances that arise within a mental apparatus that contains forces in conflict. Freud's theory explains the conflictual structural neuroses but does not adequately address the concept of a self and its disorders.

Classical theory understands phenomena such as 'orality' and 'anality' as defensive retreats from an oedipal position to regressive points on the continuum of psychosexual development. Kohut finds this explanation narrow and simplistic. He feels that it addresses only a small sector of the personality and loses sight of the complex, overriding whole. Kohut focuses on the effects, both salutary and deleterious, that the childhood milieu has upon the developing child. As he explains:

> My clinical experience with patients whose severe personality distortions I would formerly have attributed to a fixation of the drive organization at an early level of development (orality), and to the concomitant chronic infantilism of their ego, has increasingly taught me that the drive fixation and the widespread ego defects are neither genetically the primary nor dynamic–structurally the most centrally located focus of the psychopathology. It is the self of the child that, in consequence of the severely disturbed empathic responses of the parents, has not been securely established, and it is the enfeebled and fragmentation prone self that (in the attempt to reassure itself that it is alive, even that it exists at all) turns defensively toward pleasure aims through stimulation of erogenic zones, and then, secondarily, brings about the oral (and anal) drive orientation and the ego's enslavement to the drive aims correlated to the stimulated body zones.
>
> (Kohut 1977, p. 74)

The drives and the self

In Kohut's view, the primary factor in a child's development is the relationship between the developing self and its selfobjects, not unconscious libidinal or aggressive drives. When the self is weakened or enfeebled because the child's selfobjects failed in either their idealizing or mirroring functions, the child turns to its erogenous zones for stimulation. These attempts at enlivenment are often carried into adulthood, where they exist as perversions. They encompass the vast array of self-stimulating activities available to humankind.

Because the drives occupy a central position in classical psychoanalytic theory, Kohut must account for them in his psychology. Retaining the self as his central focus, he conceptualizes the drives as breakdown products of a fractured self. Kohut suggests that when disrupted, the child's affection and assertiveness fracture into the 'drive elements' of sexuality, aggression and destructive hostility.

Interpretation and resistance

Interpretation and resistance is another area where Kohut feels psychoanalysis benefits from self psychology's new explanations. Kohut believes that the interpretive process in analysis is similar to a two-step developmental process in which the self becomes structuralized. The first step involves a merger with an empathic selfobject that provides the developing self with the experience of being understood and affirmed. The merger also aids in tension regulation as the developing self participates in the selfobject's capacity to contain its own affects. Eventually affects are recognized as a signal rather than as a spreading and overwhelming experience. The second step concerns the child's experience of the selfobject's need-satisfying actions.

Kohut suggests that the interpretive process, like structuralization, is a two-step process that involves the experiences of merger and action. The merger component of the interpretive process is what Kohut calls the 'understanding phase'; the action component he calls the 'explaining phase.' Kohut describes the interpretive process as follows:

> Every interpretation, in other words, and every reconstruction, consists of two phases; first the analysand must realize that he has been understood; only then, as a second step, will the analyst demonstrate to the analysand the specific dynamic and genetic

factors that explain the psychological content he had empathically grasped.

(Kohut 1977, p. 88)

The intense rage that sometimes follows an interpretation should be understood, says Kohut, in a way that differs from the classical understanding. The classical understanding assumes that the rage is the result of a correct interpretation that has liberated primitive aggression from its unconscious confinement and brought it into consciousness. Kohut views the rage as the by-product of an injury, precipitated by the analyst's incorrect or premature explanation, rather than as an expression of primary aggression.

An analyst's view of early development has a profound effect upon his or her therapeutic conceptualizations and activities. The classical view sees the infant as a biological bundle, with no psychological self present in the early months. Development classically centers around the maturation of the erogenous zones and the vicissitudes of the affects connected with them. Kohut's focus differs. He is concerned about the developing self and its maturational experiences. The relationship of the self to its milieu and an understanding of the self as a container of affects is central to Kohut's psychology. Some of his ideas anticipate Stern's findings in the field of infant observation (1985), as in the following:

I have no doubt, in other words, that with the aid of a psychology of the self – the study of the genesis and of the development of the self, of its constituents, its aims, and its disturbances – we will learn to recognize new aspects of mental life and to penetrate into greater psychological depths, even in the areas of normal acculturation and of the structural conflicts of the classical neuroses.

How could it be otherwise? A complexly organized empathic-responsive human environment reacts to the child ab initio; and we may well discover, as we investigate early states of infancy with more and more refined psychological means, that a rudimentary self is already present very early in life.

(Kohut 1977, p. 98)

A self psychological view of anxiety, dreams and aggression

Kohut demonstrates the explanatory power of his psychology by examining the mental phenomena of anxiety, dreams and aggression.

He compares the anxiety experienced in the structural neuroses with the anxiety experienced by a weakened self. The self in a structural neurosis is intact and the anxiety, which usually presents as a vague dread, becomes increasingly clear and specific as one works with the resistances. The anxiety deepens because the castration fears that previously were defended against are now revealed and experienced.

In disorders of the self, anxiety tends to present differently. Here the anxiety is due to a preconscious concern about the fragile nature of the self. It often begins with specific concerns about wholeness and safety, reflected, for example, in a worry that a skin infection might lead to septicemia, that an insignificant lump might be cancer or that a crack in the foundation of a home might lead to its eventual collapse. The anxiety is focused and specific rather than vague or diffuse. These are concrete attempts to define the vague, broader concern about the disintegrating self. As treatment progresses, these circumscribed hypochondriacal fears generally give way to a recognition of the diffuse anxiety connected to the threatened disruption of the self. Kohut argues that mental apparatus psychology lacks a satisfactory explanation of this anxiety whereas a psychology of the self brings this understanding to psychoanalysis.

Dreams are another phenomenon Kohut uses in his argument to demonstrate the usefulness of self psychology. He describes two categories of dreams. The first is dreams in the structural neuroses. Such dreams express drive-wishes, conflicts and attempts at conflict resolutions. By following the patient's associations the analyst undoes the camouflaging dream work and uncovers the unconscious wish that stimulated the formation of the dream.

The second group of dreams contains imagery that expresses the vague tensions associated with traumatic states. In dreams of this type, the patient's associations do not lead to an uncovering of the deeper, defended layers of the unconscious, as they do with dreams of the first group. Instead, associations tend to stay at the level of manifest content and provide imagery of the disintegration that threatens the self. Kohut calls these 'self-state' dreams and likens them to the dreams of the traumatic neuroses.

As an example of the latter group of dreams, a young woman about to make a major life change was leaving a city where she had deep attachments. She reported a series of dreams in which she kept losing her luggage as she traveled to her new home. Whenever she felt relief at finding one piece, she suddenly lost another. Try as she might, it was impossible for her to gather and retain all her belongings in one safe place at the same time. Associations were to thoughts about moving and feeling disrupted. They did not deepen to reveal an unconscious drive-related wish. The meaning of the dream is contained in its manifest content, which symbolically expresses the state of her dislocated and temporarily fractured self. Kohut argues that by addressing the state of the self rather than its contents, self psychology provides clinical understandings that are unavailable to practitioners of drive psychology alone.

Aggression is yet another area where Kohut believes that psychoanalysis benefits from a psychology of the self. A basic tenet of classical theory is that assertiveness, hate and aggression are primary psychological givens, part of humankind's essential biological nature. Kohut questions the classical explanation of aggression and destructiveness. For Kohut, destructiveness is not the expression of a primary drive. Destructiveness, instead, is the product of a disintegrating self. Destructive rage is always motivated by an injury. Although the rage is primitive, it is not psychologically primary. Expanding on this idea, Kohut writes:

> In essence then, I believe that man's destructiveness as a psychological phenomenon is secondary; that it arises originally as a result of the failure of the self-object environment to meet the child's need for optimal – not maximal, it should be stressed – empathic responses. Aggression, furthermore, as a psychological phenomenon, is not elemental. Like the inorganic building blocks of the organic molecule, it is, from the beginning, a constituent of the child's assertiveness, and under normal circumstances it remains alloyed to the assertiveness of the adult's mature self.
> (Kohut 1977, p. 116)

By challenging the primacy of aggression Kohut exposes himself to the criticism that he denies the unpleasant reality of humankind's aggressive essential nature. However, he neither questions nor denies humankind's destructive capacity, but provides a new explanation for its origin. He insists that his understanding of the self, derived empathically in the clinical setting, provides a broader and deeper explanation for the human condition than does speculation-based classical theory. For Kohut, 'psychological bedrock' (that point beyond which analysis cannot penetrate) is not the threat of castration. It is not a threat to physical survival. Instead, it is the threat of the destruction of the self.

Kohut regards rage as the breakdown of the child's innate healthy assertiveness. He sees the infant as born with an assertiveness that is supported by empathic responses from its selfobject milieu. When the child is traumatically disappointed by its milieu, its assertiveness fractures into rage. Assertion, not aggression, is the primary psychological given:

> Stated in descriptive terms: the behavioral baseline with regard to aggressiveness is not the raging-destructive baby – it is, from the beginning, the assertive baby, whose aggressions are a constituent of the firmness and security with which he makes his demands vis-à-vis self-objects who provide for him a milieu of (average) empathic responsiveness. Although traumatic breaks of empathy (delays) are, of course, experiences to which every infant is unavoidably exposed, the rage manifested by the baby is not primary. The primary psychological configuration, however short-lived, does not contain destructive rage but unalloyed assertiveness; the subsequent breakup of the larger psychic configuration isolates the assertive component and, in so doing, transforms it secondarily into rage.
> (Kohut 1977, pp. 118–19)

Kohut turns next to the sexual drive. Again, he conceptualizes pathologic expressions of sexuality within the context of the self and its selfobject experiences rather than as the expression of a primary drive. From Kohut's perspective, perversions are the expressions of an enfeebled self attempting to stimulate and enliven itself through sexualized means. The perversion represents the sexualized relationship with a selfobject that failed in its function. He writes:

> The infantile sexual drive in isolation is not the primary psychological configuration. . . . The primary psychological configuration . . . is the experience of the relation between the self and the empathic self-object. Drive manifestations in isolation establish themselves only after traumatic and/or prolonged failures in empathy from the side of the self-object environment. . . . In order to escape from depression, the child turns from the unempathic or absent self-object to oral, anal, and phallic sensations, which he experiences with great intensity. And these childhood experiences of drive hypercathexis become crystallization points for the forms of adult psychopathology that are in essence diseases of the self. . . . The deepest level to be reached [in an analysis] is not the drive, but the threat to the organization of the self . . . the experience of the absence of the life-sustaining . . . empathic responsiveness of the self-object.
> (Kohut 1977, pp. 122–3)

To conclude this discussion Kohut returns to his starting point – the issues involved in determining readiness for termination – and repeats that readiness for termination depends upon one's view of illness and cure. From the classical perspective, patients' enhanced knowledge about the genetics and dynamics of their disturbance and the development of reliable control over their sexual and aggressive instincts are central therapeutic goals. From the self psychological perspective, the goal of treatment is the filling in of defective narcissistic structures and the formation of a cohesive self that functions in a joyful, fulfilling and creative way. As with Mr. M, cure is not always accomplished through the complete filling in of the defects. Rehabilitation can occur through the enhancement of compensatory structures as well.

GUILTY MAN, TRAGIC MAN

As one can see, self psychology and classical mental apparatus psychology are informed by vastly different views of humankind. Kohut calls one view 'Guilty Man' and the other view 'Tragic Man.' Guilty Man, the view from the classical perspective, sees humankind as living in accord with the pleasure principle. Guilty Man attempts to satisfy drives but is unable to do so because of environmental pressures and internal conflicts.

Tragic Man, the view from the self psychological perspective, does not live within the pleasure principle. Instead, Tragic Man seeks to express the inborn patterns of the nuclear self so that life can be lived in a creative and fulfilling way. Failures in living a fulfilled life, however, usually overshadow successes, which leads Kohut to emphasize the tragedy of unmet potential.

In summary, Kohut asserts that self psychology brings to psychoanalysis an understanding of the self that a mental apparatus, drive–defense, conflict psychology cannot provide. A psychology of the self describes how self cohesion evolves from early and later self-object experiences and culminates in the healthy expression of the self's innate nuclear program. It is a psychology in which cohesion of the self rather than drive primacy constitutes the primary psychological issue.

Chapter 8

The Restoration of the Self: Part II
Clinical considerations

THE BIPOLAR SELF

As we have seen, the self is the central configuration in Kohut's psychology. Kohut's main hypothesis, that the primary configurations that form the self are due to the child's relationships with its selfobjects, is derived from reconstructive work with his adult analysands. This work leads him to infer that the movement of the child's nuclear self, from isolated fragments to cohesive whole, depends upon the responsiveness of the child's selfobjects to its specific developmental needs. In *Analysis of the Self*, Kohut outlines these specific needs and delineates the two psychological configurations around which they center. One configuration, the grandiose self, concerns the mirroring, early maternal selfobject, whose responses accept and affirm the child's exhibitionistic narcissism. The other configuration, the idealized parental imago, concerns the merger with an idealized selfobject that brings a sense of perfection, safety and wholeness to the self. These two configurations are components of a supraordinate configuration that Kohut calls the 'bipolar self.' He expanded his earlier ideas and presented an in-depth discussion of the bipolar self in *The Restoration of the Self* (1977).

The bipolar self contains two poles, a pole of ambitions and a pole of ideals. The child's healthy, expansive, exhibitionistic narcissism constitutes one pole. In normal development the narcissism associated with this pole evolves into what eventually is experienced as ambitions. The yearning to merge with a stabilizing, tension-regulating, idealized self-object creates the other pole. In normal development the idealizing narcissism associated with this pole evolves into what eventually is experienced as guiding ideals.

The sense of continuity within the self, the sense of being the same person over time, depends upon the nature of the poles as well as upon the relationship between the poles. Kohut suggests that a tension, experienced as a sense of being pushed by the pole of ambitions and led by the pole of ideals, exists between the two poles. He calls this tension a 'tension arc' and describes it in the following way:

> I have tried to express this hypothesis by the employment of an evocative terminology. Just as there is a *gradient* of tension between two differently charged (+, –) electrical *poles* that are spatially separated, inviting the formation of an electrical *arc* in which the electricity may be said to flow from the higher to the lower level, so also with the self. The term 'tension gradient' thus refers to the relationship in which the constituents of the self stand to each other ... it indicates the presence of an action-promoting condition that arises 'between' a person's ambitions and his ideals. With the term 'tension arc' however, I am referring to the abiding flow of actual psychological activity that establishes itself between the two poles of the self, i.e., a person's basic pursuits toward which he is 'driven' by his ambitions and 'led' by his ideals.
> (Kohut 1977, p. 180; emphasis in original)

Kohut introduces a third constituent of the bipolar self. This is the area of skills and talents that exists between the two poles. This is one area where compensatory mechanisms can form, as was the case for Mr. M (see Chapter 7). Kohut summarizes the development and shape of a particular self in the following way:

> The self then is the central overriding psychological configuration. Its formation and deformation is at the heart of growth and development. It is formed out of the structure building experiences with the self-objects. The exhibitionistic–expansive self is supported by the mirroring early self-object which usually is the mother. The configuration of the idealized parental imago forms when a parent allows and even enjoys the child's idealization. This is a later development and usually involves the father. The specific form of a particular self depends upon the nature of the child's relationships with its self-objects. If there is a disturbance in the formation of one pole of the self, an attempt will be made to compensate for the weakness by strengthening the other pole. Serious self disturbance and deformation occurs when there is a failure in the development of both poles. Stated differently, the child has two chances at health. If one parent cannot fulfill its self-object function the child turns, in a

compensatory way, to the remaining parent. Pathology results when neither parent can provide the self-object functions to support and strengthen either pole of the self.

(Kohut 1977, p. 186)

Kohut acknowledges that the gross events of childhood, such as births, deaths, illnesses, disruption of families, etc., play an important role in the genesis of emotional illness. He believes, however, that the nature of the parents' personalities, whether healthy or ill, affects the psychological atmosphere and is responsible for the shape of a particular self.

The central position of the drives in classical psychoanalytic theory demands that Kohut account for them within his theory. In *The Restoration of the Self*, he breaks with analytic tradition and conceives of the drives as breakdown products of a fragmenting self rather than as biological givens. Because this hypothesis departs from classical theory in such a major way, I present it as a direct quotation:

> It is instructive in this context to examine the disintegration of the two basic psychological functions – healthy self-assertiveness . . . [and] healthy admiration for the idealized self-object. . . . When the child's self-assertive presence is not responded to by the mirroring self-object, his healthy exhibitionism . . . will be given up, and isolated sexualized exhibitionistic preoccupations concerning single symbols of greatness (the urinary stream, feces, phallus) will take over. And similarly, when the child's search for the idealized omnipotent self-object with whose power he wants to merge fails . . . then again, the child's healthy and happy wide-eyed admiration will cease, the broad psychological configuration will break up, and isolated sexualized voyeuristic preoccupations with isolated symbols of the adult's power (the penis, the breast) will take over.
>
> (Kohut 1977, pp. 171–3)

What traditionalists consider to be expressions of drives, Kohut conceives of as the breakdown or fractionation of core aspects of the self. For example, when the child's healthy self-assertiveness is not responded to appropriately, the assertiveness turns into rage and aggression. When the healthy need to be seen and admired is traumatically frustrated it turns into a sexualized exhibitionism and when the healthy need to gaze with awe at an idealized selfobject is traumatically frustrated it becomes a sexualized voyeurism. These sexualizations become entrenched and are carried into adulthood as perversions. For Kohut, perversions are not expressions of the drives but symptoms of a fragmented, sick and deadened core that attempts to enliven itself.

Kohut contends that the selfobject transference experiences mobilized in treatment are not repetitions of earlier infantile relationships. They are new experiences. They express the thwarted developmental needs that have come alive. Their reawakened presence makes possible the restoration of an arrested and enfeebled self. Kohut echoes a comment offered twenty-five years earlier (1951, pp. 164–6), namely that all repetitions are transferences, but not all transferences are repetitions.

CLASSIFICATION OF PATHOLOGY

Having established the bipolar self as a central configuration, Kohut is in a position to classify and discuss psychopathology on the basis of disturbances in the nature and shape of the self. He groups the disorders into primary and secondary disturbances. His predominant interest lies in the primary disturbances since they are the result of arrests in the formation of the self, whereas the secondary disturbances are the reactions, acute and chronic, to the exigencies of life. Kohut distinguishes five categories of primary disturbance:

(1) *the psychoses* (permanent or protracted breakup, enfeeblement, or serious distortion of the self);
(2) *the borderline states* (permanent or protracted breakup, enfeeblement or serious distortion of the self which is covered by more or less effective defensive structures); and
(3) *the schizoid* and *the paranoid personalities*, two defensive organizations employing distancing, i.e. keeping at a safe emotional distance from others.

(Kohut 1977, p. 192)

Although people with these primary disturbances can form beneficial relationships with a therapist, the disordered sector of the self cannot form stable transferences that can be therapeutically managed. Psychoanalytic psychotherapy, therefore, is not the appropriate treatment for these people. Kohut describes two narcissistic disorders in which stable transferences, that can be worked through in a psychoanalytic treatment, however do form. They are:

(4) *the narcissistic personality disorders* (temporary breakup, enfeeblement, or serious distortion of the self, manifested predominantly by autoplastic symptoms (Ferenczi, 1930) such as hypersensitivity to slights, hypochondria, or depression), and
(5) *the narcissistic behavior disorders* (temporary breakup, enfeeblement, or serious distortion of the self manifested by predominantly alloplastic symptoms (Ferenczi, 1930), such as perversion, delinquency or addiction).

(Kohut 1977, p. 193)

In some narcissistic disturbances, the activities designed to enliven a deadened self are confined to fantasy. Kohut calls these 'narcissistic *personality* disorders.' In the other group of self disturbances, fantasy life is enacted in the form of perversions, delinquencies or addictions. Kohut calls these the 'narcissistic *behavior* disorders' to distinguish their action mode of restitution from the restitutive attempts that are confined to fantasy. The dynamic issues are similar for each of these two groups, but the genetic issues differ. When at least one parent is able to provide the necessary selfobject functions, one of the poles develops in a compensatory way and offsets the weakness in the other pole. This enables people who suffer from a narcissistic personality disorder to contain the attempt at restitution and confine its gratification to fantasy. For people with narcissistic behavior disorders, neither of the early selfobjects was able to promote the development of either pole of the self. This created a diminished ability to manage affects and evolved into an uncontrolled drivenness either to revitalize a deadened self or to soothe an agitated self. Kohut believes that the narcissistic behavior disorder is the more severe type of disturbance because neither pole of the bipolar self has been sufficiently nurtured.

CLINICAL ILLUSTRATION 1

Whereas Kohut previously defined the self narrowly, as a content of the mental apparatus, he now defines the self broadly, as a central overriding construct. He presents the analysis of Mr. X to demonstrate the clinical utility of his concept of the bipolar self.

Mr. X, whose female analyst sought supervision with Kohut, had an addictive masturbatory activity and an associated homosexual fantasy that caused him great shame. He had had neither homosexual nor heterosexual experiences. His sexual life consisted of masturbating many times during the course of a day with a fantasy about the pastor at his church. The climactic moment in the fantasy occurred when Mr. X crossed his penis with the pastor's while receiving Holy Communion. There was no conscious fellatio in the fantasy, which did seem to contain a sense of deep loneliness.

History revealed that when he was a child, Mr. X's mother had idealized him, while she simultaneously deprecated her husband, Mr. X's father. She was a religious woman who read Bible stories to Mr. X, emphasizing the perfection of the relationship between Jesus and his mother Mary. Mr. X's mother idealized Jesus's intellect and emphasized his superiority to the older men. She also idealized Mr. X but supported his grandiosity only so long as he remained emotionally tied to her. She withdrew her adoration when he threatened to move away from her.

Kohut speculated that Mr. X's fantasy expressed his yearning for a strong man to replace his unavailable father, whose deprecation by his mother interfered with any idealization that might have been possible. The fantasy was the sexualized expression of Mr. X's wish to merge with an idealized, God-like man whose power would become his own. The emotional absence of Mr. X's father interfered with the development of the pole of the self that contained ideals and goals.

Kohut uses the structural model to describe the contents of Mr. X's personality and the unfolding of his analysis, as shown in Figure 8.1. He defends what seems to be the inconsistency of mixing theoretical models, while simultaneously revealing his playful scientific attitude:

> In the present instance, I chose to fit the self and its constituents into the framework of the structural model of the mind, knowing full well that in doing so I reduced the self to a content of the mental apparatus and thus temporarily abandoned the comprehensiveness of the explanatory powers of an independent psychology of the self. These are permissible inconsistencies because, to my mind, all worthwhile theorizing is tentative, probing, provisional contains an element of playfulness.
>
> (Kohut 1977, pp. 206–7)

The work in Mr. X's analysis was conducted in two stages. The first stage addressed the vertical split that maintained the facade of superiority and isolation. The second stage addressed the true nuclear self, depressed and depleted, hidden beneath the repression barrier. Kohut asserts that a psychology that focuses on conflict over incestuous wishes misses the essence of Mr. X's personality whereas a psychology that conceives of a self as a central psychological configuration can

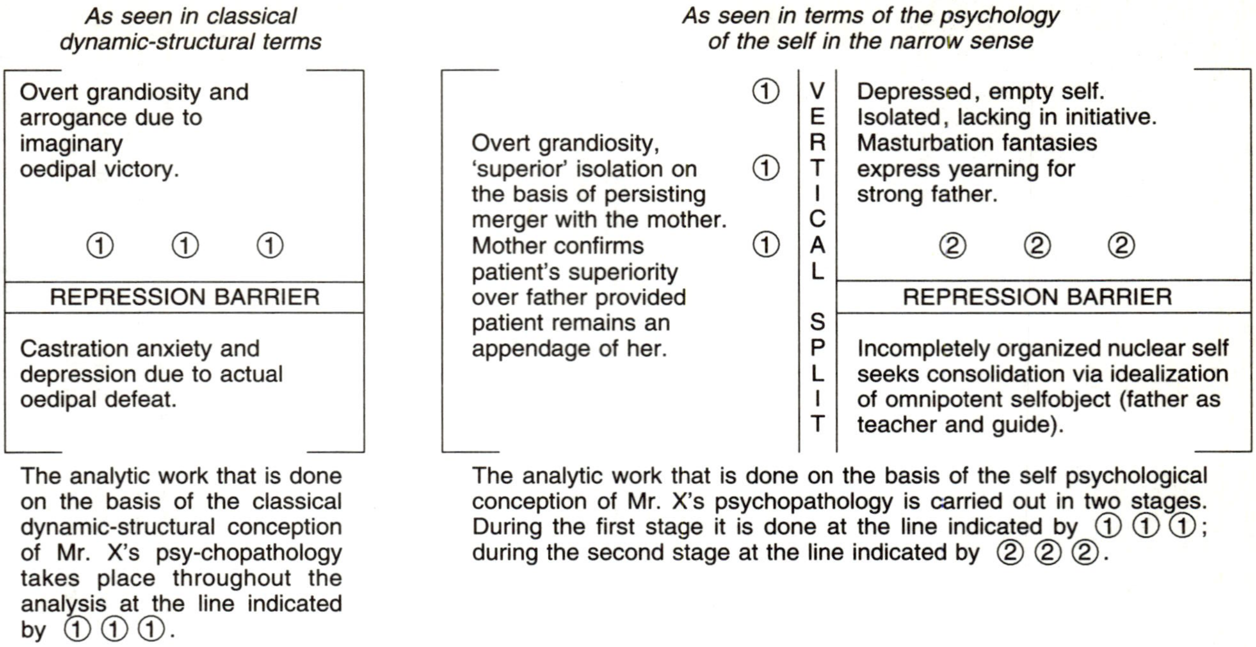
As seen in classical dynamic-structural terms
Overt grandiosity and arrogance due to imaginary oedipal victory.
① ① ①
REPRESSION BARRIER
Castration anxiety and depression due to actual oedipal defeat.
The analytic work that is done on the basis of the classical dynamic-structural conception of Mr. X's psy-chopathology takes place throughout the analysis at the line indicated by ① ① ①.
As seen in terms of the psychology of the self in the narrow sense
Overt grandiosity, 'superior' isolation on the basis of persisting merger with the mother. Mother confirms patient's superiority over father provided patient remains an appendage of her.
① ① ①
VERTICAL SPLIT
Depressed, empty self. Isolated, lacking in initiative. Masturbation fantasies express yearning for strong father.
② ② ②
REPRESSION BARRIER
Incompletely organized nuclear self seeks consolidation via idealization of omnipotent selfobject (father as teacher and guide).
The analytic work that is done on the basis of the self psychological conception of Mr. X's psychopathology is carried out in two stages. During the first stage it is done at the line indicated by ① ① ①; during the second stage at the line indicated by ② ② ②.

Figure 8.1 Kohut's characterization of Mr. X's personality and the two phases of his analysis (Source: Kohut 1977, p. 213)

address his core. Kohut summarizes the therapeutic issues in Mr. X's analysis as follows:

> Before the analytic process began to offer the patient truly effective means to fill in the structural defect, he could do no more than obtain fleeting relief through concretized erotized enactments. These found their most poignant expression in the patient's feeling suffused with male strength when he imagined the act of crossing his penis with the penis of the priest at the moment of receiving the Host. It was the task of the analysis to move this need for a firm self – particularly for the pole of the self that was able to carry his idealized goals – from its addictive–erotic representation, which provided only a temporary sense of strength, back to the underlying need to reactivate the relation with the idealized self-object.
>
> (Kohut 1977, pp. 217–18)

The vertical split, indicated by (1) in Figure 8.1, played a prominent role in Mr. X's disturbance. It created the disavowed split-off sector, on the left side of the diagram, that contained elements of unmodified grandiosity. The disavowal was necessary because it protected Mr. X from the shame and embarrassment associated with the grandiosity.

The first phase of Mr. X's analysis addressed the disavowed grandiosity and its relationship to his mother's need to merge with her grand and idealized son. Mr. X learned that his arrogance and superiority, the predominant experience of himself, did not flow from his authentic self. It came from a part of himself that was an extension of his mother. The analytic work in this area helped diminish the haughty, isolated arrogance that covered Mr. X's hidden true self.

Once the vertical split healed, Mr. X moved into the second phase of his analysis. He gradually became aware of the empty, depleted, deprived and depressed self that lay beneath the horizontal barrier (2) as shown in Figure 8.1. He came to know that this hidden self had always been present and that it was his more authentic self. In addition, fragments of a self based on Mr. X's thwarted childhood relationship with his idealized father lay hidden beneath the repression barrier. The disturbed relationship Mr. X had with his father prevented the formation of a firm pole of idealizations. In the analysis, the thwarted need for a pole that carried masculine ideals was reactivated and expressed through the emergence of an idealizing transference. The working-through process centered about this transference, which led to a strengthening of the idealized pole of the self.

Kohut asks what he considers a disturbing question: Is it possible for there to be multiple outcomes for a given analysis? Could an analyst's focus on one pole over the other create varying outcomes? He answers emphatically that each self has its own specific configuration based upon its unique relationships with its childhood selfobjects. An analysis conducted empathically will be in tune with the shape of the particular self in question. The transferences that emerge will be pathognomonic for that self:

> In the overwhelming majority of cases, however, the course of the analysis, if correctly pursued, is essentially predetermined by the endopsychic factors . . .
>
> The essential transference (or the sequence of the essential transferences) is defined by preanalytically established internal factors in the analysand's personality structure, and the analyst's influence on the course of the analysis is therefore important only insofar as he – through interpretations made on the basis of correct or incorrect empathic closures – either promotes or impedes the patient's progress on his predetermined path.
>
> (Kohut 1977, pp. 216–17)

CLINICAL ILLUSTRATION 2

A patient of mine further demonstrates Kohut's concept of the bipolar self. This patient's psychotherapy was unusual in that we met several times a week for one, two or occasionally three weeks punctuated by interruptions of two to six weeks. To engage a therapeutic process with this man it was essential to accept his erratic schedule, necessitated by work-related travel. Although the disruptions seemed to cause my patient no overt distress, we eventually came to understand the deeper issues expressed in his nomadic way of life.

Winston, a tall, charming, forty-one-year-old British man, had expected to come for only a few sessions to settle a troubling pattern he had discovered in himself. A likeable and seemingly sensitive person, he off-handedly dismissed the import of feelings, which gave him an air of emotional shallowness. Despite this seeming shallowness, however, he quickly moved into an active therapeutic process.

In terms of his problem, Winston noticed that, inevitably, after a relationship with a woman had intensified, he found a trivial imperfection in her that became a reason to end their relationship. He had recently gone through this with three women in a short time and realized something was wrong with him.

Despite Winston's claim that his early life in England was wonderful, we quickly discovered that he had lived a life of disguised loneliness. His early years were spent under the guidance of three nannies who were present respectively from birth to three years, from three to seven and from seven to eleven. The nannies did not enjoy the company of either Winston or his two siblings. They acted in a friendly way toward the children when the parents were present but were cold and distant when alone with them. Strict disciplinarians, they hurried the children to bed early in the evening. Winston recalled the many nights he longingly watched other children play outside after he had been sent early to bed. An obedient boy, he stayed in his room and learned to entertain himself, inventing games to keep occupied.

Winston was sent to boarding school at the age of eight, living at home only for the school holidays. He recalled the pangs of loneliness he felt the week before returning to school and the homesickness of the first days at school. Parents were, however, allowed to take the children home for one day every four weeks.

Life at home was formal. Between the ages of three and seven the children, who were with their parents from 5 to 5.30 each evening, were required to stand when their father entered the room. Winston's father, who had recently died when Winston entered psychotherapy, was described as a special person, deeply loved by many. He possessed an unusual capacity to relate to people of all social levels. Winston loved his father dearly and felt they had a wonderful relationship. The feeling between them was deep, yet their intimacy was never openly expressed. A slap of the hands in passing was the extent of their physical contact. They spoke solely of business or sports, never about themselves or each other. Although his family tended to suppress their feelings, Winston felt unimpeded in his ability to mourn his father and, in fact, he and his sister were the only members of the family able to cry at the funeral. The rest were stoic.

His mother was a distant, intrusive, judgmental woman who dismissed other people's feelings off-handedly. She was a frightful gossip, and someone to whom appearances seemed to mean more than did people. Winston believed he might have fled England to distance himself from her. Although Winston had come for 'just a few sessions to help untie the knot in my brain,' he rapidly became engaged in a treatment process. He was intensely curious, eager to talk about himself and looked forward to every session. I directed my initial comments toward his presenting complaint. I noted that although the woman in his life was ever-changing, nonetheless he never was without the *presence* of a woman. It seemed that he had created an aura of a woman for a constant companion and, I suggested, this might have served as a counter to an underlying loneliness. This idea caught Winston's attention and opened exciting new doors for him. He spontaneously began to review his childhood and quickly saw the lonely existence he had lived as a boy.

Winston's experience when a woman fell in love with him was instructive. He yearned to be loved by women and described his remarkable ability to ensnare them, each time hoping he had found the perfect woman for whom he searched. But whereas he hunted for a woman's adoration, he became terrified when it emerged. We discovered this was the point when he found her inevitable imperfection and withdrew. He did not actually leave her, however, until he had started a relationship with another woman. This pattern had begun when he was eighteen and had always been the same. Winston had not been alone since late adolescence.

Since it seemed pivotal, we explored Winston's experience of being adored. Although adoration was what he sought and worked for, the actual experience seemed overwhelming. It made him feel both intensely excited and embarrassed. The only way to regain his comfort was to distance himself. This experience reminded him of another situation. Winston was a superb athlete, yet it was unbearable for him to hear his accomplishments praised. He recounted memories of walking off the field, head down and embarrassed, after playing remarkably well. In association, he recalled that his parents, fearing he would become conceited, rarely acknowledged his many accomplishments.

Reviewing the emotional life of his family, Winston spoke of another embarrassment. Open affection toward anyone – girl, woman or family member – brought ridicule and humiliation from parents and sibs alike. 'Love her, do you? My, my,' his family would taunt. Winston realized also that it was his family's censure he feared when he thought about a woman's 'imperfection.' He needed their approval and feared their criticism.

Winston asked why he had his problems when so many others were also raised with the help of nannies but seemed to fare better. In search of an answer, we reviewed his life with the nannies and realized that they were chosen by Winston's mother. They were extensions of her. Their unattuned personalities reflected his mother's unempathic idea of childhood. Winston thought others might have fared better because their nannies were loving women. Some were with families for fifteen years, while Winston had had three cold nannies by the time he was eleven.

Although Winston sought treatment for a single problem, I considered several questions in my attempt to understand him. Why, for example, was praise, as well as adoration, an intolerable experience? What was the similarity? What was the meaning of Winston's nomadic life? Why could he not commit himself to a single person? Were closeness and intimacy intolerable for him? To answer these questions, I will consider the genetic factors that helped shape the self and use that understanding to explain the dynamics of Winston's current life. In this consideration, three features of his life seem remarkable.

The first was Winston's presenting complaint, his constant need for adoration and his retreat when it emerged. Although he lacked an enduring relationship with a single woman, it seemed to me that he did have an enduring relationship with a fantasy creature, composed of the many women he had known. Over the years, all the women blended into one constant, though faceless, womanly presence. I believe that one answer to the question of Winston's inability to engage in a lasting relationship lies in the multiple losses he experienced as a child. His mother's distant personality, her assignment of his care to the changing nannies and his life away from home at an early age – all were traumatic. Winston protected himself against further hurt by avoiding the vulnerable state a commitment would create. His attachment to the ethereal womanly presence fulfilled his lonely need for company while simultaneously keeping him safe from the threat of a loss. The second striking feature of Winston's life related to his work. With fluid attachments and a shallow emotional life, Winston moved easily and quickly as his company transferred him to new countries. He had learned as a child to disavow and deny his affective life. Valued as strength of character by his stoical childhood milieu, disavowal became a valued part of himself. Carried into adulthood the disavowal enabled his nomadic life of incessant travel. The capacity to bear disruption and isolation without complaint was now valued in the milieu of his firm and handsomely rewarded.

Winston's choice of work had several elements. By establishing a sense of mastery over a nomadic life, it recreated the trauma of childhood while simultaneously providing an illusion of control. Nomadic life also protected him by preventing any person or place from becoming too important. In this regard, Winston was similar to people who experienced parent loss during childhood. They protect themselves from the threat of attachments which expose them to another loss. Winston's initial interest in a few consultative sessions rather than a sustained involvement reflected this protectiveness.

The third remarkable feature in Winston's life was the contrast between his sensitivity, his ease of engagement, his capacity for introspection and his presenting emotional shallowness. I believe the shallowness was a facade that protected Winston from exposure to further injury. Having grown up in an unempathic, emotionally suppressive environment, he expected nothing different as his life progressed. He had learned to treat feelings with a 'stiff upper lip,' as though they did not matter. In treatment the facade melted rapidly, suggesting that the hope for a responsive milieu never died. It lived in hiding.

Winston's emotional shallowness served another function. It protected him against affects he had not learned to experience with comfort and safety. The source of this problem lay with the selfobjects of Winston's childhood milieu, who feared their own affective experiences. Love, warmth, pride, anger – the gamut of human experience was frightening for them. In this milieu, affects were managed through avoidance and suppression, denial and disavowal. Missing was the mirror function of the attuned selfobjects, comfortable with their own affects, able to affirm and validate a child's experience. Whereas affirmation of affect enhances the capacity for affect management, shameful humiliation for feelings such as love, warmth, loneliness and pride forces affect under the defensive cover of denial and disavowal. Emotional shallowness ensues.

With this understanding we can now approach the issue of Winston's experience when he was adored or praised. Winston's wish for adoration expressed his unending quest for the missing gleam in his mother's eye. The unmodified need of the grandiose self for affirmation of its grandeur was the result of selfobjects who were unable to appropriately participate in, reflect and thereby modulate the exhibitionistic narcissism. Winston's wish for praise had the same origin as his wish for adoration: affirmation of the unmodified grandiosity. His difficulty with this affirmation had two sources. One related to the intense excitement he experienced when the wished-for affirmation was realized. Affirmation, whether in the form of praise or adoration, brought a threatening excitement that Winston could manage only through withdrawal. To protect himself from this stimulation, he left women when they adored him and he avoided praise whenever it came. The other related to the shame attached to the wished-for affirmation. Exhibitionistic grandiosity is especially vulnerable to shame and embarrassment. It must be comfortably accepted by the selfobjects of childhood in order to be integrated into the personality.

The concept of a bipolar self carries the danger of reification, as I discuss in Chapter 13. When approached with the attitude of the playful scientist, experimenting with different ideas, however, it can be a useful conceptual tool. I do not consider the bipolar self to be a concrete model. I use it merely as a guide to help me organize my understanding and am ready to change any portion when it no longer explains the data. My conceptualization of the bipolar self for Winston was that the pole of ambitions (derived from the gradual maturation and modulation of grandiosity) was weakened, as evidenced by his endless pursuit of adoration. He learned to withdraw in an attempt to protect himself against his overstimulating excitement when the disavowed wish for affirmation was realized. This contributed to his inability to sustain a relationship as an adult. To stabilize himself during childhood and to compensate for the effect of his unmirrored and unmodified grandiosity, Winston turned to his second parent. Winston's father was available and allowed himself to be quietly idealized, which enabled psychological structures to form around the pole of ideals. Derived from his father, Winston's ideals held an elevated position in his personality and possessed a guiding quality. They were a source of narcissistic enhancement when he lived in their accord. Remember that Winston's motivation to seek help was stirred by his ideals. He realized he had hurt other people. He valued decency, courageously owned his hurtfulness and wanted to change his behavior. At that time, he had no expectation that he could be empathically perceived and helped for himself.

I turn now to a brief summary of the treatment where the therapeutic effort centered on a repair of the defective pole, the unmirrored sector of the self. Uncomfortable with affects, Winston managed them through withdrawal, disavowal and denial. In our work, I encouraged him to experience his affects and identified them as they emerged. In response, his facade of emotional shallowness quickly dissipated, his hidden capacity for introspection surfaced and he became curious about himself. As he spontaneously reviewed his boyhood life the first affect to emerge was loneliness. He had never realized he was a lonely child. He had accepted the myth that his was a happy life. He soon articulated, however, what he had long suspected: children were social legitimizers for his parents' way of life, rather than a joy, cherished for themselves. Winston cried openly for the lonely boy he had been and to his surprise he welcomed his tears. Tearfully he recovered a screen memory that he carried throughout our work. In this memory Winston's parents had taken him to a trailer in the country and left him there with a nanny for a summer vacation. He poignantly remembered imploring them not to leave as their car traveled down the road and out of sight.

Winston's capacity to observe himself developed at a rapid rate. It was as though, unbeknownst to him, he had been waiting for this experience. As he understood the stoic loneliness of his boyhood he developed a capacity for empathy with himself. His empathy soon extended to others as he realized, with a sense of horror, that he had been unable to appreciate the feelings of the women he had left. He reflected on how he had learned to live his life alone. As he said, 'No one would ever guess that of me, because I am so friendly and outgoing, but it's absolutely true. I'm always alone on the inside.' He was delighted that this hidden part of himself was becoming revealed.

I introduced Winston to the many feelings he had not been encouraged to know as a boy. Opportunity arose to address his disavowed exhibitionism when Winston spoke of the embarrassment he had experienced when he played well athletically. I suggested that feeling proud was a problem for him, adding that comfort with one's pride was the outcome of a healthy childhood environment. We then explored the experience of his exhibitionism as a child and as an adult.

Winston also spoke of the experience of feeling angry with people. He said he never argued and wondered whether people spoke of anger in relationships. Similarly, he was unsure of whether he ever felt love. Certainly he never spoke of it in a relationship. Winston knew himself as a kind, generous person and felt sad when he realized how deprived he had been. He began to feel that he might be missing an important part of life since relationships did not deepen for him.

In a kaleidoscopic way, Winston talked about the vast range of affects, the repertoire of feelings missing from his childhood. In an effort to integrate what he had been experiencing I attempted to link my understanding of his current experience with my comprehension of his early life. I made a dynamic–genetic interpretation when I said that he had been talking about love, pride, anger, loneliness – all feelings that were part of being human. They were feelings that had been difficult for him to experience and difficult to share with another. I added that all the feelings he had been experiencing in our treatment were strong feelings that children learn to experience with growing comfort when the caretakers are able. For Winston, as a boy at home and then away at school, there were no able caretakers who could help him become comfortable with his feelings. On the contrary, he was taught to bury what he felt. The result was that feelings were unpleasant and went underground. Further, he developed a way of being alone inside himself and now, as a man traveling the world, he kept to himself on the inside, despite that fact that he knew hundreds of people. Winston responded, saying that he realized what a lonely person he had been and what a waste of a fine life it had been, or could have been, if he had not come for help.

Winston became curious about an attachment to a person and for the first time in his life considered the possibility of changing the nomadic nature of his life to allow a relationship to form. Though much work remained, a repair in the sector of Winston's unmirrored affective life was occurring. He had begun to engage affects that had been split off because of the missing mirror experience of childhood.

THE OEDIPUS COMPLEX AND PSYCHOLOGY OF THE SELF

The new view Kohut offers from his self psychological perspective is overarching and places drive–defense psychology in a new context. It reminds me of the difference between studying a valley from its floor and from atop the mountain range that forms it. The view from the valley floor is limited, confined by the defining mountains. The view from the mountain top, on the other hand, places the valley within the context of its defining surround. From the broader perspective, the centrality of the valley diminishes and the defining mountains take on new meaning. So it is with Kohut's psychology of the self. His view adds the broader, overarching perspective of the self, as a defining element in mental life, to the confined view of the drives as the primary motivators in human psychology. Because his is a new, evolving and controversial view, Kohut was continually confronted with the objections of his colleagues whose view has been sequestered by the confines of rigid theory. In *The Restoration of the Self*, Kohut engages this controversy directly, beginning in this way:

> The classical theory of drives and objects explains a good deal about the child's oedipal experiences; par excellence it explains the child's conflicts and, in particular, the child's guilt. But it falls short in providing an adequate framework for some of the most important experiences of man, those that relate to the development and vicissitudes of his self. To be explicit . . . these theories fail to do justice to the experiences that relate to the crucially important task of building and maintaining a cohesive nuclear self.
> (Kohut 1977, pp. 223–4)

Kohut saw support for his new ideas in the oedipal material that emerged at the end of analyses with some of his patients who had narcissistic personality disorders. Initially, he thought the emerging oedipal configurations were repetitions of the unresolved oedipal conflicts of childhood which the now strengthened self was able to revive and resolve. Surprisingly, however, the oedipal material that emerged did not contain the intensely charged memories about parents and siblings that Kohut expected would be associated with the revival of the old oedipal configurations. Instead, the associations and oedipal fantasies involved Kohut and members of his family. His interpretation of this material is that these were new oedipal experiences, not the revival of old configurations. He hypothesizes that the enfeebled self of the oedipal child was not able to engage and experience the oedipal struggle, whereas the newly strengthened self of his adult analysand is now able to experience the oedipal phase for the first time.

Kohut felt that he could study the nature of the oedipal phase, in an environment uncontaminated by inappropriately responding selfobjects, through the emergence of this new oedipal material. He observed that the oedipal phase, experienced in the analysis for the first time, seems to be accompanied by a sense of joy. The anxiety traditionally associated with the oedipal complex seems to be missing. To account for this unexpected finding, Kohut suggested that the previously fragmentation-prone self has been restored to a firm, cohesive self able to safely experience the affects of the oedipal phase.

Kohut differs with Freud, who asserts that the oedipal child's world of incestuous wishes is responsible for the affects of the oedipal phase, whereas the external milieu has little significance. Kohut says that the oedipal phase can be understood *only* within the context of the child's experience of its selfobject milieu. Regarding the child's milieu, empathic parents react to the sexuality and competitive assertiveness of their oedipal child on two levels. On one level, the parents offer a counter-response to the child's sexuality and competitiveness. They attempt to modulate the impulses and civilize the child. On another level, the parents express pride in their child's developmental achievement. The parental pride supports the child's emerging self and contributes to the child's joy over its own vigor, assertiveness and appropriate sexuality.

On the counter-responsive level, parents are stimulated by the child's sexuality and antagonized by its competitiveness. They grasp the meaning of their child's behavior and respond in aim-inhibiting ways to both the sexuality and the assertiveness. The empathic parent is neither traumatically overstimulating in response to the sexuality nor heavy-handed in response to the child's aggression. Kohut describes the process when he suggests that empathic parents help the child build up internal structures that modulate the drives. He adds that when modulating structures fail to develop, a weakening of the mental apparatus ensues, creating a person 'spurred on by his drives and shackled by castration anxiety and guilt' (1977, p. 233).

Parents who are not able to respond empathically to their oedipal children do not see the sexuality and assertiveness in terms of its developmental totality. The emerging vigor and vitality associated with the sexuality and assertiveness are not correctly understood. The child's oedipal features develop in a distorted way when the parental echo to the libidinal and aggressive strivings is missing during the oedipal phase. The result of the absent echo is an unaffirmed, shaky and fragmentation-prone self.

Healthy parents enjoy their child's vigor and assertiveness. They recognize it as a developmental achievement. A father in narcissistic balance does not feel challenged by his son's assertiveness. He enjoys it and sees his son as a 'chip off the old block.' He allows his son to merge with him and with his strength. The result is a firming of the boy's self and a strengthening of his sense of masculinity. Kohut describes the oedipal experience for the child of narcissistically balanced parents:

> What, in other words, is the Oedipus complex of the child who entered the oedipal phase with a firmly cohesive self and who is surrounded by parents who themselves have healthy cohesive and continuous selves? It is my impression, on the basis of inferences that I believe can be drawn from the observation of the quasi-oedipal phase at the end of some successful analyses of narcissistic personality disorders, that the normal child's oedipal experiences – however intense the desire for the heterogenital parent, however serious the narcissistic injuries at recognizing the impossibility of their fulfillment; however intense the competition with the homo-genital parent, and however paralyzing the correlated castration anxiety – contain, from the beginning and persisting throughout, an admixture of deep joy that, while unrelated to the content of the Oedipus complex in the traditional sense, is of the utmost developmental significance within the framework of the psychology of the self. I believe . . . this joy is fed from two sources . . . (1) the child's inner awareness of a significant forward move into a psychological realm of new and exciting experiences, and of greater importance – (2) his participation in the glow of pride and joy that emanates from the parental self-objects despite – indeed, also because of – their recognition of the content of their child's oedipal desires.
> (Kohut 1977, pp. 235–6)

Kohut's new understanding of the oedipal phase is based upon his observation of the oedipal experience of his analysands. He sees the oedipal era as a time of potential strengthening rather than a time of vulnerability and weakness. When experienced with an appropriately responding self-object, the oedipal phase is a period of joy rather than anxiety. Kohut questioned the ubiquity of the oedipal conflict in human experience and wonders whether the oedipal configuration of classical analysis is actually the expression of pathological development. He wrote:

> Could it not be . . . that the normal Oedipus complex is less violent, less anxious, less deeply narcissistically wounding than we have come to believe – that it is altogether more exhilarating and, to speak in the language of mental apparatus Guilty Man, even more pleasurable? Could it be that we have considered the dramatic desires and anxieties of the oedipal child as normal events when, in fact, they are the child's reactions to empathy failures from the side of the self-object environment of the oedipal phase?
> (Kohut 1977, pp. 246–7)

The classical concept of the oedipal phase as an era of hostile aggressiveness and enhanced sexuality has mistaken secondary for primary phenomena. Kohut suggests that the oedipal era cannot be fully understood without considering the relationships of the oedipal child with its selfobject environment. He contends that narcissistically intact parents make an affirming and strengthening contribution to the self of their child. The intact selves of these parents do not experience their child's affection and competitiveness as isolated, dangerous and threatening. Unchallenged and unintimidated by their child's oedipal liveliness, such parents are able to respond to the totality of their oedipal child. On the other hand, the child's self tends to fragment when its selfobjects are out of touch with its forward movement. In such a situation, the healthy oedipal assertiveness fractures into an aggressive hostility and the healthy affection breaks down into desperate sexualized attempts at enlivenment. The self of this child is enfeebled, the poles of ambitions and ideals weakened. In adult life, the experience of an enfeebled self is the guiltless depression of Tragic Man. Although mental apparatus psychology is well able to describe the mechanism for guilty depressions, it lacks an adequate explanation for the guiltless empty depression of an enfeebled self.

THE ANALYTIC SITUATION

Regardless of their theoretical orientation, analysts agree that the unique structure of an analysand's personality emerges spontaneously in an atmosphere of analytic neutrality. The question is, what constitutes analytic neutrality? Kohut had quite definite ideas about neutrality and what he calls the 'average expectable analytic milieu' (1977, p. 258). He opposed the analytic stance that equates neutrality with non-responsiveness and ventured several explanations for analytic stiffness. He speculated that the pre-psychological training of medical psychoanalysts biases their analytic activity. Medically trained psychoanalysts tend to see neutrality as the creation of a 'clean' environment with no contamination coming from the side of the analyst. According to Kohut, analytic stiffness and non-responsiveness are a misunderstanding of analytic neutrality:

> [M]an can no more survive psychologically in a psychological milieu that does not respond empathically to him, than he can survive physically in an atmosphere that contains no oxygen. Lack of emotional responsiveness, silence, the pretense of being an inhuman computer-like machine which gathers data and emits interpretations, do no more supply the psychological milieu for the most undistorted delineation of the normal and abnormal features of a person's psychological makeup than do an oxygen-free atmosphere and a temperature close to the zero-point supply the physical milieu for the most accurate measurement of his physiological responses.
> (Kohut 1977, p. 253)

Kohut believed that analysts are unusual in their empathic abilities, for their natural inclination is to react to their analysands with warmth. Theoretical bias, however, makes it difficult for many analysts to behave in a relaxed and natural way. Many actually feel guilty when they are themselves with their patients. Their natural inclinations come into conflict with the dictates of their theory. Observing this, Kohut comments, 'In consequence, a certain stiffness, artificiality, and strait-laced reserve are not uncommon ingredients of that attitude of expectant "neutrality" analysts bring to the analytic situation' (1977, p. 254). The rationale for analytic non-responsiveness lies in the classical idea that frustration of the unconscious wish forces the drive elements of the wish into consciousness, where they can be brought under control of the ego. In this theory, the analyst's responsiveness and warmth are understood as gratification of the wish and should be avoided.

Despite its claim to neutrality, analytic non-responsiveness is not neutral. The analyst who responds to an analysand's question with silence and no explanation for not providing an answer is rude and hurtful. It is not an average expectable environment. Instead, it is grossly depriving and at times repeats the traumatic experience with the selfobjects of childhood. Analysands often respond to this hurt with rage and withdrawal. The analyst operating from drive–defense theory often misunderstands the rage and sees its emergence as confirmation of the correctness of an interpretation. The reactive rage mistakenly confirms the theory. The analytic attitude of muted responsiveness and reserve is often the appropriate one, especially in situations where children have been overstimulated by the adult environment. This attitude, however, is most often adopted out of obedience to the basic tenet of non-contamination of the transference rather than out of harmony with the analysand's psychological core. Kohut surmises that the analysand would most likely experience this attitude as unempathic were it not that the analyst's tone softens unconsciously despite conscious theoretical convictions.

Although he emphasizes the import of a warm responsive milieu, Kohut insists, lest he be misunderstood, that the core of the analytic experience is the reconstructive–interpretive approach:

> Even the most sensitively responsive behavior from the side of the analyst . . . cannot replace the reconstructive–interpretive approach based upon the analyst's conscious grasp of the patient's structural defects in the self, and of the self-object transferences that establish themselves on the basis of these defects.
>
> (Kohut 1977, p. 259)

The analytic setting informed by a psychology of the self requires an appropriate responsiveness and an understanding and acceptance of the emerging exhibitionism and idealizations. In the course of classically informed analyses, analysands with narcissistic disorders experience an emergence of their arrested narcissistic needs, but these needs are often misunderstood. Informed only by a drive–defense psychology, the analyst mistakes the mobilization of an idealization for a defensive maneuver. Remobilized exhibitionism is similarly misunderstood and not accepted in the context of its developmental history. The rejection of these manifestations of the emerging narcissistic configurations in the analysis repeats the faulty response of the selfobjects of childhood and fragmentation ensues. The analysand responds with lethargy and rage. The rage is misunderstood as the reactivation of infantile aggression, and the lethargy is interpreted as guilt over the destructive wishes.

From Kohut's perspective, the goal of the treatment, which in turn affects the analytic ambience, is the working through of the traumatic failures of the early selfobjects as they emerge in the transferences and become understandable through reconstructions. It is not the confrontation of the analysand with his or her bedrock hostility in an effort to tame and control the unconscious aggression. Kohut answers the misunderstanding that infers he suggests a cure through love or through 'being nice' when he writes:

> To summarize my views on the analyst's attitude in the analytic situation, I will say first that it must never become the goal of the analyst to provide an extra measure of love and kindness to his patients – he will provide substantial help to his patients only through the employment of his special skills and through the application of his specialized knowledge. The nature of his specialized knowledge, however – his specific theoretical outlook – is an important factor in determining the way in which he conducts himself vis-à-vis his patients.
>
> (Kohut 1977, p. 261)

EPILOGUE

In his final thought, Kohut returns to the central point of his 1959 paper. What, he asks, is the essence of psychoanalysis? What defines the nature of the field? His answer lies not in a particular theory or technique but in the activity that enables the analyst to understand his or her patient. That activity is the analyst's empathic immersion into the inner life of the analysand. Kohut asserts that empathic immersion by the open-minded analyst avoids theoretical bias. Theorizing guided by empathic immersion makes new understandings possible.

Kohut ends his discussion in *The Restoration of the Self* with a demonstration of what he considers to be an appropriate scientific attitude. He notes that, in all he has written on the psychology of the self, he has purposely not defined the self. He explains his reason for this omission in the following:

> My investigation contains hundreds of pages dealing with the psychology of the self – yet it never assigns an inflexible meaning to the term self. . . . But I admit this fact without contrition or shame.

The self . . . is, like all reality . . . not knowable in its essence. . . . We can describe the various cohesive forms in which the self appears, can demonstrate the several constituents that make up the self . . . and explain their genesis and functions. We can do all that, but we will still not know the essence of the self as differentiated from its manifestations.

These statements . . . express my belief that the true scientist – the playful scientist as I put it before – is able to tolerate the shortcomings of his achievements – the tentativeness of his formulations, the incompleteness of his concepts. Indeed, he treasures them as the spur for further joyful excursions. . . . A worshipful attitude toward established explanatory systems . . . becomes confining in the history of science – as do, indeed, man's analogous commitments in all of human history. Ideals are guides, not gods. If they become gods they stifle man's playful creativeness; they impede the activities of the sector of the human spirit that points most meaningfully into the future.

(Kohut 1977, pp. 310–12)

Chapter 9

The two analyses of Mr. Z

In 1979, Kohut published a paper describing two analyses he had conducted with the same patient but from two different theoretical perspectives. The first analysis, conducted within the frame of drive–defense theory, occurred before Kohut had developed his hypotheses about the self. The patient, Mr. Z, returned five years later for further treatment and the second analysis was informed by Kohut's new theories. The analyses, each lasting four and a half years and each conducted at a frequency of five sessions a week, gave Kohut the opportunity to compare the theoretical perspectives in a clinical setting.

Kohut reports that Mr. Z was a handsome man in his mid-twenties when he first sought treatment for a series of vague complaints that included a feeling of social isolation and of difficulty forming relationships with women. His academic work, as measured by grades, was good, but he felt he was not functioning to his full ability. He had mild somatic complaints: sweaty palms, extrasystoles and periods of either constipation or diarrhea.

Mr. Z was an only child who lived with his widowed mother following the death of his financially successful father. He described a close relationship with an important male friend. They attended movies and concerts together, often accompanied by Mr. Z's mother. It was after this friend abandoned him for a relationship with a woman that Mr. Z sought treatment.

The first year and a half of Mr. Z's life appeared to have been happy, and a core of vitality seemed to have ensued from the early relationship with both his parents. Mr. Z's father became seriously ill, however, and was hospitalized when Mr. Z was three and a half years old. His father met and fell in love with a nurse while in the hospital and left home to live with her. While his father was away, Mr. Z slept in his father's bed. When he returned, one and a half years later, Mr. Z slept on a couch at the foot of the parental beds, where he was exposed repeatedly to the primal scene.

Mr. Z began to masturbate when father returned home. The content of his masturbatory fantasies was suggested by themes in *Uncle Tom's Cabin*, a book his mother had read to him while his father was away. The fantasies involved being sold as a slave to women who used him like an animal, allowed him no initiative, ordered him about and treated him harshly. Mr. Z reported a homosexual relationship, at the age of eleven, with a thirty-year-old camp counselor whom he idealized, in which there was minimal genital play. He also reported that, as an adult, he had masochistic masturbation fantasies in which he submissively performed tasks for a domineering woman, although he never enacted these fantasies in reality.

The first analysis began with Mr. Z demanding Kohut's total attention. Kohut understood and interpreted this demand to be Mr. Z's wish to have the analysis repeat the experience of his doting mother who, in the absence of a rival father or competing siblings, devoted all her attention to him. Mr. Z vigorously opposed these interpretations and was furious with Kohut for making them. In fact, the first year and a half of the analysis was dominated by Mr. Z's rage over his frustrated sense of entitlement and his wish to be admired. The rage suddenly stopped, however, as did his assertion that his demands were justified. Kohut suggested that the change was due to Mr. Z's working through his narcissistic delusions. Mr. Z rejected that explanation, but he did so calmly and attributed his diminished rage to a soothing statement Kohut had made before he delivered one of his interpretations. According to Mr. Z, Kohut had prefaced his interpretation with, 'Of course it hurts when one is not given what one assumes to be one's due.' Kohut did not understand the meaning his comment held for Mr. Z and persisted in his belief that Mr. Z's diminished rage was the result of his working through his narcissistic demands.

In the first analysis Kohut believed that the causes of Mr. Z's complaints lay in the conflicts associated with unconscious infantile sexuality and aggression. Kohut believed that Mr. Z's insistence that he was special and without a rival grew out of the childhood experience of his father's prolonged absence, which left him alone with his mother. Mr. Z's persistent narcissism, expressed in his sense of specialness, was understood as a denial of the painful awareness that his father had, in fact, returned to possess his mother sexually. Mr. Z's 'specialness' protected him against an awareness of his competitiveness toward his father and against the accompanying castration anxiety. Mr. Z's narcissism and his denial were seen as defensive maneuvers, enacted in the transference.

Kohut interpreted Mr. Z's intense relationship with his mother as a retreat to a preoedipal position. The retreat protected him from the castration anxiety he would have experienced if he had assumed a non-regressive hostile–competitive stance with his father. Kohut understood Mr. Z's homosexual relationship with the older camp counselor as the defensive enactment of the pre-oedipal relationship with the mother. In the first analysis Kohut repeatedly rejected Mr. Z's emerging narcissistic needs. He understood and interpreted them as a resistance against the deeper fears associated with Mr. Z's masculine assertiveness and his competition with men. Kohut did not understand and accept the narcissism as the mobilization of arrested configurations.

Eventually the narcissistic features receded, Mr. Z's transference demands became more realistic, and he became assertive in his work. Aggressive thoughts directed toward Kohut appeared and Mr. Z developed an interest in Kohut's private and sexual life. Toward the end of the analysis, Mr. Z reported a dream that he would remember years later, during the termination phase of his second analysis. The dream was as follows:

> [He was] in a house, at the inner side of a door which was a crack open. Outside was the father, loaded with gift-wrapped packages, wanting to enter. The patient was intensely frightened and attempted to close the door in order to keep the father out.
>
> (Kohut 1979, pp. 407–8)

After working with the dream, Kohut and Mr. Z concluded that it referred to Mr Z's ambivalent attitude toward his father. They surmised that Mr. Z feared retaliatory castration by his beloved father. Mr. Z responded defensively by retreating to the pre-oedipal attachment to his mother and by adopting a submissive homosexual attitude. Kohut describes his thinking at the end of the first analysis:

> I had no doubt that Mr. Z's vast improvement was indeed based on the kind of structural change that comes about as a result of bringing formerly unconscious conflicts into consciousness. To my analytic eye, trained to perceive the configurations described by Freud, everything seemed to have fallen into place. We had reached the oedipal conflict, the formerly unconscious ambivalence toward the oedipal father had come to the fore, there were the expected attempts at regressive evasion with the temporary exacerbations of preoedipal

conflicts, and there was ultimately a period of anticipatory mourning for the analyst and the relationship with him, abating toward the end, as the dissolution of the bond of trust and cooperation was in the immediate offing. It all seemed right, especially in view of the fact that it was accompanied by what appeared to be the unquestionable evidence of improvement in all the essential areas of the patient's disturbance.

(Kohut 1979, p. 408)

In retrospect, Kohut recalls one feature that seemed strange. The termination seemed lifeless, despite the fact that Mr. Z was an intense man whose affects were available to him. Aside from his sadness over leaving Kohut and the analysis, there was little vitality in the material.

Mr. Z contacted Kohut nearly five years later complaining of having experienced little change in his life. He lived alone, in his own apartment, but although he had had several relationships with women, he had experienced no special attachment. The relationships had been shallow and unsatisfying. He had been doing well in his work, though he did not enjoy it. Work was a necessary burden that brought no joy. The masochistic fantasies never completely disappeared, and Mr. Z called upon them to enliven his sexual experiences. In addition, Mr. Z's mother had had a psychotic change in her personality and had become overtly paranoid. Kohut thought this had something to do with Mr. Z's coming back for treatment but later he learned that the mother's illness had had a salutary effect upon Mr. Z.

Although treatment did not begin immediately, Mr. Z felt better after the initial contacts. Awakened to the presence of narcissistic needs, Kohut hypothesized that Mr. Z's immediate well-being came from a transference that Kohut had not considered in the first analysis. Kohut now believed that Mr. Z had established an idealizing transference, similar to what he had experienced when he had turned from his mother to the idealized camp counselor. Mr. Z reported a dream at the beginning of the second analysis that confirmed Kohut's hypothesis about an idealizing transference. He dreamed of a dark-haired man. His associations were an idealized amalgam of his father, the counselor and Kohut. During the second analysis Kohut did not interfere with the idealization as he had before. The idealizing transference soon was spontaneously replaced by a mirror transference of the merger type. Mr. Z became demanding and insisted upon perfect empathy, just as he had in the first analysis. He reacted with rage at the slightest misunderstanding of his emotional states. This time, however, Kohut had a different perspective. He no longer viewed narcissism as a defensive maneuver. Instead he saw it as a valuable replica of a childhood condition that was coming alive in the analysis. Kohut believes that his changed attitude prevented the rages of the first analysis, which he believes were precipitated by his insistence that the narcissistic demands were defensive. In the second analysis, Kohut understands Mr. Z's demanding behavior as the repetition of the relationship with his over-involved mother who was willing to provide whatever Mr. Z wished, so long as he maintained his allegiance to her. Kohut describes the change in his analytic attitude:

> I had in the first analysis looked upon the patient in essence as a center of independent initiative and had therefore expected that he would, with the aid of analytic insights that would enable him to see his path clearly, relinquish his narcissistic demands and grow up. In the second analysis, however, my emphasis had shifted. I had acquired a more dispassionate attitude vis-à-vis the goal of maturation, and assuming that growth would take care of itself, I was now able, more genuinely than before, to set aside any goal-directed therapeutic ambitions. Put differently, I relinquished the health and maturity morality that had formerly motivated me, and restricted myself to the task of reconstructing the early stages of his experiences, particularly as they concerned his enmeshment with the pathological personality of the mother. And when we now contemplated the patient's self in the rudimentary state in which it came to view in the transference, we no longer saw it as resisting change or as opposing maturation, but on the contrary, as desperately – and often hopelessly – struggling to disentangle itself from the noxious selfobject, to delimit itself, to grow, to become independent.
>
> (Kohut 1979, p. 416)

The early work of the second analysis focused on Mr. Z's experience of his mother. In the first analysis, Kohut explained Mr. Z's idealization of his mother as an expression of his incestuous love toward her. In the second analysis, Kohut realized that the wonderful picture Mr. Z had of his mother was, instead, the picture she herself had conveyed to the world. Those close to her, however, realized that she enslaved them and stifled their moves toward independence. Mr. Z's report that his mother bestowed endless love upon him was amplified during the second analysis. Together, Kohut and Mr. Z found that she did bestow endless love but the love came with the uncompromising condition that Mr. Z submit to his mother's total domination and not have important relationships with other people. Seen within this light, his father's relationship with the nurse and move away from home took on new meaning. His father's relationship was a flight to save himself from his suffocating wife, but at the sacrifice of his son.

Mr. Z's growing understanding of the psychotic nature of his mother's personality was accompanied by severe anxiety and resistance. He could no longer idealize her, and her loss as an archaic selfobject created intense anxiety. Massive disavowal during childhood countered Mr. Z's awareness of his mother's strangeness and enabled him to maintain her as an idealized selfobject, a tie that protected him against the experience of annihilation anxiety.

The second analysis paid attention to the mother's personality and revealed the effect of her bizarre involvement with Mr. Z. She experienced her son as an appendage, rather than as a center of his own initiative. She assumed that his intense relationship with her would never change. As Mr. Z confronted the bizarre elements of his mother, the idealized aura of their relationship, fostered by the mother, gradually diminished. For example, Mr. Z recalled his mother's minute inspection of his feces, which continued until he was six years old. He noticed how that inspection merged into a minute inspection of his skin that continued well into his adolescence. His mother searched for blemishes in Mr. Z's skin and extracted blackheads whenever she found them. As she did this she spoke of the strength of her fingernails and her extraordinary ability to perform the extractions.

The stories of these bizarre experiences hardly surfaced during the first analysis. On the rare occasions when they did, Kohut understood Mr. Z's report of his mother's exaggerated interest as an expression of Mr. Z's defensive narcissism. Kohut emphasized Mr. Z's overvaluation of his own productions. The memory of his mother's intense interest was seen as an expression of childish grandiosity. The second analysis, in contrast to the first, focused on the depression and the hopelessness that his mother's suffocating attitude created. In the second analysis, Mr. Z came to realize that his mother's interest was not in him but in her control over him and in his attachment to her as an enhancing appendage. He recalled that his mother allowed him no privacy as a boy, entering his room unannounced at all times of the day. His domain was her domain, and her rage over his attempts at freedom gave him no room to protest. Her domination created a sense of total submission on his part. Although his mother appeared normal to the world outside, her hollow core and the rigid domination she exerted were known by those close to her.

Kohut marvels at the absence of this material in the first analysis. Though the material was there, it failed to claim his attention. Answering the puzzling question of why that was so he writes:

> I believe that we come closest to the solution of this puzzle when we say that a crucial aspect of the transference had remained unrecognized in the first analysis. Put most concisely: my theoretical convictions, the convictions of a classical analyst who saw the material that the patient presented in terms of infantile drives and of conflicts about them, and of agencies of a mental apparatus either clashing or cooperating with each other, had become for the patient a replica of the mother's hidden psychosis, of a distorted outlook on the world to which he had adjusted in childhood, which he had readily accepted as reality – an attitude of compliance and acceptance that he now reinstated with regard to me and to the seemingly unshakable convictions that I held.
>
> (Kohut 1979, p. 423)

Mr. Z's improvement in the first analysis was due to his compliance, in the transference, with Kohut's convictions about the oedipal complex. The same, of course, could be said about the second analysis, but Kohut asserts that Mr. Z's compliance was deeply explored and worked through in the second treatment, making that enactment less likely.

The realization that Mr. Z's mother was mentally ill took several years. Mr. Z's initial response was one of great relief and joy. He was delighted to have a witness to what he previously knew by himself. Eventually, however, this realization was accompanied by depression and severe disorganizing anxiety. The second analysis addressed Mr. Z's underlying depression rather than his wish to gain pleasure by gratifying his infantile drives. Kohut describes his theoretic orientation during the second analysis:

> Where we had formerly seen pleasure gain, the sequence of drive demand and drive gratification, we now recognized the depression of the self that, wanting to delimit and assert itself, found itself hopelessly caught within the psychic organization of the selfobject. We realized not only that neither his masturbation nor his involvement in the primal scene had ever been enjoyable, but that a depressive black mood had pervaded most of his childhood. Since he could not joyfully experience, even in fantasy, the exhilarating bliss of growing self-determination and independence, he tried to

obtain a minimum of pleasure – the joyless pleasure of a defeated self – via self-stimulation. The masturbation, in other words, was not drive-motivated; was not the vigorous action of the pleasure-seeking firm self of a healthy child. It was his attempt, through the stimulation of the most sensitive zones of his body, to obtain temporarily the reassurance of being alive, of existing.

(Kohut 1979, p. 425)

With intense shame and humiliation, Mr. Z recovered memories of his lonely childhood and the times he dragged himself through the day, looking forward to the night when, alone in bed, he would be able to masturbate. He also recalled a period of anal stimulation when he smelled and tasted his feces. Kohut felt that Mr. Z was able to tolerate the recovery of these humiliating memories because they occurred within the empathic resonance of another human being who was able to help him understand their function as feeble attempts to provide himself with a feeling of vitality. With Kohut's help, Mr. Z discovered that his behavior was neither disgusting nor evil. The primal scene experience also took on a new meaning. It was no longer understood as an expression of healthy curiosity that came to grief because of incestuous wishes. It was now understood as intensely overstimulating and as being engineered by the mother, who wanted Mr. Z to be enmeshed in her experience.

The second analysis entered a second phase when Mr. Z turned from an almost exclusive concern about his mother to thoughts concerning his father. He focused on his father's submission to his dominating mother as well as his father's weakness, expressed most blatantly when the father left home and abandoned Mr. Z to life alone with his mother. Although a sense of hopelessness persisted, it was neither as intense nor as overriding as before. Mr. Z's depression diminished and elements of vitality began to appear.

This was the point at which Mr. Z became intensely curious about Kohut's life. Kohut interpreted this as the revival of Mr. Z's childhood curiosity, connecting it to Mr. Z's curiosity about his parents' sexual life. Mr. Z became depressed and insisted that he was being misunderstood. Despite his appeals, Kohut did not tell Mr. Z about his life. He did, however, reassess his understanding of Mr. Z's curiosity. Kohut surmised that the curiosity was not an expression of sexual voyeurism but rather related to Mr. Z's need for a strong father. At its heart, Mr. Z's question was not about sexuality but about whether Kohut was a strong and active man who was not subdued sexually or in any other way by a dominating woman. Kohut realized also that Mr. Z's homosexual relationship with the camp counselor was not truly sexual but rather expressed his yearning for a relationship with a strong man.

Mr. Z was reassured by Kohut's courage and strength when he did not provide answers to his intensely demanding questions. His depression diminished, and he began to flesh out the personality of his father, who previously had been a shadowy figure. Mr. Z was relinquishing the archaic selfobject tie to his mother and turning toward a strong father. Intense anxiety accompanied this move, however, since a major sector of Mr. Z's personality was based on the illusion of his mother's strength. The realization that his mother was severely damaged carried a dreadful sense of isolation and annihilation, and Mr. Z struggled with a wish not to see what had become apparent.

An idealization of Kohut emerged, followed by positively inflected memories of his father. Mr. Z recovered the memory of a ski trip with his father when he was nine years old. On that trip, Mr. Z discovered that father was an able skier and a man who functioned well in the world. Mr. Z recalled meeting a woman during the trip who seemed to have a special relationship with his father. Mr. Z speculated that his father had been having a relationship with this woman and that she might have been the nurse with whom his father had had the affair. There was no way to substantiate Mr. Z's speculation, but he recalled that upon returning home he mentioned nothing to his mother when she asked about the trip. It was as though Mr. Z and his father shared a special unspoken understanding. Kohut felt that Mr. Z's childhood need for a man whom he could idealize and about whom he could feel proud had been revived in the analysis. This material emerged last in the analysis, and this, Kohut speculates, was because the material represented the deepest layers of that which had been repressed.

As part of his argument, Kohut considers whether the material about Mr. Z's father's interest in a woman was actually a defensive cover for the oedipal conflicts of Mr. Z's childhood. If these were indeed hidden oedipal concerns, one would have expected Mr. Z's mood, as he recovered and described the memories, to be one of depression and hopelessness in the face of his overpowering rival father. Kohut concludes that these memories were not a defensive cover since they contained no associations of hopeless rivalry with either father or analyst. On the contrary, Mr. Z maintained a sense of optimism and vitality associated with his connection to the analyst-father whom he now experienced as a strong masculine figure. Mr. Z's mood was one of pride in his father's maleness, and joy over the father's ability to free himself from the enslaving mother.

The termination phase soon followed. Mr. Z remembered the dream of the first analysis in which his father, who was loaded with gifts, had tried to enter the partially opened door while Mr. Z attempted to keep him out. In the first analysis, Kohut had interpreted the dream as the expression of Mr. Z's ambivalence about his castrating father. Through the combination of additional associations in the second analysis and his new theoretical perspective, Kohut came to understand the dream as the expression of Mr. Z's difficulty in managing the overwhelming excitement he felt at the psychological return of his father. The gifts the father carried were the gifts of masculinity and psychological strength. Closing the partially opened door was Mr. Z's attempt to regulate the excitement he experienced at the return of the long-lost father who carried these gifts. The dream expressed the psychoeconomic imbalance precipitated by the psychological return of the yearned-for paternal presence.

Kohut speculates that memories of strength relating to the father had been hidden in a walled-off sector of Mr. Z's psyche and had to wait for the completion of analytic work concerning the mother before they could be unearthed. The healthy tie to the father threatened the troublesome but seemingly life-sustaining illusion of his mother's strength. Mr. Z's precarious psychological vitality depended on his attachment to his adoring, but enslaving, mother who extracted a severe price for her adoration. If, as a boy, Mr. Z had acknowledged an interest in his father, she would have withdrawn her sustaining interest.

As termination progressed, sadness about losing Kohut emerged. Mr. Z also regretted the lost opportunity to develop a friendship with his father, who was now dead. Mr. Z became angry with Kohut for having failed him in the first analysis. He felt hopeful, though, and thought about marrying a woman and having children, particularly a son. Mr. Z's empathy and tolerance toward his parents expanded. He became able to view his mother from an unmerged position, with both his separateness and his maleness intact. He recognized her real assets without the distortion of the earlier idealization and appreciated the firm core she had given him through her mothering when he was a small child. Kohut summarizes the second analysis this way:

On the whole I believe that I now understood how the structure of Mr. Z's self as it became clearly outlined during the last weeks of the analysis was genetically related to the personalities of his parents. His most significant psychological achievement in analysis was breaking

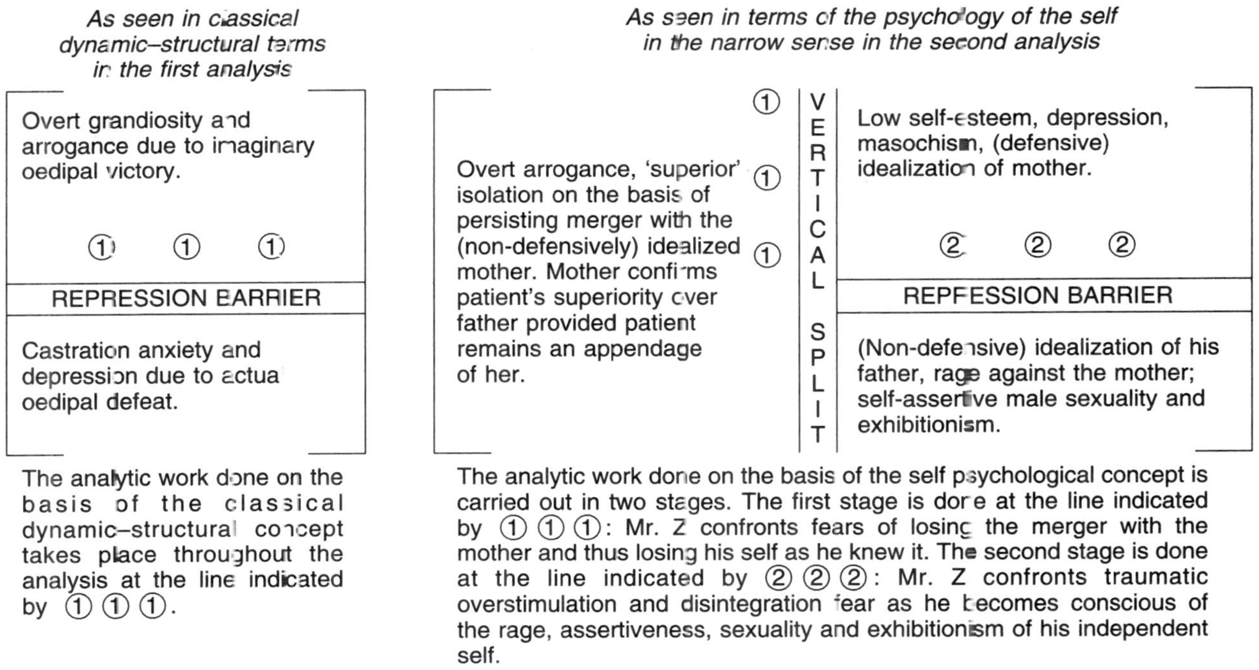

As seen in classical dynamic–structural terms in the first analysis	As seen in terms of the psychology of the self in the narrow sense in the second analysis
Overt grandiosity and arrogance due to imaginary oedipal victory. ① ① ① REPRESSION BARRIER Castration anxiety and depression due to actual oedipal defeat.	Overt arrogance, 'superior' isolation on the basis of persisting merger with the (non-defensively) idealized mother. Mother confirms patient's superiority over father provided patient remains an appendage of her. ① ① ① V E R T I C A L — ② ② ② REPRESSION BARRIER S P L I T — (Non-defensive) idealization of his father, rage against the mother; self-assertive male sexuality and exhibitionism.
The analytic work done on the basis of the classical dynamic–structural concept takes place throughout the analysis at the line indicated by ① ① ①.	Low self-esteem, depression, masochism, (defensive) idealization of mother. ② ② ②

The analytic work done on the basis of the self psychological concept is carried out in two stages. The first stage is done at the line indicated by ① ① ①: Mr. Z confronts fears of losing the merger with the mother and thus losing his self as he knew it. The second stage is done at the line indicated by ② ② ②: Mr. Z confronts traumatic overstimulation and disintegration fear as he becomes conscious of the rage, assertiveness, sexuality and exhibitionism of his independent self.

Figure 9.1 Kohut's diagram of the two analyses of Mr. Z (Source: Kohut 1977, p. 446)

the deep merger ties with his mother. . . . The working-through of his transference relationship to me enabled him to reestablish a link with his father's maleness and independence, and thus the emotional core of his ambitions, ideals, and basic skills and talents was decisively altered, even though their content remained unchanged. But now he experienced these assets of his personality as his own, and he pursued his life goals not in masochistic compliance – as had been the case following his first analysis – but joyfully, as the activities of an independent self.

(Kohut 1979, pp. 443–4)

The two analyses of Mr. Z shown in Kohut's diagram (Figure 9.1) gave Kohut the unusual opportunity of returning to an old problem with new solutions. Using the new lens of self psychology, Kohut viewed Mr. Z differently than during the first analysis, when his vision was informed by classical theory. Strengthened by the therapeutic successes he experienced with his psychology of the self, Kohut soon began work on his final essay, *How Does Analysis Cure?*

Chapter 10

How Does Analysis Cure?: Part I
Theoretical reflections

THE RESTORATION OF THE SELF: RESPONSES AND AFTERTHOUGHTS

As noted earlier, Kohut's work was enthusiastically welcomed in some quarters and severely criticized in others. His harshest critics contemptuously labelled it non-analytic. Kohut, deeply troubled, felt that he had been precise in his thinking and lamented the absence of serious scientific thought and non-contentious study on the part of some of his critics. His shift away from the traditional drive-processing mental apparatus psychology and toward a psychology concerned with the effects of the childhood selfobject milieu upon the formation of the self is one probable source of the intense antagonism. Taming the drives by expanding the domain of the ego is neither the goal of psychological development nor the definition of mental health, as Kohut understood it. For him, the goal of development and therefore the definition of emotional health is the establishment of an intact self, capable of maximally expressing one's innate talents and skills and creating a fulfilling life. As we have seen, Kohut presented this new pragmatic definition of health in *The Restoration of the Self* (1977), where he emphasized the enhanced functioning of an intact self over the complete resolution of conflict or control over drives. This new definition of health forces a redefinition of the goals of an analysis and a rethinking of the criteria for termination.

Kohut's critics, however, misunderstand what he wrote, arguing that he advocated the premature termination of analyses. That misunderstanding, as well as his wish to present new information, prompted Kohut to write *How Does Analysis Cure?* (1984). Published posthumously under the editorship of Arnold Goldberg in collaboration with Paul Stepansky, *How Does Analysis Cure?* is a rather unusual book. For as he wrote, Kohut was aware that he was dying. Guided by his ideal of rigor and playfulness in scientific thought, supported by a staunch group of analysts who validated his conceptualizations, and freed from the sting of ostracism by his classical analytic colleagues, Kohut here presents his final statement about his psychology. The earlier ambivalence arising out of political concerns is gone. He redefines emotional health, places castration anxiety and the Oedipus complex in a new light, outlines the process of analytic cure as he understands it, redefines defense and resistance, and introduces a new categorization of the selfobject transferences.

In *How Does Analysis Cure?* Kohut devotes himself to a discussion of psychoanalysis, as he had done in all his previous work. The psychodynamic psychotherapist, however, faces the task of how to read and apply Kohut's valuable conceptualizations and technical insights to the conduct of psychotherapy. To address this task it is useful to join the controversial discussion, for a moment, of whether psychotherapy is distinct from or essentially the same as psychoanalysis. This question is a variant of the more meaningful question, 'What are we doing, anyway?' Perhaps less intellectual, the latter question is probably the more useful, for one needs a clear understanding of what one is doing before one procedure can be distinguished from another. In addition, if we understand our task clearly we are in a better position to determine what we need to perform that task.

Kohut's conceptualizations are immediately useful in the current task of resolving the above questions, and I turn to Arnold Goldberg's paper, 'Self Psychology and the Distinctiveness of Psychotherapy' (1980), for an application of Kohut's insights. In his paper Goldberg asserts that a reasonable theory of psychotherapy is needed. Confusing is the fact that while frequency of sessions and position in space vary in psychodynamic psychotherapy and psychoanalysis, the operative therapeutic techniques are similar. The understanding of defenses, re-examining distortions, interpreting dreams and transferences, abreactions, genetic reconstructions and the whole technical armamentarium are common to both procedures. This commonality is one source of the conceptual disarray. Distinctions based on method are not helpful. Instead, they lead to turf arguments about who should be doing what. As Goldberg writes, 'The technical maneuvers are not of primary concern so much as our attempting a theoretical stance for the results' (1980, p. 67).

Goldberg is in favor of defining psychotherapy in terms of goals rather than method. To define the goal of treatment Goldberg applies his knowledge of the self to a diagnostic differentiation between an injured self and a disorganized self. He asserts that the appropriate goal of treatment is different for each of these two selves. The injured self is deformed as a result of a narcissistic injury but, because the empathic responsiveness of the selfobject milieu was sufficient, it is not disorganized at its core. The essential health and cohesion of the injured self dictate a treatment that Goldberg asserts aims at 'modifications, enlargements, or filling in of defects of the symbol of the self. This is a discrete change in a basically unchanged self: a repair' (1980, p. 62). He suggests that the focal repair of an injured segment of the self is the work of psychotherapy.

The situation is different for the disorganized self, which, because of the faulty early responses of its selfobject milieu, is disorganized at its core. Goldberg suggests that the proper goal of treatment in this situation is a reorganization of the self. Further, he suggests that reorganization is the work of psychoanalysis and asserts that the extent of the work to be done

> supports all the conditions for the conduct of an analysis, such as frequency of appointments, etc. A task like reorganizing a faulty self-symbol needs everything going for it, and making such an effort with less frequent contact adds a probably insurmountable burden.
> (Goldberg 1980, p. 69)

In summary, Goldberg claims that the proper therapeutic procedure for a given patient or client is determined by goal rather than by technique and, he emphasizes, the goal is determined by the state of the self. The answer to the question 'What are we doing, anyway?' is a function of whether the prescribed treatment is for repair or for reorganization. In addition, Goldberg's distinction between psychotherapy and psychoanalysis based on goal rather than method has the salient effect of relieving the psychotherapist from the burden, fueled by one's therapeutic ambition some of the time and by pressures from one's clinic or agency at other times, of accomplishing an improbable task.

I travel this momentary tangent to demonstrate further the utility a psychology concerned with issues of the self has for all therapists, as well as to make this useful distinction between psychotherapy and psychoanalysis. As I have asserted, Kohut addresses the psychoanalytic process throughout his work but his conceptualizations are applicable to the psychotherapeutic process as well. At the end of Chapter 11 I present a psychotherapy case to demonstrate this applicability.

SHOULD SOME ANALYSES OF SEVERE PERSONALITY AND BEHAVIOR DISORDERS REMAIN INCOMPLETE?

In the first part of *How Does Analysis Cure?*, Kohut discusses the major differences between self psychology and traditional theory. He defines mental health as he understands it and responds to his critics who misunderstood the termination of Mr. M's 'incomplete analysis' in *The Restoration of the Self* (1977). Kohut's critics believe he advocates terminating analyses early to protect patients from experiencing painful and distressing regressions, even if they are left with structural defects. Kohut wishes to correct that misunderstanding and locates the root of the problem in his failure adequately to convey his new definitions of psychological health and psychoanalytic cure.

To clarify the misunderstanding, he first repeats the basic tenets of his theory, contending that in the treatment of analyzable narcissistic personality disorders there is a spontaneous mobilization of thwarted childhood selfobject needs. The defective self attempts to complete its development through the mobilization of specific selfobject transferences. As in the analogous situation in classical analysis, the mobilization of these transferences is accompanied by resistances that are dealt with by interpretation. The defects in the self become structuralized via transmuting internalization and the working through of the selfobject transferences.

Kohut next presents his new definition of mental health. He asserts that the goal of the self, and the optimal outcome for the analytic process, is the establishment of a whole non-defective self capable of realizing the potential of its innate skills and talents. The establishment of a whole self leads to a creative and fulfilling life. Guided by this new definition, Kohut suggests that it is possible for analyses to be terminated despite their supposed incompleteness, as he explains through the following dynamic.

Development is never free from trauma, and the self, even in the face of serious and repeated trauma, searches for ways to ensure psychological survival. The self searches for new solutions to the frustration of its developmental needs. When one selfobject is traumatically frustrating and unable to satisfy essential narcissistic needs, the developing self turns to other available selfobjects. Kohut notes that during childhood some people are able to free themselves from seriously disturbed primary selfobjects, such as a psychotic mother. In a restitutive move that characterizes the resilience of the self, such people attempt to form a new relationship with another potential selfobject, such as the father, aunt, uncle or any other available caretaker. When the new selfobjects are reliable and healthy, the move is psychologically lifesaving. The new selfobjects fulfill essential narcissistic needs by reflecting the child's expansiveness in appropriate ways, allowing crucial idealizations to form and echoing a sense of shared humanity. Through its compensatory turn to the lifesaving second selfobject, the child is able to overcome the defects associated with the traumatic primary selfobject. As I mentioned in Chapters 7 and 8, Kohut calls the internalizations that develop around the second selfobject compensatory structures. These are structures that compensate for the defects created by the experience with the failed primary selfobject.

For people with narcissistic personality disorders, however, the rescue attempt fails because the compensatory selfobjects are unreliable and deficient, although to a lesser degree, in their selfobject functions. Though compensatory structures do indeed form, they are unstable and unreliable. Mr. M, whose controversial termination Kohut presented in *The Restoration of the Self* (1977), is such a person. He freed himself from his toxic mother but required an analytic experience to strengthen the unreliable compensatory structures that formed in relation to his idealizable but rejecting father.

Stabilization of compensatory structures through an analytic experience is a major therapeutic stratagem for Kohut, who, unlike his classical predecessors, does not insist upon the revival and thorough working through of the primary trauma. He believes that no positive gain can possibly come from that work since the failed selfobject is psychologically useless and the self has already extricated itself at great cost. He sees no value in excavating all the terrible trauma associated with the defective primary selfobject. He feels strongly that structure-building and consolidation of the self come from the revival of thwarted narcissistic needs mobilized in the specific selfobject transferences experienced with the analyst. The self, strengthened through the analytic process, will be able to consolidate the weakened compensatory structures, which eventually become important sources of narcissistic nourishment and sustenance. Describing this basic tenet, Kohut writes:

> But, to underscore the crucial issue, it is not possible to reactivate traumatic situations of infancy and childhood to which the self had on its own responded constructively during its early development. Even if the revival of these situations were feasible, moreover, no good purpose would be served if we could in fact bring it about.

In emphasizing this final point, I intend to clear up the misunderstanding of my friendly critic regarding certain passages in *The Restoration of the Self*. I argued in 1977, and I would reiterate now, that those traumatic aspects of its early selfobjects from which the nuclear self was able to withdraw successfully during its development are not reviveable in the narcissistic transference. They cannot be revived because the developing self had turned away from them early in life and, since it was able to shift to different sources of structure formation – sources that culminated in the formation of compensatory structures – it has no subsequent need for them.

(Kohut 1984, pp. 43–4)

Kohut's understanding that the self strives to ensure its survival and seeks its structural rehabilitation guides his definition of mental health and influences his goals for an analysis. He defines mental health, as I have emphasized throughout, as the possession of a structurally whole and/or rehabilitated self. Kohut is content to end an analysis when the self, bolstered by its compensatory structures, is firm, consolidated and capable of joyfully experiencing life. He does not insist upon the perfectionistic completion of goals held dear by various psychoanalytic theorists, as he describes:

I believe we can state with assurance that it is not a measure of pathology but a sign of resourcefulness and health when a self – nondefensively – demonstrates in the transference that it had, already during its early development, turned away from hopeless frustrations and found new paths or at least made partially successful moves in the new direction. The attempt to push such a self in therapy toward areas from which it had severed connections not only is doomed to failure, but also betrays a gross misunderstanding of the patient. By insisting that his analysand's disease conform to the specific mold that he holds to be universal and by insisting, furthermore, that the analysand submit to the particular procrustean therapeutic process that the analyst considers the sine qua non of true analysis – be it the resolution of the Oedipus complex, the reliving of the emotions of the paranoid–depressive position, the abreaction of the trauma of birth, the reexperiencing of an early injury to the self, or any other theory-limited panacea – the analyst who undertakes such an attempt puts obstacles in the patient's path to recovery.

(Kohut 1984, pp. 44–6)

For Kohut, then, termination of an analysis is appropriate when the structural restoration of the self is sufficient to make enhanced functioning possible, rather than when the analyst's preconceived theoretical issues have been considered.

Kohut's critics misunderstand his emphasis upon the functional rehabilitation of the self. They charge that he protected his patients from getting 'too upset' by terminating prematurely, before the chaotic depths can be reached. However, Kohut in reality was not afraid of emotional turmoil. In fact, throughout his work, especially in *Analysis of the Self*, he describes severe psychotic-like regressions that occur in his patients and provides the calming reassurance that with proper understanding the regressions can be analytically valuable and in time will safely abate. I believe that a portion of the rage-filled criticism Kohut receives relates to the injured therapeutic ambition some of his critics experience when he suggests avoiding unnecessary emotional chaos.

RE-EXAMINATION OF CASTRATION ANXIETY

In *How Does Analysis Cure?* (1984), Kohut presents his final understanding of castration anxiety. He stresses that his understanding has evolved from observations of transferences that have emerged during his clinical work. In drawing conclusions from his observations he acknowledges a basic assumption that informs his theorizing. The analytic process proceeds from the surface to the depths and the unfolding transference sequences repeat development but in reverse order. The most recently formed configurations emerge first and the earlier configurations appear later.

Kohut describes an oedipal phase that appears at the end of successful analyses of people with narcissistic personality and behavior disorders (1977). He believes that for these people, the strengthened self has become able, for the first time, to engage the oedipal issues. Because they have not been experienced before, the developmental issues of the oedipal phase that emerge in the analysis are unaffected by the trauma of unempathic oedipal selfobjects. Kohut calls this developmental period the 'oedipal stage' and distinguishes it from its pathological form, the oedipal complex.

From his observations, Kohut describes a three-stage sequence of the transferences that emerge during the oedipal stage of an analysis. Each transference is preceded by a stage of resistance illustrated in the following schema:

1 stage of initial resistance, which is generally severe;
2 *transference stage* of the oedipal complex dominated by experiences of severe castration anxiety;
3 phase of severe resistances;
4 *transference stage*, marked by fears of disintegration anxiety;
5 phase of resistance marked by mild anxiety, that differs from castration anxiety and alternates with a sense of joyous anticipation; and
6 *transference phase* of the oedipal stage, marked by a developmental step toward a gender-differentiated self.

Kohut postulates a dynamic for the normal oedipal stage and its pathologic outcome, based upon his observations of the oedipal drama as it emerges, untraumatized, in the clinical setting. In this dynamic, the healthy oedipal child enters the oedipal era with the experience of having been responded to by its selfobjects in appropriate ways. There has been no rejection of the child's need for confirmation of its vitality and assertiveness by a mirroring selfobject. The need to be soothed and uplifted by an idealized selfobject has not been frustrated and the need for the sustaining presence of an *alter ego* has also been met. The child anticipates that, as always before, it would be responded to by understanding selfobjects, and enters the oedipal stage with the exuberance of taking a new step that is characterized by feelings of intense affection and assertiveness. This is the story of the normal oedipal stage.

In the formation of an Oedipus complex, which Kohut believes is the pathological result of experiences with selfobjects that fail, the oedipal child is in for a surprise because the previously attuned parents are unable to respond with the same attunement as before. These parents are either stimulated by the child's intensified affection and respond preconsciously to the child in overstimulating ways or are challenged by the child's intensified assertiveness and respond preconsciously with a hostile–competitive attitude in response to the child's assertions. In his reconstructions, Kohut finds that the faulty parental responses are rarely verbal. Parents usually become confused by the child's new affects and withdraw from the child in a state of inhibition. The previously strong self of the normal oedipal child weakens in response to the parental stimulation, challenge and/or withdrawal. The weakened self then fragments, and the non-sexual oedipal affection and non-hostile oedipal assertiveness break down into overt sexuality and hostility. Kohut's description of the oedipal experience differs markedly from the classical position. He understands the oedipal complex to be a response to an unempathic environment rather than the expression of biologically based drives that are entirely internal and not affected by the environment. He describes the active dynamic for the oedipal girl and boy:

> [Oedipal] tensions occur when, following the break-up of its affectionate and assertive attitudes, the child experiences the pathological sexual drivenness and destructive hostility which arise pari pasu with the fragmentation or enfeeblement of its self. Subsequent to an oedipal phase that is marred by the failure of the parents to respond healthily to their child, a defect in the child's self is set up. Instead of the further development of a firmly cohesive self able to feel the glow of healthy pleasure in its affectionate and phase-appropriate sexual functioning and able to employ self-confident assertiveness in the pursuit of goals, we find throughout life a continuing propensity to experience the fragments of love (sexual fantasies) rather than love and the fragments of assertiveness (hostile fantasies) rather than assertiveness and to respond to these experiences – which always include the revival of the unhealthy selfobject experiences of childhood – with anxiety.
>
> (Kohut 1984, pp. 24–5)

Kohut's clinical approach to the transference neuroses is the same as in traditional psychoanalysis. The oedipal transferences are mobilized in the analysis and worked through via the systematic analysis of the defenses and the interpretation of the transferences. The goal of the classical analyst is to help the patient learn about and master his or her infantile lust and hostility. Classical theory teaches that the deepest levels of the psyche have been reached when the patient experiences his or her unconscious impulses, wishes and drives. Kohut's position is quite different, however. He holds that the oedipal complex forms within the matrix of a disturbed oedipal selfobject experience. For him, the core analytic work addresses the depression and narcissistic rage, associated with the oedipal child's flawed selfobject matrix, that always lies beneath the surface hostility and sexuality.

Kohut takes issue with the classical hypothesis that suggests the oedipal complex is a normal event in psychological development. While the ubiquitous nature of the oedipus complex is often cited as proof of its normality, Kohut insists upon making the distinction between ubiquity and normality. The frequent, even ubiquitous, nature of the oedipal complex is not evidence that it is normal. It is evidence that it is ubiquitous. Kohut asserts that the imperfection of selfobjects is ubiquitous. It is the imperfect responses of imperfect selfobjects, during the oedipal stage, that account for the ubiquitous appearance of the oedipal complex.

THE PROBLEM OF SCIENTIFIC OBJECTIVITY AND THE THEORY OF PSYCHOANALYTIC CURE

Before he can address the question of how analysis cures, Kohut finds it necessary to look at the analytic environment and its impact on the analysand. The classical position requires that the analytic environment be neutral so that the contents of the unconscious can emerge in the form of uncontaminated transferences. Kohut strongly disagrees with this position, arguing instead that the analytic environment cannot be neutral and, as such, the environment invariably affects the analytic process. Expanding the discussion of scientific objectivity he had begun in *The Restoration of the Self*, Kohut turns to the history of science and the changing ideas about scientific objectivity to further explain his disagreement with the classical position. The prevailing scientific attitude that informed Freud's thinking at the close of the nineteenth century was a science modeled after the methods of Newtonian physics. It dealt with observations of large particles of matter. Experiments were conducted, observations made and data collected without the observer having any apparent impact upon the observed. The data were considered pure and thought to represent Truth. Freud extended that orientation to the science of psychoanalysis in which the analyst was the neutral observer who had no effect upon the observed. Kohut's term for a psychoanalysis that studies the macro-agencies of the mental apparatus, such as the ego, id and superego, and overlooks the analyst's significance in the analytic situation is 'large particle' psychoanalysis.

Kohut suggests that his own perspective is similar to the model of a twentieth-century Planckian physics that studies micro-particles and understands that, at the molecular level, the observing instrument, by virtue of its presence in the environment under study, does have an impact upon the observed. It is important to note that Kohut refers here to the consequences of the analyst as a listening presence rather than to the analyst's impact upon the analytic environment through his or her countertransferences. Although he addresses countertransferential issues elsewhere (1971, 1984), he calls attention here to the effect a listening, understanding milieu has upon an analysand.

Kohut notes (1984, p. 216) a passing comment of Freud's that did acknowledge the analyst's non-countertransferential influence upon the analysand. In this famous statement Freud suggests that the analyst is not in a position to affect the patient until the patient has established a proper rapport with the analyst. Freud writes:

> It remains the first aim of the treatment to attach him to it and to the person of the doctor. To ensure this, nothing need be done but to give him time. If one exhibits a serious interest in him, carefully clears away the resistances that crop up at the beginning, and avoids making certain mistakes, he will himself form such an attachment and link the doctor up with one of the imagos of the people by whom he was accustomed to be treated with affection.
> (Freud 1913, pp. 139–40)

Freud's comment points to the area of influence Kohut feels Freud overlooked. This is, of course, the selfobject milieu which is central to the self psychological understanding of the analytic process. Addressing the impact the listening, understanding selfobject milieu has upon the analysand, Kohut writes:

> We need an orientation that acknowledges and then examines the analyst's influence in principle as an intrinsically significant human presence, not his influence via distorting countertransferences. The former kind of influence characterizes the psychoanalytic situation in general, but is exemplified par excellence in the working through process. Let me restate my last point most unambiguously. If we are in a situation in which a human being listens to us in order to understand us and explain us to ourselves, and we know that such listening and explaining will go on for a long, at first seemingly unlimited, time, we are not in a situation that can be properly defined as being neutral. On the contrary, it is a situation that, in its psychological impact on us is the very opposite of neutral – indeed it is a situation that may be said to provide us with the most crucial emotional experience for human psychological survival and growth: the attention of a selfobject milieu, that is a human surrounding that, via empathy, attempts to understand and participate in our psychological life. . . . Indeed, the analyst focuses his attention on the inner life of his patient, and the successes and failures of his understanding are the essential motor of the psychoanalytic process.
> (Kohut 1984, pp. 37–8)

Kohut argues that scientific objectivity is a myth, better understood as a relative objectivity, and calls for a new understanding of the analyst's role in the analytic environment. The analyst, rather than a mythologized neutral non-influencing observer, affects the process by his or her listening presence. In fact, it is the empathic presence of the analyst that invites the mobilization of dormant selfobject needs and functions as a 'motor' in the curative process.

THE NATURE OF THE PSYCHOANALYTIC CURE

Kohut's discussion of analytic cure is an excellent example of his didactic style. He uses his mastery of classical theory to facilitate a comparison of the classical positions with his own. He observes that cure, according to Freud's topographic model, is the result of an increased awareness of the contents of the Unconscious. In Freud's model, illness is due to the untamed drives and wishes sequestered within the Unconscious by forces that form the repression barrier. Cure comes as repression is diminished and the contents of the Unconscious are brought to awareness. In this model, the essence of cure lies in the expansion of knowledge. Cure, as Kohut understands it, does not lie in the expansion of knowledge, although an enhanced scope of self-awareness usually does develop.

Freud's tripartite model brought a change to the theory of cure. Freud's model was a machine-like apparatus, composed of several agencies that were in conflict over the expression, management and control of the drives. In this model, cure is the result of the ego's expanding its domain to gain dominance over the drives, which, in turn, lessens the need to retreat defensively from the guilt and anxiety generated by the drive derivatives. Kohut contrasts this model with his own perspective, where ego expansion does occur as a consequence of an analysis but is not necessarily the essence of the cure. In Kohut's model, ego expansion is a secondary result.

Elements of cure

What, then, is Kohut's theory of cure? How does self psychology understand the curative process? For Kohut, the curative process consists of three elements. The first two are technical and involve first, the analysis of defenses, and second, the working through of the unfolding transferences. Although these first two technical elements are the same as in classical psychoanalysis, the self psychological approach to defense, which I will describe later, and Kohut's understanding of the transferences (1966, 1968, 1971, 1977) differ significantly from the classical position.

The third element, in Kohut's understanding of analytic cure, differs radically from the classical position. Yet this element is the most important. Kohut considers it 'the essential one because it defines the aim and the result of the cure' (1984, p. 66). The third element is the establishment of empathic communication between the self and its selfobjects on mature adult levels instead of the level of repressed or split-off unmodified narcissistic needs. This shift in the goal of an analysis comes from Kohut's understanding of the development of normal narcissism and the importance of selfobjects. Drawing upon his clinical observations, he asserts that the need for selfobjects exists throughout life. He argues that through an analysis, the self is freed from the early needs that bind it to archaic selfobjects. Through an analysis, the *unmodified needs* for merger with an idealized selfobject and/or mirroring by an affirming selfobject are diminished. The need for selfobjects and their functions never vanishes, however, but rather persists throughout life. Unfettered by the bondage that tied it to archaic selfobjects, the self after analysis is freer to chose selfobjects at higher levels of maturity.

The goal of an analysis, in Kohut's view, is the enhanced ability of a strengthened self to choose healthier sustaining selfobject experiences. As can readily be seen, this view differs radically from that of the classical position, which works toward the Western value-laden goals of separation and independence. Kohut's thinking about the perpetual need for selfobjects has evolved from the thoughts he expressed in his early work when he still operated within the conceptualizations of ego psychology. In 1971, Kohut conceptualized the adult personality as an autonomous organization, 'an organization that had relinquished its ties to its selfobjects, that had overcome the need for a nurturing selfobject milieu' (1984, p. 218). Freed from the Western ethic of 'independence' and 'autonomy,' Kohut is able to perceive the lifelong need for selfobjects. The *sine qua non* of the analytic cure becomes the gradual establishment of empathic contact with mature selfobjects rather than 'autonomy.'

Strengthening through optimal failures

Having defined the essential goal and outcome of an analysis, Kohut turns his attention to the process that strengthens the self during an analysis. As he had noted earlier, non-traumatic failures on the part of the selfobject analyst are essential to the analytic process. In this regard Kohut makes the following technical recommendation:

[T]he quietly sustaining matrix provided by the spontaneously established selfobject transference to the analyst that establishes itself in the early phases of analysis is disrupted time and again by the analyst's unavoidable, yet only temporary and thus nontraumatic, empathy failures – that is, his 'optimal failures.' In response to the analyst's errors in understanding or in response to the analyst's erroneous or inaccurate or otherwise improper interpretations, the analysand turns back temporarily from his reliance on empathy to the archaic selfobject relationships (e.g., to the remobilization of the need for merger with archaic idealized omnipotent selfobjects or remobilization of the need for immediate and perfect mirroring) that he had already tentatively abandoned in the primary selfobject transference of the analysis. . . . Having noticed the patient's retreat, the analyst must watch the analysand's behavior and listen open-mindedly to his associations. By listening open-mindedly, I mean that he must resist the temptation to squeeze his understanding of the patient into the rigid mold of whatever theoretical preconceptions he may hold, be they Kleinian, Rankian, Jungian, Adlerian, classical-analytic, or, yes, self psychological, until he has more accurately grasped the essence of the patient's need and can convey his understanding to the patient via a more correct interpretation.

(Kohut 1984, pp. 66–7)

Warning against the practice of applying any explanatory theory with an orthodox rigidity, Kohut emphasizes that empathic immersion into the experience of the analysand creates the optimal analytic environment. He acknowledges that a listener must have theories to guide and order what is heard and experienced but, he warns, the theories are to be helpers, not masters. Theories are to be held in the background, where they serve as organizers, while one listens openly to each experience of the analysand without forcing that understanding into a rigid mold dictated by the theory *du jour*. Nevertheless, the analyst, no matter how open-minded, will eventually misunderstand the analysand. No harm will come if the analyst can remain open to the possibility that he or she might be wrong and can allow the patient to set him or her right. The error will become an 'optimal failure' if the analyst is able to recognize the misunderstanding and recognize the patient's response of withdrawal, rage, anxiety, etc. The analyst's task becomes, then, to acknowledge, non-defensively, the mistaken understanding and the patient's reaction to it and then to interpret, non-critically, the dynamics of the patient's retreat. This will occur many times in the course of an analysis. As Kohut describes:

> Each optimal failure will be followed by an increase in the patient's resilience vis-à-vis empathy failures both inside and outside the analytic situation; that is, after each optimal failure new self structures will be acquired and existing ones will be firmed. These developments, in turn, lead to a rise in the patient's basic level of self-esteem, however minimal and by itself imperceptible to analysand and analyst each such accretion of structure may be.
> (Kohut 1984, p. 69)

Empathic resonance and non-traumatic frustration

Kohut notes that two events are necessary for the normal developmental process to build a healthy self. The first is the experience of a basic attunement between the self and its selfobjects. The second is the repetition of non-traumatic failures with the selfobjects which Kohut calls 'optimal frustrations.' This two-step developmental process has two consequences:

1 Optimal frustration, through the process of transmuting internalization (Kohut 1971), is responsible for the creation of new internal structures.
2 These new internal structures enable the self to shift from the need to merge with idealized, mirroring and alter ego selfobjects, in order to feel whole, to an ability to be sustained by the empathic resonance of the selfobjects in adult life. The self-esteem functions, once performed by the merged selfobjects of childhood, eventually are provided by the adult selfobject milieu of family, friends, work and culture.

Kohut summarizes the analytic cure this way:

> A treatment will be successful because . . . an analysand was able to reactivate, in a selfobject transference, the needs of a self that had been thwarted in childhood. In the analytic situation, these reactivated needs were kept alive and exposed, time and again, to the vicissitudes of optimal frustrations until the patient ultimately acquired the reliable ability to sustain his self with the aid of the selfobject resources available in his adult surroundings. According to self psychology then, the essence of the analytic cure resides in a

patient's newly acquired ability to identify and seek out appropriate selfobjects – both mirroring and idealizable – as they present themselves in his realistic surroundings and to be sustained by them.
(Kohut 1984, p. 77)

The analytic process brings structure and firmness to the self, but it does not bring freedom from the need for selfobject experiences. Kohut draws the analogy between the need for empathic resonance in psychological life and the need for oxygen in physical life. Both are vital. The successful analysis does not bring independence from objects. On the contrary, it enables the self to choose healthier, more appropriate selfobjects and to make better use of them for its lifelong narcissistic needs.

Surveying the nature of the analytic cure, Kohut contends that analysis provides a 'corrective emotional experience' rather than a gaining of insight. The defects in the self are corrected via the experiences of being understood, in an empathic manner, and non-traumatically frustrated in a structure-building, 'optimally' frustrating way. Kohut maintains that the term 'corrective emotional experience' is a useful one despite its unfortunate association with Franz Alexander's ill-fated misunderstanding of the analytic process. Lest he be misunderstood, Kohut emphasizes that he is not suggesting a corrective emotional experience through love, empathy and understanding. To begin with, empathy is the tool an analyst uses to gather data, not the active agent of cure. Secondarily, but not less important, the same empathy that gathers data provides a beneficial effect since the experience of being empathically understood is, as Kohut notes, the oxygen of psychological life. To lessen the fears of those concerned that the experience of being empathically understood forever binds the patient to the analyst, Kohut notes that empathic resonance reactivates a developmental push which moves the patient toward new modes of narcissistic sustenance outside the analytic situation.

Chapter 11

How Does Analysis Cure?: Part II
The therapeutic process reconsidered

THE SELF PSYCHOLOGICAL REASSESSMENT OF THE THERAPEUTIC PROCESS

The analytic setting: the analyst's attitude, the analytic ambience and the theory of cure

Since change in theory ultimately brings change in technique, we must ask, what technical change does Kohut's new theory bring? Is the analytic attitude any different as a result of his theory? Does the ambience in the consulting-room change?

Kohut believes that the analytic approach toward patients with disorders of the self is the same as the approach of traditional psychoanalysis. His new awareness of his patient's narcissistic needs, however, has altered his attitude toward the expression of those needs as they emerge in the transferences and creates a new ambience in his consulting-room. With his new understanding, Kohut as analyst considers himself to be the target of arrested selfobject needs. He now understands the reactivated needs for merger with an idealized object, affirmation by a mirroring object or twinship with a humanity-conferring alter ego as positive events, welcomed as movement along a previously obstructed developmental path. He neither rejects nor censors these blossoming expressions of arrested narcissism. Instead, he explains them as legitimate needs, gone into hiding because of traumatic frustrations during childhood, that are coming alive because of the treatment. The reactivated selfobject needs are greeted as a positive movement in the analysis.

The drive psychologist, in contrast, sees the idealization of the analyst and the grandiose–exhibitionistic wish as defensive maneuvers, mobilized to protect the patient against the guilt and anxiety associated with the underlying sexual and aggressive drives. Understood as defenses, these reactivated selfobject needs are thought to oppose the analytic work that uncovers the drives. Since drive–defense theory mistakenly assumes these narcissistic developments to be blocking maneuvers, the correct drive–defense technique is to counter these seemingly unwelcome defensive movements.

Drive–defense psychology and self psychology carry very different therapeutic attitudes. By accepting the narcissistic transferences, with their underlying selfobject needs, Kohut creates a friendlier atmosphere in his consulting-room. To create the friendlier atmosphere, the self psychologically informed analyst does not behave differently. No special activity is necessary beyond understanding and accepting the reality of the patient's experience and allowing the often humiliating selfobject needs to emerge. Classical theorists conceive of the expressions of arrested narcissism as defensive movements and adopt a subtly suspicious, critical attitude that favors the uncovering of the hidden forces over the reality of the patient's experience.

Kohut cites 'The Two Analyses of Mr. Z' (Kohut 1979) to demonstrate how his analytic attitude changed as a result of his awareness of selfobject needs. He notes, in retrospect, that his work contained a subtle sense of rejection and censure when he understood the expressions of narcissistic needs as escapist regressions from the 'real issues.' The ambience of the analytic setting changed and a friendlier, less moralistic atmosphere was established when he understood and accepted his patients' narcissistic needs as valid and legitimate. With Mr. Z, for example, Kohut understood that the arrested childhood narcissistic needs were the primary factor in Mr. Z's disorder and that their mobilization in the analysis enabled the resumption of development. Understanding Mr. Z's selfobject needs as primary and not defensive, Kohut could welcome their appearance as progressive moves in the analysis. In a telling passage Kohut describes the changed ambience in his consulting room:

> If there is one thing I have learned during my life as an analyst, it is the lesson that what my patients tell me is likely to be true – that many times when I believed that I was right and my patients were wrong, it turned out, though often only after a prolonged search, that *my* rightness was superficial whereas *their* rightness was profound.
>
> (Kohut 1984, p. 94)

Technical considerations: understanding, explaining and the therapeutic impact of erroneous interpretations

The question of what effects a cure can be addressed from two perspectives: one describes the reactivated developmental processes that bring about the cure, and the other describes the technical considerations that activate the developmental processes. Throughout the bulk of his work, Kohut addresses the first perspective in great detail. He describes how analysis cures through the reactivation of arrested developmental processes. In *How Does Analysis Cure?* (1984) he turns his attention to the second perspective, the technical considerations that activate the process. Here he addresses the practical issues of what the analyst actually does to reactivate the dormant configurations and help them move along their developmental path.

To answer the 'how to' question of what the analyst does, Kohut asks the perplexing question of how, if his (Kohut's) theories are correct, is it possible that oedipal neuroses are treated successfully by analysts using traditional theories? How might we explain the successful treatment of narcissistic disorders by analyses employing other, even divergent, theories?

Kohut offers the work of a Kleinian analyst to address the technical considerations of this seeming paradox. He presents a vignette in which the analyst tells her patient that she must cancel an appointment in the near future. At the session following the announcement, the patient is silent and does not respond to the analyst's request to say what she is experiencing. The analyst responds to the withdrawal in a warm tone, saying that she believes her announcement of the cancellation has changed the patient's perception of her from the previously experienced good, warm breast to the now bad, cold and non-feeding breast. In addition, the analyst said, the patient has come to feel a sadistic rage and wants to pull the analyst to pieces by biting and tearing at her. To defend against these impulses, the analyst adds, the patient has inhibited her activity, especially her oral activity, so that now she cannot speak. The patient relaxes. She expresses some biting fantasies toward the analyst and feels better. Both agree that the analyst has been restored to her previous position of the good breast.

Kohut suggests that the interpretation might have been equally effective if it had been expressed in oedipal terms, explaining that the patient feels abandoned by a mother who is locking the bedroom door in order to have intercourse with the father. It could also have been effectively presented in self psychological terms, explaining that the patient's self-esteem has been lowered by the announcement of the analyst's absence just as her self-esteem was lowered in childhood when the supportive and affirming cook was abruptly fired by her cold distant mother.

Does this mean Kohut is an eclectic for whom anything is acceptable? On the contrary, Kohut believes that only one interpretation is correct although all might have a beneficial effect. How is that possible?

Kohut refers to Edward Glover's attempt to answer the question in Glover's well-known paper (1931) describing the therapeutic effect of an inexact interpretation. Kohut disagrees with Glover's assessment that the beneficial effect of the inexact interpretation is due to the patient's suggestibility. Kohut feels that whereas the articulated content of an interpretation might be incorrect, the essential communicated message can be correct. In the vignette of the Kleinian analyst, the essential message, expressed by the analyst with humanity and warmth, conveys the understanding that the patient is deeply upset because the appointment has been canceled. The analyst's appreciation of her patient's upset is the essence of what the patient has heard. The dynamic explanation of the upset is not essential and can be expressed in Kleinian, Freudian or self psychological terms. The analyst, however, cannot communicate her understanding and create its reparative response if her message is conveyed without appropriate warmth or in words that do not appreciate the upset.

Kohut uses this vignette to demonstrate that a complete technical intervention contains two components:

1 an *understanding* component; and
2 an *explaining* component.

In practice these two components or phases of an interpretation are interconnected and often come together in a single intervention. Kohut notes that some patients need an especially long period of understanding alone before they can be presented with explanations.

The vignette of the Kleinian analyst is a specimen intervention. Kohut uses it to dissect the understanding phase from the explanatory phase. The Kleinian analyst correctly understands her patient's disrupted experience over the missed appointment and conveys that understanding despite what Kohut feels is an incorrect dynamic explanation. The analyst's 'off the mark' explanation is tolerable for the patient because the core experience has been understood. Inexact interpretations are beneficial because they participate in the correct first phase of the two-phase interpretive process. Despite their inexactness, 'off the mark' explanations contribute to the laying down of psychological structure. How, Kohut asks, is it possible that only the first step of the two-step interpretive process can be effective in laying down structure? How can understanding alone build structure? Is this not simply a variation of cure through love, kindness and understanding?

To answer, Kohut cites his core tenet, namely that the process that builds psychological structure is initiated by optimal frustration. That being the case, how is the analyst's communication of her understanding an optimal frustration? Kohut answers:

> It is frustrating because, despite the analyst's *understanding* of what the patient feels and his *acknowledgement* that the patient's upset is legitimate . . . the analyst still does not *act* in accordance with the patient's need. Thus, in the case of the Kleinian analyst, the regularity and continuity of the sessions will still be interrupted by the analyst's forthcoming absence. It is *optimally* frustrating because the communication is still in compliance with the patient's need – though to a lesser degree. It is optimal *frustration* rather than optimal *gratification* because, through the analyst's more or less accurate understanding, an empathic bond is established (reestablished) between analyst and patient that substitutes for the de facto fulfillment of the patient's need. All these components, it should be noted, still remain part of the understanding phase of the basic therapeutic unit.
>
> (Kohut 1984, pp. 102–3)

In the understanding phase of an intervention, the analyst communicates her awareness that the patient has experienced an upset with the analyst. The upset is the frustration. The analyst's communication of her understanding diminishes the traumatic intensity of the frustration which makes it an *optimal* frustration. Kohut examines the optimal frustration in detail and concludes that it contains a sequence of three microscopic events:

1 *Need*. The reactivation of early narcissistic needs is experienced in the selfobject transference with the analyst. (In the vignette we are studying, the revived need for a continuous merger with an idealized selfobject is expressed in the wish for the analyst to be continuously present.)
2 *Disruption*. A disappointment of the reactivated narcissistic needs by

the selfobject ensues. (In this vignette, the disappointment of the revived selfobject needs is precipitated by the analyst's announcement of the coming cancellation.)
3 *Repair.* The empathic bond between the self and the selfobject is re-established. (Repair is effected by the analyst's communication of her understanding that the announcement of the cancellation had disrupted the patient's internal state.)

Kohut contends that this sequence of need–disruption–repair, as part of an optimal frustration, occurs in healthy development as well as in the analytic situation. It is ubiquitous and occurs in the traditional as well as in the self psychological psychoanalytic situation:

> I believe that psychoanalysis – traditional psychoanalysis – has *always* achieved its successes via the three step process that I have laid out and that the only real forward move provided by self psychology is its expansion of psychoanalytic theory, specifically, its theoretical elucidation of the whole area of the reactivation of thwarted developmental needs in the transference via the discovery of the selfobject transferences.
> (Kohut 1984, p. 104)

Setting aside the often snide question of whether something is, in fact, 'analytic,' Kohut turns to the question of what is a true analytic intervention. For him, it must include both the understanding and explaining components of the interpretation. Both are essential to the analytic process. This raises yet another question. If structure-building can occur with the optimally frustrating understanding phase alone, why is the explanation phase necessary? What is its function and what does it add to the process?

To answer, Kohut examines the explanation phase and delineates yet two more elements:

(a) *The dynamic element.* This is a statement, made by the analyst, that explains the patient's current emotional reaction in terms of the revived developmental needs that are now experienced in the transference.
(b) *The genetic element.* This is a statement, made by the analyst, that considers the patient's early life experiences and uses them to explain the origins of the current transference experience.

The following is an expanded version of the complete interpretation for the specimen situation we have been studying. In it the analyst responds to her patient's withdrawal after announcing the upcoming cancellation.

1 *Understanding phase*:
   'You don't feel like talking to me because you were upset by my announcing that we will miss a session soon. It seemed offhanded and abrupt and you felt hurt.'
2 *Explanation phase*:
   'You feel this way because:'
   (a) Dynamic statement:
   'You have come to count on me for a feeling of safety and wholeness and feel disrupted when you are cut off.'
   (This statement provides an explanation of the idealizing transference and the experience of its rupture.)

   and

   (b) Genetic statement:
   'You are especially sensitive to this kind of disruption because when you were little you, like all children, needed the consistent, uninterrupted presence of your mother in order to feel safe and whole. Your lonely and depressed mother was taken away from you frequently – often without much notice – to go on her long trips to spend time with her mother, leaving you with that series of nannies, none of whom really knew you very well.'
   (This statement explains, in a non-judgmental way, the original need for the idealized selfobject and the traumatic disruptions that occurred during childhood, sensitizing the patient to the current disruption.)

To return to the function of the explanation phase, Kohut believes that this phase increases the impact of the understanding phase. In doing so it qualitatively changes the nature of the entire interpretation. The complete genetic–dynamic explanation has a twofold effect upon the patient:

1 The patient's trust in the reality of the empathic bond with the analyst is strengthened as the analyst conveys the depth of his or her understanding. This experience also deepens the patient's empathic understanding of him- or herself.
2 The two-step genetic–dynamic explanation provides a lasting way for the patient to think about the meaning of the patient's transference experience. Over time, the understanding phase, by

itself, tends to become vague and disconnected. The addition of the complete dynamic–genetic explanation enables the patient to think about his or her transferential experiences within the context of the patient's life story. Understood in context, the disruption has greater meaning and even enables the patient to comprehend similar experiences in other situations when the analyst is not present. The dynamic–genetic explanation is an important tool in the working-through process.

Repeated many, many times in the course of an analysis, this two-step interpretive unit, understanding followed by explanation, is the technical element that Kohut believes leads to psychoanalytic cure. This technical maneuver is the same in any analysis where transferences are interpreted and worked through, regardless of the analyst's theoretical orientation. This maneuver is not unique to a self psychologically informed treatment.

Can new structures be created?

The building of psychological structure is the essential element in the curative process. Kohut asks whether the structures formed during an analysis are new or whether they are rehabilitated structures, present from childhood but in a weakened state. He answers that totally new structures cannot be created, for a nuclear self cannot be established *de novo*. The structures of an analysis are rehabilitations of old, faulty, shaky structures. Analytic treatment cannot provide what was not there originally. This understanding carries diagnostic and prescriptive implications. It posits that a patient must possess the rudiments of a self for a psychoanalytic treatment to be effective. Accessibility to an analytic cure requires the capacity to reactivate the arrested narcissistic needs of childhood within transferences that are mobilized in the analytic situation. The analytic treatment Kohut outlines is not effective for people who are psychotic in either an overt or covert way.

SUMMARY OF KOHUT'S ESSENTIAL ELEMENTS OF AN ANALYTIC CURE

There follows a summary of the elements Kohut considers essential to the analytic cure, in outline form. It is intended to provide a visual representation of the material and a concise way to think about cure as Kohut conceives it.

1 *Psychological health*: Kohut's new definition of health with its corresponding new goal of analytic treatment.

   (a) Psychological health, according to Kohut, is expressed in a functional continuum, from one pole of the self to the other. It is the result of a healthy, structure-promoting childhood or the result of a successful analysis in which the structures, thwarted during childhood, develop through the remobilization of arrested narcissistic configurations.

   (b) Psychological health is expressed through a life in which the functional continuum and wholeness of the self enable the expression of one's innate talents and skills which, in turn, become enhancing sources of narcissistic fulfillment.

2 *Structure-building processes*: the reactivated developmental processes responsible for the newly strengthened structures.

   (a) Rehabilitation of the defective structures occurs through the *mobilization* of the arrested narcissistic needs that now appear in the form of selfobject transference experiences with the analyst.

   (b) *Transmuting internalization* (initiated by optimal frustrations) is the process responsible for strengthening the self once the above-noted mobilization occurs.

3 *Technique*: the two-phased intervention which fosters structuralization.

   (a) *Understanding phase of the intervention*: the analyst obtains data about the patient's inner life, through empathic immersion into the patient's affective experience, and communicates that understanding to the patient when appropriate. Although empathy is the analyst's data-gathering tool, not a therapeutic technique, the patient's experience of being empathically understood is essential to psychological life. It secondarily carries therapeutic benefit.

   (b) *Explanation phase of the intervention*: the analyst adds an understanding of the patient's early experiences (genetic reconstructions) to the understanding of a current situation. In a non-intellectualized way, the analyst explains how a particular early experience has been replayed in the dynamic of the current situation. Explanations, even though sensitively delivered, are slightly removed from the immediacy of current experience. They add a cognitive element to the understanding. This allows the patient to think about his or her experience within the context of their life, aids the working-through process and ultimately strengthens the self.

The self psychological approach to defense and resistance

Although it is self-evident, I will repeat the axiom that an understanding of the forces that create an illness informs the rational attempt to treat it. Let us turn, for a moment, to an example from physical medicine. When locally invaded by bacteria, the body protects itself against a generalized infection by encapsulating the invading bacteria in a defensive structure such as an abscess. The abscess wall, however, protects the invading bacteria from the full effect of the body's immune response, enabling the bacteria to grow in the protected environment of the defensive structure. Informed by this understanding, the technique for treating an abscess is to open the wall and drain its contents.

Just as our understanding of the process of abscess formation determines its treatment, so our in-depth understanding of a given psychological state dictates our approach to its treatment. One's theory of the mind determines one's clinical approach to a psychological issue. With this appreciation, I turn to the technical management of defense and resistance in psychoanalysis. The psyche responds to the threatened invasion of troublesome feelings and affect states with a range of defenses. In the clinical situation, the defenses are called resistances. Historically, defense and resistance analysis has occupied a central position in the psychoanalytic armamentarium and has been guided predominantly by Freud's models of the mind. I will first discuss the classical approach to defense and resistance and then turn to Kohut's understanding of these psychologically protective maneuvers.

Freud's topographic model conceived of an Unconscious that contains drive-wishes, walled off from consciousness, similar to the way toxic contents of an abscess are walled off from the body. According to this theory, the technique for treating mental illness resembles the medical treatment of an abscess. The protective structure, which in the case of mental illness is composed of the defenses and resistances, is to be pierced and the toxic contents (the drive-wishes and associated disturbing affects) are to be exposed. Defense and resistance analysis – piercing the defensive armor surrounding the toxic unconscious material – is a major component of traditional analytic technique. Freud formalized this medical approach when he suggested that analysts should 'model themselves during psycho-analytic treatment on the surgeon, who puts aside all his feelings, even his human sympathy' (1912, p. 115).

Later, Freud's structural theory introduced the concept of psychic agencies (1923). According to that model, cure requires that the ego tame the unconscious drives. Analytic technique, in this model, involves educating the patient about the existence of the drives as they present themselves in the transference and in other enactments. Because the drive-wishes are laden with anxiety and guilt, however, the patient protects him- or herself against an awareness of the drive-wishes by employing various unconscious characterologic defenses. The classical analyst sees the patient's emerging defenses as a resistance to progress of the analysis since they oppose the knowledge of the drives. The analyst's listening is guided by a sensitivity to the presence of resistances. The analyst's major technical thrust focuses on overcoming the resistances by identifying their existence and interpreting their defensive function. For the classical analyst, the analysis of defense and resistance is an end in itself. The underlying depressions and the thwarted psychological development of a defective self that Kohut considers to be the core of the personality are not a central focus.

Freud's traditional models explain mental processes such as slips of the tongue, dreams, inhibitions and various symptoms, but they do not explain the complex mental states of humankind. They provide an adequate explanation for neither the formation of personality nor the effects of arrests upon the formation of the self. Although ego psychologists extended the structural model when they considered developmental issues and paid attention to the stunted growth of an arrested ego, they still emphasized the functions of the ego, rather than the core depletion.

For the self psychologist, in contrast, illness is the result not of unconscious drives but of an arrest in the development of the self. The therapeutic effort is not to expand knowledge and increase the ego's domain. For the self psychologist, cure is effected by the rehabilitation of the enfeebled structures of the self. Rehabilitation occurs through the mobilization of the selfobject transferences, understood as expressions of selfobject needs and explained within their historical context. Kohut considers the traditional approach to defenses and his own changed perspective:

> [T]he analysis of drive-wishes, defenses, and resistances has long constituted a therapeutic end station. Analysts ... have not

traditionally focused on this constellation as a transitional issue pointing to more significant, underlying problems of the patient. Instead they have concentrated on it at length in the belief that once drive-wishes, defenses, and resistances were thoroughly analyzed and worked through, everything else would follow. Needless to say, self psychology, in both its conception of scientific objectivity and its governing theoretical commitments, takes issue with this traditional belief . . .

My personal preference is to speak of the 'defensiveness' of patients . . . and not of their 'resistances.' . . .

Thus, the analyst – and especially the self psychologically informed analyst – who has achieved a degree of therapeutic mastery will only very rarely look at his patient in terms of his drive-wishes and defenses; . . . Defense motivation in analysis will be understood in terms of activities undertaken in the service of psychological survival, that is, as the patient's attempt to save at least that sector of his nuclear self, however small and precariously established it may be, that he has been able to construct and maintain despite serious insufficiencies in the development-enhancing matrix of selfobjects of childhood.

(Kohut 1984, pp. 114–15)

In a major shift away from the classical perspective, Kohut sees his patients' protectiveness as their best attempts to keep their selves safe from the anticipated destructiveness and intrusions of the old, failed selfobjects. He does not consider their protections to be a resistance against the progress of the analysis. Instead, he sees the protectiveness as the healthiest means available to ensure the safety and wholeness of the self until that hoped-for time when the self can resume its stunted growth.

Kohut calls the employment of the characterologic protective maneuvers 'the principle of the primacy of self preservation.' He believes that preservation of the psychological self is the basic thrust of every person and, in an effort to preserve itself in a toxic environment, the self hides beneath a protective facade. From compliance to aggression, from withdrawal to competence, the self uses any and all forms to keep itself hidden and safe. During the course of treatment the specific nature of these protections is elaborated. The so-called resistances, then, are present to keep the self safe, not to defend against the awareness of the drive-wishes.

Although this understanding might seem similar to the traditional psychoanalytic technique of unearthing defenses, in fact it is quite different. The purpose of the elaboration of the protective facade, from a self psychological perspective, is not to expand the ego's knowledge in an effort to help it gain mastery over the drive-wishes. Instead, the goal is to help the patient realize the extent to which the integrity of the self has been threatened and to understand and explain how things came to be the way they are. The analytic work emphasizes the function the defenses serve to keep the self whole and safe from the destructive effects of the failed selfobjects. The analyst's empathic understanding of the protective maneuvers enhances the selfobject bond and aides in the forward movement of the treatment. Kohut describes his attitude regarding the protective maneuvers of the self when he writes:

> Is the patient's hiding of the needs of his defective self as they become activated in the transference analogous to the way in which the traditional analyst sees the analysand opposing the pain and anxiety that he would have to face if he allowed his drive-wishes toward the father-analyst to emerge? Decidedly not. All these so called 'resistances' serve the basic ends of the self; they never have to be 'overcome.'
>
> (Kohut 1984, p. 148)

Clinical illustration

One of my patients demonstrates the applicability of Kohut's conceptualizations in the conduct of a psychodynamic psychotherapy. Goldberg's (1980) differentiation between an injured self and a disorganized self is useful in this discussion, where I focus on a defensive posture that protected an injured self. Once I recognized the protection for what it was I was able to reach the depths of the injury. A repair was eventually effected and the self returned to its developmental track.

Cindy was a passive, nearly inept woman, barely able to make decisions in the conduct of her daily life. She looked and acted like a frail child, asking anxiously how to understand simple situations. A bright woman, she felt no ability to provide her own answers. It was as though she had no mind of her own. In time, I noticed that she adopted this 'brainless' stance whenever she was stimulated by a strong affective experience. The exact nature of the affect seemed irrelevant. Her 'brainless' response seemed stimulated by the intensity of the affect rather than its content.

Cindy, the second child in a sibship of four, was born to a covertly psychotic mother who functioned socially but who was overwhelmed and irrational in her mothering. Cindy's mother did not understand and could not respond appropriately to Cindy's childhood inquisitiveness, playfulness and intelligence. In fact, her mother was enraged at evidence of Cindy's competence. Cindy's mother had an intense tie to her own mother and sister. The three (mother, grandmother and aunt) functioned as a single organism with their own set of rules and culture. Any family member who acted outside the family culture met with either overt rage or a deadly, silent withdrawal. Obedience and compliance were rewarded; initiative and independence were punished.

Cindy's psychologically overwhelmed mother had a maid who helped care for the four children. The maid was a warm, reassuring, quiet but strong woman who loved and enjoyed the children. Cindy had many fond memories of the maid, who rescued her from frightening situations, in contrast to her mother, who seemed to make terrors worse. Cindy's father was another responsive presence in the home. He was caring, full of life and an antidote to her toxic mother.

Cindy was sixteen years old when, tragically, her father died. In her characteristic way, Cindy's mother was unable to confront the tragedy. Although Cindy's father lived for several days following his myocardial infarct, her mother was unable to tell any of the children how seriously ill he was. They were not allowed to visit with him in the hospital and Cindy laments the lost opportunity to say good-bye. When her father did die, Cindy's mother sent for their pediatrician, who injected the children with a sedative.

While alive, Cindy's father was a domineering presence. Larger than life, he seemed to possess the answer to all Cindy's questions. Although in reality he was probably controlling and overbearing, Cindy remembers him as an affirming, non-malignant force to whom she turned, in a compensatory way, to overcome her mother's destructive emotional inadequacies. Father's precipitous death was devastating. It created a profound, long-lasting disruption. For years Cindy was unable to acknowledge the reality of his loss. She maintained the tie to her beloved father through magic, rituals and her characterologic stance of the helpless know-nothing child, in need of another to be her brain.

Cindy was able to retain the feeling of her father's presence as long as she lacked a brain of her own. Her marked passivity also helped Cindy maintain her troubled tie to her rageful mother, who rejected Cindy whenever she appeared strong and competent. Although terrifying, Cindy's tie to her mother was better than the isolation she would have experienced alone. To keep her self safe, while she was tied to her mother, Cindy hid beneath the masquerade of the brainless, helpless child.

Classical theory would frame this constricted woman's marked passivity as a defensive retreat from her sexuality, strength and competence. This defense would be seen as Cindy's unconscious attempt to protect herself against her mother's fantasied rage which, in turn, would be her mother's retaliatory response to Cindy's love for her father and competitive feelings toward her mother. Cindy's regressed behavior would be understood by the classical analyst as the statement, 'I'm no threat to you, mother, I'm a helpless little girl.'

Another level of Cindy's paralyzing passivity would be understood as the expression of a self-imposed punishment. The fantasy motivating the need for punishment would be her belief that it was she who had caused her father's death. In this fantasy, his death would be Cindy's punishment for her incestuous and murderous drive-wishes. The goal of a classical treatment would be to provide the ego with an awareness of the unconscious wishes so that the ego could gain mastery over the drives. To accomplish this, treatment would focus on Cindy's repeated defensive attempts to keep the drive-wishes, expressed in the transference and other resistances, out of awareness.

The self-psychologically informed approach is fundamentally different. Although a long time passed before I grasped the full meaning of Cindy's remarkable passivity and ineptness, I did understand that her passivity protected an enfeebled and hidden self. I did not assume that her passivity was a defensive retreat from her drive-wishes, which needed to be exposed. I did not understand Cindy's fantasy life as the elaboration of unconscious drives. Instead, following Kohut, I understood Cindy within the context of her selfobject milieu.

The understanding phase of this treatment, in which Cindy communicated her depression and the terrifying experience of her psychotic mother, lasted many years. Eventually, Cindy came to understand the depth of her mother's illness and its impact upon her psychological development, including her need to be 'little' in order to be safe.

As we worked, Cindy spoke often of Dorothy in Frank Baum's *The Wizard of Oz*. She identified with Dorothy, the young woman lost, searching for wholeness and the safety of home. Cindy understood Dorothy's travel mates as fragments of a broken self: the Scarecrow without a brain; the Tin Man without a lively, feeling heart; and the Lion without courage. She longed for the wizard who, like her omnipotent father, could magically put her back together.

The predominant transference in the treatment was an idealization which I understood initially as the remobilization of Cindy's arrested need for an idealized selfobject. The idealization, however, was remarkable in that it did not change over time. I had predicted its gradual diminution as structure accrued but it was unrelenting in its sameness. Eventually I realized that the idealization did not exist in the service of renewed growth. Rather, it was part of a vast facade that protected a terrified and weakened self.

Together, we learned that being inept, brainless and 'little' kept Cindy safe from the rages of her psychotic mother. It also helped maintain the life-sustaining connection to her lost father. The transference, in which I had all the answers and Cindy had none, was *not* a defensive retreat from the dangers associated with Cindy's unconscious drives, nor was it due to the mobilization of idealizing selfobject needs. Instead, it was an effort on Cindy's part to feel whole and safe by enacting, in the transference, the childhood memory of her lost father. In addition, Cindy's childlike state created a refuge from the threat of her psychotic mother.

I was able to work effectively with the transference only after I understood its protective function in relation to Cindy's mother and the life-sustaining tie it maintained to her father. A mourning process, delayed many years, began once we started to work with this aspect of the father transference. While mourning, Cindy gave voice to the injured self gone into hiding. She proclaimed: 'I've come to realize that I went mad when my father died. When he died, I climbed into the coffin with him. That seemed to be the only safe place.'

As treatment progressed, it became increasingly clear how being little kept Cindy safe. It was a masquerade that provided a haven until her injured self could gain the necessary repair and strength to work through the loss of her father. Cindy had countered the toxic effects of her psychotic mother through the compensatory turn toward her father. His death threw Cindy back to the tie with her mother, who seemed to be the source of wholeness. This wholeness was an illusion, however, since her mother's destructiveness was interminable.

As repair of the injured self progressed, Cindy gradually loosened the tie to her psychotic mother. She grasped the reality of her mother's destructiveness and mourned for the mother she did not have. Strengthened, Cindy turned to the overwhelming trauma of her father's death. We spent many years working with the toxic effects of Cindy's psychotic mother, but the loss of her father might have been the more difficult issue for her to engage. This was because Cindy had protected herself from her mother's toxicity through an early life-saving turn toward her father and the nurturing maid. Father was Cindy's second and best chance for life and health, which made his premature death especially devastating. He was the compensatory parent who provided sanity and safety.

Treatment moved rapidly once we were able to address the depth of Cindy's experience of her father's death. Her need for the idealization that seemed to keep her safe diminished. This change announced itself around a vacation I was about to take. In a new experience, Cindy was openly angry with me for going away and soon she became angry with me for many things. At first her rage was diffuse, then it focused on feeling betrayed and abandoned. Feelings about her father's illness and death emerged that Cindy had not known before. She no longer needed to disavow the profound experience of her father's death. In mourning and despite her pain, Cindy began to feel whole.

Of interest are her associations about the Wizard. He was no longer the magical person; he was simply a foolish man behind the curtain, frantically pulling strings. Having repaired the injured self and having mourned her magical father, Cindy was free of the bonds that kept her 'little'. She no longer needed the protective function of the idealization. She felt like a competent person, able to speak for herself, in the world, with confidence. She believed she would develop her talents and live life fully in the future. Like Dorothy, whose slippers transported her home, Cindy felt able to direct her own life. As she commented during one session, 'Now I'm a whole person. I have a heart and a brain and a soul.'

The self psychological perspective enabled me to grasp the *health* inherent in Cindy's defensive stance. Guided by the beacon-like image of a terrified, injured self, attempting to stay safe, I understood Cindy's passivity as the life-sustaining facade that it was. I did not conceive of it as a retreat from unconscious drives. From this position we were able to repair the injured self which freed itself from its imprisoning fortress and returned to its developmental track.

Chapter 12

Last words

Kohut died on October 8, 1981, three days after extemporaneously delivering his presentation, 'On Empathy' (1981), to the Fifth Annual Conference on Self Psychology held at Berkeley, California. Approaching the conference, Kohut knew death was imminent and that this presentation would be his last. What would he choose to discuss? What issue merited his last words? Curiously, he returned to the topic of empathy, the seminal topic he introduced in his 1959 paper. Why did he do this?

Kohut was deeply troubled that his conceptualization of empathy had been thoroughly misunderstood by his critics. He also felt that the concept had been abused by the mistaken claim of others that empathy cures, which is not his position at all. He was so troubled by the misunderstanding that he felt a 'serious obligation to set the record straight' (1981). Emphatically he asserted his wish to provide an 'antidote to the sentimentalizing perversions in psychotherapy about curing through love, through compassion, to just being there and being nice' (1981).

To accomplish his task, Kohut discusses empathy on several levels before he concludes with the essential point he wishes to make. He turns first to his original delineation of empathy as a definer of the psychological field (1959) and restates his earlier thesis that just as the external world is studied through the extrospective instruments employed by the various sciences, so the internal world is studied, by the psychological observer, through the instrument of empathy. The analyst uses the empathic instrument to obtain information about a patient's world of complex mental states. The analyst immerses him- or herself in the perception of the patient's experience and then reflects upon the nature of that experience. Repeating himself, Kohut emphasizes that empathy is the means by which the psychological observer gathers information about the inner world of human experience. Empathy is the data-gathering instrument. It defines the field the psychologist studies just as the histologist's microscope defines the field the histologist studies. If histology is that field accessible to study by the microscope, psychology is that field accessible to study by empathy.

At this level of understanding, empathy is not an action but a definer of a particular field. It is nothing else. Since empathy defines the psychological field, only information obtained empathically belongs within the field of psychoanalytic study. By defining psychoanalysis in this way, Kohut excludes principles from other fields that might intrude into it. He is especially concerned about the intrusion of biological principles, such as Freud's introduction of the biological instincts, into psychoanalysis. On the next level of understanding, Kohut speaks of empathy as an informer of appropriate action. In this consideration he notes that if one wishes to know how to act toward another, one needs to put oneself in the other's shoes. Appropriate action is informed by knowledge of the other. Such knowledge can be used for good or for evil. Clearly, one needs to know the other in order to be helpful. One also needs to know the other in an intimate way if one really wants to be hurtful, for in order to be hurtful one needs to know the other's vulnerability.

As an example of action informed by empathy, Kohut related how Nazis used their understanding of their victims' vulnerabilities to inflict the greatest possible emotional pain. In a very different vein, Kohut describes the mother who uses her empathy to know and respond to her children. He suggests that, in a similar way, analysts use their empathy to know their patients and inform their analytic actions. Empathy, Kohut insists, is an informer of action regardless of the intent.

The next level of empathy Kohut considers is, he believes, the most difficult to explain. He has argued that empathy is not an action, yet he believes that empathy carries beneficial effect and induces a broad therapeutic benefit. According to Kohut, the paradox that empathy is not a therapeutic act yet has a therapeutic effect is the source of the confusion surrounding his writings. With ironic emphasis, he asserts that the presence of empathy in the surrounding milieu is essential to psychological existence, regardless of whether the empathy is used for good or for evil purposes. Empathy, whether for good or for ill, acknowledges the existence of the other. It affirms their humanness. Although the destructive use of empathy is especially terrifying, Kohut maintains that the empathyless environment is even worse. It brushes one off as though one had no existence at all. In this regard, he asserts that one of the gravest horrors the Nazis inflicted upon their victims was the total disregard for their victims' humanity.

To further his point about the essential nature of an empathic human environment, Kohut tells the story of the astronauts who lost control of their ship after it had become disabled. Before the problem could be diagnosed and repaired, they were given the choice of orbiting forever in space or attempting a return to Earth, where they would probably incinerate upon entry. Kohut recounts that the astronauts decided, without question, to return to Earth. They preferred to risk incineration rather than have their remains circle forever in uninhabited space. Kohut asserts that this choice enacts the deep human wish for contact with an empathic human environment and expresses the great fear of isolation in a perpetual lifeless space.

Kohut contends that the connection with an empathic human environment is essential to human psychological existence. He surmises from his analytic work that 'the loss of an empathic milieu, the loss of an understanding milieu, not necessarily of the correct action, but the loss of *any* understanding' (1981, p. 531) creates disintegration anxiety, which is the most severe and disabling of all anxieties. The loss of an empathic milieu is disabling because it carries the loss of that most basic human need, validation of one's psychological existence – even if the validation occurs within a hurtful context. In this regard Kohut asserts that whereas horrible parental misunderstandings create terrible emotional scars, he believes that the worst suffering stems from the subtle absences of caretakers who are absent by virtue of their empty, quietly vacuous personalities. It is the emptiness of the caretaker that leads to the worst suffering. With deep feeling, Kohut quietly asserts that the hidden psychosis of a caretaker who disregards the reality of the child's existence and treats the child as a thing or as an extension of him- or herself creates an 'anaerobic' psychological milieu. Children of such caretakers cannot describe what is wrong because they assume that the milieu in which they grew up is normal. These children quietly feel guilty in wishing for what their caretakers cannot provide. In his concluding point Kohut suggests that empathy has a developmental line. It progresses from early forms of empathy, expressed in the caretaker's body-close holding, touching and smelling, to the still close but slightly more distant experience of holding through words and facial expression. To illustrate this point, Kohut tells of the adventuresome young child who leaves his mother's side to explore a new area. The child stops and turns back to see his mother's affirming and encouraging smile before proceeding. Kohut suggests that the mother's proud, reassuring smile represents a higher form of empathy. It replaces the body-close experience of holding and touching with the in-tune, but experientially more distant, smile of pride and belief in the child's capacity.

Kohut maintains that the movement from a lower-level experience of empathy to a developmentally higher-level experience has its parallel in the treatment situation. Initially, the patient experiences an earlier form of empathy through the experience of being 'held' in the empathic merger by the understanding of the analyst. For some people this takes a long time but eventually the next step can be taken and a move to a higher form of empathy becomes possible. As the patient progresses on the developmental path, the analyst responds and moves from the developmentally lower-level form of 'experience-near' empathy to a higher-level, slightly 'experience-distant,' form of empathy. The higher-level form is expressed when the analyst adds an explanation to the previous lower-level, 'experience-near,' understanding.

Concluding, Kohut underscores the complexity of empathy. Empathy contains elements of the experience-near understanding admixed with the higher-level, experience-distant explanation which adds an appreciation of how the complicated story of the past is alive in the sensitivities, hurts and reactions of today. Offered with care, the explanation is still a form of empathy, but on a higher developmental level. The analyst still observes the inner world but expresses it on a verbal secondary process level. So convinced is Kohut of the developmental nature of empathy and of the import of movement along its continuum, by both patient and analyst, that he declares this to be the single most important point he makes in *How Does Analysis Cure?* (1984). He writes:

> [A]nalysis cures by giving explanations – interventions on the level of interpretations; not by 'understanding,' not by repeating and confirming what the patient feels and says, that's only the first step; but then the analyst has to move and give an interpretation. In analysis an interpretation means an explanation of what is going on in genetic, dynamic and psychoeconomic terms . . . I believe that the move from understanding to explaining, from confirming that the analyst knows what the patient feels and thinks and imagines (that he's in tune with his inner life), and the next step of giving interpretations is a move from a lower form of empathy to a higher form of empathy.
>
> (Kohut 1981, p. 532)

Always the clinician, Kohut concludes with a clinical vignette that is an example of his relating to a patient at the lowest level of empathic understanding while still remaining an analyst. He tells of a very vulnerable woman who was seriously suicidal. He recounts that when this woman lay down on his couch for the first time she said she felt as though she were lying in a coffin, the lid of which had just closed with a sharp click. She was deeply depressed, and Kohut acknowledged that at times he thought he would lose her. At one frighteningly desperate point, Kohut asked how she would feel if he gave her two fingers to hold, just for a little while, while she was talking. 'Would that help you?' he asked. He describes the experience this way:

> Doubtful maneuver. I am not recommending it, but I was desperate. I was deeply worried. . . . And now I'll tell you what is so nice about that story. Because an analyst always remains an analyst. I gave her my two fingers. She took hold of them, and I immediately made a genetic interpretation to myself. It was the toothless gums of a very young child clamping down on an empty nipple. That was the way it felt. I didn't say anything. I don't know whether it was right. But I reacted to it even there, to myself, as an analyst. After this one occasion that was never necessary anymore. I wouldn't say that it turned the tide, but it overcame a very, very difficult impasse at a given dangerous moment, and gaining some time that way we went on for many, many more years with a reasonable success.
>
> (Kohut 1981, p. 535)

Why does Kohut present this, of all vignettes, as his last clinical statement? What does he have in mind? Why open himself to further charges of being 'non-analytic?' Is he not attempting here to treat through love and kindness? Why confuse the very issue he feels an obligation to set straight?

First, Kohut prefaces the recounting of this story with the statement that he is not a 'stodgy analyst.' He finds that his experience and broadened understanding bring him greater freedom in his work. The vignette relayed here is one example.

I believe the point of Kohut's iconoclastic vignette, however, is to demonstrate that empathy does have multiple forms which are experienced in differing ways by patient and analyst. Earlier in his presentation Kohut asserts that the single most important point he makes in *How Does Analysis Cure?* is that empathy exists on a developmental continuum resulting in developmentally earlier and later forms of empathy. He suggests that in normal emotional growth mother and child move forward along that continuum. The mother moves from the holding, touching, body-close early forms of empathic communication to the later form of empathy typified by her encouraging 'smile-at-a-distance' that communicates her awareness of her child's many feelings as he attempts to move out on his own as well as her reassuring belief in his ability to do so. In similar fashion, patient and analyst move forward along a developmental continuum. As the patient matures, the analyst moves from providing the patient with the lower-level form of empathy in which the patient is 'held' in the empathic merger with the analyst's understanding to providing the higher-level empathic experience of the secondary process, verbal explanation.

The explanation phase of the intervention, as Kohut explains in *How Does Analysis Cure?*, adds a cognitive element to the understanding phase. It enables the patient to understand him- or herself within the context of their own history. By adding the cognitive element, the sensitive explanation creates a modicum of internal structure. It allows the patient to understand and eventually manage him- or herself in the analyst's absence. The understanding phase alone eventually becomes vague and fades from memory. The explanation phase of the two-phase intervention makes the intervention analytic.

As Kohut recounts the vignette he says that 'what is so nice about that story' is that it shows how 'an analyst always remains an analyst.' What does he mean? I believe he means that he retained his function as an analyst even though he related to his patient at the developmentally earliest level of empathy. At a desperate time, when words seemed ineffective, he provided his patient with a tangible connection to help her establish the psychological continuity she lacked. Nevertheless, he retained his function as an analyst by internally moving to the second phase of the intervention, the explanation phase. Internally Kohut added the developmentally higher-level secondary process explanation, which he chose not to share with his patient at that moment, to his lower-level experience-near understanding. Clearly, empathy has different functions and meanings for patient and analyst. For the analyst, it is a method for gathering data on different levels of maturity, as well as an informer of appropriate analytic action. For the patient it is the breath of life.

Thus Kohut ended his remarkable career. Beginning with his study of Aschenbach's deterioration in Thomas Mann's *Death in Venice*, he pursued a course marked by growing courage and the development of ideas that enabled him to view old facts with new eyes. Tragically, his life was cut short at the peak of his abilities and, consequently, we are deprived of the unknown directions his thoughts might have traveled. Nevertheless, Kohut gave psychoanalysis new direction, and his ideas, as embodied in his psychology of the self, must continue to develop without him. I have attempted to convey the evolution of Kohut's ideas so that students of psychoanalytic psychotherapy can benefit from his erudition. I believe that through his scientific attitude and his understanding of narcissism, Heinz Kohut has offered humankind a new window into itself. I close with his final public words, a call to future generations of psychoanalytic practitioners:

> So with that I think I will now close. I'm very glad you waited for me. I'm quite sure this will be the last self psychology meeting that I will attend, but I wanted to do my utmost to be able to go through with my promise. So let's all hope for a good future for the ideas embodied in self psychology.
>
> Good-bye.
>
> (Kohut 1981, p. 535)

Chapter 13
Critique and conclusions

In a critique of Heinz Kohut's work one must be mindful of the fact that his is an unfinished 'work-in-progress.' Like Freud's, Kohut's ideas are ever-evolving, but his early death aborted his participation in that evolution. Because Kohut's ideas are evolving, one must ask, 'When, in Kohut's development, does he discuss this particular issue? Where is he in his thinking and where is he headed?' when one considers a particular idea. At the same time, one must be careful not to dismiss problems in Kohut's work with stultifying justifications such as, 'He hadn't got there yet.' Such a response closes debate, petrifies theory and further aborts the evolution of ideas. What, then, is the appropriate attitude to hold as one approaches the task of critical review? In my critique of Kohut's work I adopt the spirit Kohut suggests for the scientific endeavor:

> These statements . . . express my belief that the true scientist – the playful scientist as I put it before – is able to tolerate the shortcomings of his achievements – the tentativeness of his formulations, the incompleteness of his concepts. Indeed, he treasures them as the spur for further joyful excursions. . . . A worshipful attitude toward established explanatory systems . . . becomes confining in the history of science – as do, indeed, man's analogous commitments in all of human history.
> (Kohut 1977, pp. 310–12)

Turning to the task at hand, I believe that Kohut, like Freud, developed concepts of enduring value. Freud's concept of the dynamic unconscious is one of humanity's enduring contributions. Regardless of semantic issues surrounding a description of the Unconscious, the effects of unknown emotional forces within the mind are ever-present and undeniable. Similarly, I believe that some of Kohut's concepts will be enduring although they have not yet had the chance to stand the test of time.

I begin with a summary of Kohut's contributions, the first of which is his delineation of empathy as a definer of the psychoanalytic field. Kohut frees his conceptualizations from the intruding biases of non-psychological concerns when he defines the psychoanalytic field as the science that studies the inner life of humankind solely through the instruments of introspection and empathy. Kohut's use of empathy alone, to gather data about the inner lives of his patients, leads him to new hypotheses and conceptualizations. The first of these is the hypothesis that narcissism is normal and has a healthy course of development. This view frees narcissism from the judgmental attitude that considers it to be an obnoxious form of regressive psychopathology. Kohut asserts that narcissism changes form as it develops, beginning with specific early configurations (the idealized parental imago and the grandiose self) that eventually evolve into the establishment of ideals and ambitions.

Through reconstructions with his adult patients Kohut learns that specific needs are related to the early forms of narcissism. These needs include the need for an object to idealize, the need to be affirmed, valued and echoed by an object and the need to feel an alikeness and kinship with another. Kohut asserts that these needs are essential to the development, survival and vitality of the developing child. He further asserts that objects that provide the developing self with these essential psychological functions are experienced as part of the self. Since they are experienced as part of the self, Kohut calls these objects selfobjects and the needs selfobject needs. He calls the yearning for and the experience of the fulfillment of the selfobject needs a selfobject transference.

I predict that Kohut's definition of empathic immersion as *the* analytic method of data-gathering, his delineation of narcissism as a healthy aspect of normal development, his concept of selfobject needs that persist throughout life and his conceptualization of the selfobject transferences will be enduring contributions to psychoanalysis and to humankind.

My first criticism of Kohut's work is a stylistic one. He is difficult to read, especially in his early writings. His style is intensely Germanic. One searches his lengthy sentences looking for the verb that will bring sense and order to what he is saying. In reading Kohut I am reminded of what he writes when he describes the psychology responsible for the pleasure of music. He notes that the composer first states a musical premise, creates a disruptive tension by disorganizing the premise and then restores order by returning to the recognizable melody. Reading Kohut is like that. One must persevere through the discord of his convoluted sentence to obtain the restorative reward at the end.

Cocks (1994), in his compilation of Kohut's correspondence, notes the vast discrepancy between the way Kohut spoke and the way he wrote. As I note earlier, Kohut was an eloquent and lyrical speaker. He prided himself on his ability to speak extemporaneously, yet coherently, on many topics. Why should his writing be so different from his speaking? Cocks speculates, and I agree, that Kohut's early writing reflects his anxiety about what he proposes. Concerned about potential criticism, Kohut qualifies his points in an anxious and almost too cautious way that, in turn, makes reading difficult.

Kohut is ambivalent about the relationship of his ideas to the central explanations offered by classical theory. Aware that his ideas threaten the psychoanalytic establishment, he takes great pains to present his work as an extension rather than a replacement of Freud's thinking. Growing courage, a coterie of supportive colleagues, illness and the knowledge of an early death, however, eventually help diminish Kohut's ambivalence in relation to the analytic community. Curiously, the struggles of his professional life validate the hypotheses of his work. His anxiety over possible condemnation and abandonment by his mainstream psychoanalytic colleagues, because of his new ideas, reflects the truth of his observation that the need for a supportive, responsive and affirming milieu never ends. Like matter, the early selfobject need does not vanish; it simply changes form.

Nevertheless, Kohut's ambivalence dogs him throughout many of his writings, especially in the earlier years, and is responsible for a number of confusions in his work. Ornstein and Ornstein describe this quality of Kohut, 'who was still with one foot in the old and one foot – initially reluctantly – in the new conceptual frame' (1995, p. 387).

As I note earlier, when considering a particular issue within Kohut's work one must ask, 'When in Kohut's development does the issue arise?' This is certainly the case when we consider Kohut's ambivalence concerning the relationship of his theory to classical theory. The axis of this ambivalence is the central role that the dual-instinct theory, exemplified by the oedipal configurations, plays in traditional psychoanalysis relative to its place in Kohut's psychology.

In *The Restoration of the Self* (1977), Kohut clearly differentiates a psychology of the self from the classical 'drive–defense, mental apparatus' psychology. He proposes that a defective self lies at the heart of most psychopathology. The deepest work of an analysis, therefore, uncovers and works through an underlying depression related to the defective self rather than reveals a conflict over instinctual drives. Kohut asserts that the aggression and sexuality, long understood to be at the core of oedipal psychopathology, are actually breakdown products of a self that has been weakened by the earlier inappropriate responses of its selfobject milieu. What the classical analyst sees as primary sexual and aggressive drives Kohut sees as the secondary expressions of a fragmented self. Possessive affection breaks down to driven sexuality, and assertiveness fractures into aggression and destructive hostility.

Unfortunately, Kohut confuses the clear picture he paints in *The Restoration of the Self* (1977) when he refers to the breakdown products of affection and assertion as 'drives elements.' The confusion emanates from Kohut's definitional exclusion of the drive concept from psychology. He identifies 'the drives' as an intruding biological principle, not available to empathy or introspection, therefore not a part of psychology.

Concerned about condemnation by the analytic community, Kohut makes anxious and ambivalent comments such as: 'we are not necessarily denying the truth of the classical theory of the central position of the oedipus complex, but only the universal applicability of this theory' (1977, p. 223), or 'It does not indicate any lack of respect for the great explanatory power of the classical formulations . . . to enrich the classical theory by adding a self-psychological dimension' (1977, p. 227).

Kohut's anxiety seems to stay with him until shortly before his death. Even in his posthumous work *How Does Analysis Cure?* (1984), Kohut is not unambivalent in his assertion that the central classical concept of oedipal psychopathology is not truly psychological. He comes close when he writes, 'At present, however, the psychological approach [data collected via empathy], with all its limitations, is the *only* [italics mine] useful one for investigating the inner life of man, including his psychopathology' (1984, p. 32).

Kohut strengthens as he nears death, and in 'Introspection, Empathy and the Semicircle of Mental Health' (1981b), the posthumously delivered paper he was to have presented in November 1981, he explicitly writes, 'the drive concept . . . has had significant deleterious consequences for psychoanalysis' (1981b, p. 553) and 'the drive concept did not belong in a system of psychology' (1981b, p. 554). In a definitive statement Kohut writes:

Self psychology has freed itself from the distorted view of psychological man espoused by traditional analysis because, having accepted the fact that the field-defining observational stance of introspection and empathy is absolute and indeed axiomatic, it does not pose as biology or psychobiology but accepts itself as psychology through and through.

(Kohut 1981b, p. 556)

Finally, in 'On Empathy' (1981), the address delivered three days before his death, on 8 October 1981, Kohut unequivocally declares:

I do not believe, however hard it was tried, that there is a possibility to create such a misalliance as psychobiology, or biopsychology or something on that order. It was tried and the results of this attempt led to the worst distortions of the perception of man that psychoanalysis is guilty of: the introduction of the drive.

(Kohut 1981b, p. 529)

In addition to his own internal struggle, intense external pressures pushed for Kohut to integrate his ideas with classical theory. He responded to these pressures with the insistence that he needed to devote his time, uninterrupted by concerns over integration, to the development of his own ideas. The time-consuming scholarly work of integration, he replied, would be done by his colleagues and students. In retrospect it is apparent that Kohut's illness, which he concealed, was the cause for his urgency about time. Needless to say, his response engendered severe criticism.

I turn now to a discussion of the methodological problem Kohut creates when he limits the field of psychoanalysis to data obtained through empathy and introspection alone. This definition of the field protects psychoanalysis from the deforming intrusion of principles from other disciplines and from the distorting morality of cultural values and biases. However, it also isolates and potentially deprives the psychoanalytic endeavor of valuable information that is available from other fields. The study of development is but one example of how the protective wall of Kohut's definition isolates psychoanalysis. Although developmental concepts sit at the heart of Kohut's theory, the microscopic elements of early development are not available for study. They cannot be studied through reconstructions from adult analyses alone, for, as Kohut notes, we cannot be empathic with states that are too dissimilar from our own. The infant's critical early states are unavailable to the psychoanalyst. At best we are confined to adultomorphisms. The field of infant research, however, with its ingenious methods of investigation, does have access to the information we seek. Its observations are rich and can provide psychoanalysis with valuable information and explanations. Kohut had not quite opened himself to its findings at the time of his death. The study of early development is an area where the principle of complementarity can usefully be applied. Basch addresses the isolation of psychoanalysis from the rest of the scientific community and speaks to the value of complementarity when he writes:

> If my experiences do not necessarily equip me to understand a given patient's experiences, and if the patient, blinded by repression or disavowal, cannot enlighten me, what will enable me to make a plausible inference as to the meaning of what I hear sitting behind the couch? . . . The more I know about how we are designed to function – what neurophysiology, infant research, affect theory, cognitive psychology, semantics, information theory, evolutionary biology, and other pertinent disciplines can tell me about human development – the better I am prepared to be empathic with a patient's communication at a particular time in his or her treatment.
>
> (Basch 1995, p. 372)

I turn now to a consideration of difficulties inherent in Kohut's theory itself. I believe that he encounters a problem when he creates his model of the bipolar self. Although it is a useful model, he exposes himself to the problem inherent in all models, the problem of reification. Despite Kohut's assumption of the role of playful scientist, history suggests that useful models are idealized over time and their contents become treated as 'Truth' rather than as provisional pictorial statements. When such concretization occurs, the playful utility of a model's plasticity ends and creative thinking freezes. Kohut criticizes the reification inherent in Freud's tripartite model, especially the reification of the ego by Hartmann and the ego psychologists. However, he exposes himself to the same criticism.

Kohut's bipolar self, a self with a tension arc between the poles of ambitions and ideals, is an unusual conceptualization for him in that it is concrete. It is especially unusual in that Kohut assiduously avoids concretizing the self within a definitional system. He reflects his epistemological pride over this attitude when he writes:

> My investigation contains hundreds of pages dealing with the

psychology of the self – yet it never assigns an inflexible meaning to the term self. . . . But I admit this fact without contrition or shame. The self . . . is, like all reality . . . not knowable in its essence. . . . We can describe the various cohesive forms in which the self appears, can demonstrate the several constituents that make up the self . . . and explain their genesis and functions. We can do all that, but we will still not know the essence of the self as differentiated from its manifestations.

(Kohut 1977, pp. 310–12)

Although Kohut claims the attitude of the playful scientist and proposes his model within that spirit, I fear that such a model quickly outlives its usefulness. It becomes reified. This has been the case with the bipolar self, which seems to have been abandoned as an operational concept by the majority of self psychologists. It is curious, too, that whereas Kohut's model differs from Freud's hydrodynamic model in content, it is similar to it in form. Both are based on laws of physics; both are experience-distant.

Another difficulty in Kohut's theory relates to his singular focus on transmuting internalization as *the* major process responsible for growth-promoting internalizations. In Kohut's early work (Kohut 1960; Kohut and Seitz 1963), he describes 'passage through the object' as another process responsible for internalizations. Remember that in 'passage through the object' Kohut suggests that the child identifies with the calming, soothing, non-conflictual qualities of the parent. Kohut suggests that because these qualities are non-conflictual they are 'taken in' and 'reside' in the non-conflictual, non-transference 'area of progressive neutralization.' Although this concept opens a number of questions, it does point in the direction of other structure-building processes that are just as important and effective as transmuting internalization. Mysteriously, Kohut neglects 'passage through the object' as a subject for further development and emphasizes, without explanation, his concept of transmuting internalization instead.

The concept of transmuting internalization has its origin in Freud's hypothesis that the qualities of a libidinal object are internalized following its loss. Freud describes this process in 'Mourning and Melancholia' (1917). Kohut extends Freud's concept to include the internalization of idealizations following disappointments. Kohut describes how these internalizations occur when an idealized selfobject is partially lost after the selfobject has temporarily failed in one of its functions.

I have no question that optimal frustrations participate in the process of internalizations and account, in part, for emotional growth. For example, a child cannot learn to ride its bike if its parent cannot let go and allow it to experience the simultaneous terror and joy of balance on its own. The parent's letting go is a frustration. Protection from that frustration will deprive the child of its opportunity for forward movement.

Although optimal frustrations and the subsequent transmuting internalizations do establish structure, other processes account for internalization as well. Beebe and Lachmann, drawing upon their experience as infant researchers, therapists and analysts, acknowledge these other processes when they write:

> In contrast to this model of [transmuting] internalization, we (Lachmann and Beebe, 1992, Beebe and Lachmann, 1994) have emphasized that the patient acquires expectations of mutuality through ongoing regulations and the repair of disruptions. Furthermore, though 'disruptions' may lead to 'internalizations,' there are other means by which internalization occurs. Mutual and self-regulation and heightened affect are also represented and internalized (Beebe and Lachmann, 1994).
>
> (Lachmann and Beebe 1995, p. 377)

The above criticisms all refer to commissions, but Kohut is also criticized for omissions. Noticeable among these is the absence of an in-depth consideration of normal sexuality. Kohut's colleagues, students and others, however, attracted by the explanatory power of his ideas, continue to work and expand the theory of self psychology with regard to this and other topics.

Self psychology, in fact, is evolving in several directions and has now entered what is being called the 'post-Kohutian' era. The current diversity in the field is attested to by the appearance of papers such as 'Three Self Psychologies – or One' (Lachmann and Beebe 1991) and 'Self Psychology after Kohut: One Theory or Many?' (Shane and Shane 1993). An entire volume of the journal *Psychoanalytic Dialogues* has been dedicated to the questions raised because 'a single voice has been replaced by a multiplicity of voices in complex relationships to each other' (Mitchell 1995, p.351).

Some of those voices address a new tributary of psychoanalytic thought that understands the therapist to be more than the recipient target of the patient's transference needs and wishes. In this view, the therapist is thought to be an active participant in co-constructing the psychic reality of the consulting-room. This interactional model is called by various names: Beebe *et al.* (1993) call it a dyadic systems perspective; Hoffman (1991) calls it social constructivism; and Atwood and Stolorow (Atwood and Stolorow 1984; Stolorow *et al.* 1987; Stolorow and Atwood 1992) call their interactive model intersubjectivity theory.

Since Kohut's work alone is the topic of this book, I will not explore the debates and issues currently alive within self psychology with the exception of one issue that attempts to extend Kohut's work. I wish to consider the recent discussion that asks the question, 'What therapeutic stance and behavior fosters growth and promotes internalizations?'

The discourse begins with Kohut's hypothesis (1984) that optimal frustration, as I have already discussed, initiates the process of internalization. Several authors continue the debate. Bacal (1985) asserts that 'optimal responsiveness' on the part of the selfobject therapist provides a crucial experience within the treatment setting, Tolpin (1988) identifies 'optimal affective engagement' and Shane and Shane (1994) assert that 'optimal restraint' is critical in the therapeutic endeavor.

One should note that the adjective 'optimal' is an operative word in this discussion. 'Optimal' is used by all the above authors as an adjective to describe a type of therapeutic behavior. Their suggested therapeutic behaviors provide 'the correct amount of' responsiveness, engagement, or restraint. Kohut, however, uses the adjective 'optimal' to describe an accidental, unavoidable, but, one hopes, manageable event within the treatment setting. Kohut's 'optimal' does not imply the provision of a special therapeutic behavior. It does not qualify an action. It qualifies a frustration and is part of a psychoeconomic concept related to structure building.

Kohut obviously cannot participate in this discussion but his work suggests his conviction that the optimal and appropriate therapeutic stance requires no special activity or provision. Kohut asserts that his non-judgmental acceptance of his patient's psychic reality, his in-depth understanding of his patient's experience and his sensitive explanations of that experience when appropriate promote internalizations and foster growth.

In closing, I wish to address the question, 'How does Kohut's work benefit the practitioner of psychodynamic psychotherapy?' The answer is to be found in the new atmosphere of the consulting-room, for that is where Kohut's insights and conceptualizations coalesce. Convinced that the defective self is responsible for his patient's sufferings, Kohut listens to the self and hears its struggles to survive. He understands his patient's protective maneuvers as attempts to safeguard the hidden self rather than as obstacles to self-knowledge. Kohut's shift from a psychology of hidden drives to a psychology of the driven self changes the therapeutic encounter from a subtly adversarial experience to a friendly partnership. His alliance with the threatened self creates an ambience of safety. The therapeutic setting becomes a place where humiliating needs can be understood, where old traumas can be explored and where the hidden, injured or disorganized self is safe to emerge and resume its stunted growth.

Heinz Kohut changed the psychotherapeutic landscape by emphasizing empathic immersion as the primary mode for understanding people in pain. For Kohut theory is a guide and not a god. It can be changed or discarded when it is not useful. With empathy as his guide, Kohut redefines the central issues of normal development and of emotional distress. He shifts the focus of concern from a threat posed by instinctual drives to the driven state of the threatened self. As therapists, what we hear changes when we hold the self and its experiences as our central focus. The needs of the self are ubiquitous. Our grasp of those needs enhances our therapeutic effectiveness with the people who come to us for help.

Many treatments are now available. How does one select an appropriate therapy from the vast armamentarium? When informed by an understanding of the self, the task is less daunting. One asks questions such as 'What are the core issues that bring this person to see me now?' and 'Is this a person with an essentially stable self suffering from a trauma to a specific sector of his or her personality, or does this person hide a defective self behind a series of protective devices aimed at psychological survival?' The questions are easy to ask. The answers are more difficult, but, guided by a knowledge of the self, as outlined by Kohut and the self psychologists who work to extend the theory, I believe it is now possible to define, prescribe and pursue an enlightened course of treatment. In view of the current vitality of the field it seems that Kohut's final wish, 'So let's all hope for a good future for the ideas embodied in self psychology' (1981, p. 535), is being realized.

Glossary

Bipolar self: Kohut's model of a self with two poles and an intermediate area between the poles. Ambitions represent one pole, ideals represent the other. The area between the poles is the area of innate skills and talents.
Disavowal: Defense mechanism in which something is seen but not conceived. Disavowal is present in the experience of knowing about something and not knowing about it at the same time. The split between knowing and not knowing is responsible for actions that seem out of character.
Drives: Freud's conception of the basic biological forces that motivate human mentation and behavior. The two drives, often referred to as the instinctual drives, are the sexual drive and the aggressive drive.
Dynamic point of view: One of several ordering principles Freud used in his attempt to describe psychological phenomena. The dynamic perspective describes how psychological forces, with their origins in the past, affect thoughts, fantasies, wishes, needs and behavior in the present.
Economic point of view: One of several ordering principles Freud used in his attempt to describe psychological phenomena. The economic perspective describes the intensities of affect and is useful in discussing how those affects are managed psychologically. Originally Freud conceived of the intensities of affect in terms of energies that were processed by a mental apparatus.
Ego: One of the agencies of the mental apparatus. It is conceived of as having an executive function, mediating between the forces and demands of the id and the moral prohibitions of the superego. Theoretically, the ego consists of a series of functions that protect the personality from being overwhelmed by its internal drives, impulses and needs, and enables a relatively comfortable life in the external world. Although a portion of the ego is thought to be conscious, the

majority of the ego's functions are conceived of as being unconscious. Among its functions are various defenses, as delineated by Anna Freud in *The Ego and Its Mechanisms of Defense*, as well as skills, talents and relational abilities. At times 'ego' has been used to describe the experiential aspect of the personality. In this context it has historically been used synonymously with 'self.'

Ego autonomy: Ego functions that are free of inhibiting neurotic conflict and therefore available to the psyche for appropriate use.

Experience-distant theory: Explanatory statements about emotional experiences that are abstract and removed from the affects associated with the experience. Experience-distant understanding is a cognitive understanding which is referred to as higher-level theorizing.

Experience-near theory: Explanatory statements about emotional experiences that remain close to the feelings and clinical phenomena of the event being described. Experience-near understanding is an affective understanding which is referred to as lower-level theorizing.

Genetic point of view: One of several ordering principles Freud used in his attempt to describe psychological phenomena. The genetic perspective describes the origins and history of wishes, fantasies, needs and behaviors that are encountered in the present.

Grandiose self: Kohut's conceptualization of one of the two original attempts to restore the disrupted state of primary narcissistic bliss. Characterized by exhibitionism, expansiveness and a sense of omnipotence, this unconscious configuration changes form in the course of normal development, ultimately fueling the pole of ambitions.

Horizontal split: Kohut's reference to the repression barrier of Freud's mental apparatus (see *repression barrier*).

Id: One of the agencies of the mental apparatus. It is conceived of as being completely unconscious and contains the drives, wishes and fantasies that press for expression. In classical theory, the contents of the id, as they push for expression, are responsible for the conflict.

Idealized parental imago: Kohut's conceptualization of one of the two original attempts to restore the disrupted primary narcissistic bliss. It is characterized by a yearning for an omnipotent object to whom one can attach in an effort to feel whole, safe and firm.

Infantile sexuality: Freud conceived of the sexual drive as a normal phenomenon. It appears first in infancy and moves through a series of developmental phases as it matures. In the experience of infantile sexuality, bodily experiences such as hunger and excretory functions become suffused with pleasurable sensations as the various mucous membranes are stimulated in the course of their physiologic use. These pleasurable sensations become an end in themselves and are the origin of the erotic experience. During neurologic maturation the preferred organ of stimulation changes from the mouth to the anus to the genitals. Each organ preference becomes the focus of a developmental era or phase in the course of psychological maturation. Hence, infantile sexuality has three phases: the oral, anal and genital phases.

Internal object: see *object representation*.

Libido: Freud's concept of the psychic energy associated with the sexual instinct. It is an economic term that deals with quantities of energy. It does not suggest appetite. Libido can be invested either in the internal psychic representation of an object or in the self. When it is invested in an object it is called object libido; when invested in the self it is called narcissism.

Metapsychology: A highly abstract conceptual tool used to form and discuss psychoanalytic theory. It consists of a set of theoretical assumptions and a language to describe those assumptions. It is so named because academic psychology in the late nineteenth and early twentieth centuries, when Freud did his major conceptual work, equated 'mental' with 'conscious.' The phenomena of Freud's interest were unconscious and therefore they were considered 'beyond the realm of psychology,' hence Freud's psychology was metapsychology.

Narcissism: The libidinal investment of the ego or the self.

Object libido: The energy of the sexual drive that is directed toward external loved objects (see *libido*).

Object representation: An enduring schema of a particular person, akin to an enduring memory, formed from a multitude of experiences, impressions and images of that person.

Optimal frustration: A psychoeconomic concept of an external loss or disappointment of such magnitude that it can safely be experienced without overwhelming the variable emotional capacities of the person. It does not lead to the traumatic state where the capacity of the psyche is overwhelmed by affect. On the contrary, in small manageable segments frustration leads to growth.

Pleasure principle: Based on Freud's assumption that the human organism seeks to maintain a homeostatic state, this is an internal regulatory principle that seeks to eliminate the tension that disturbs the steady state. Disturbing tension, usually due to an increase in sexual or aggressive pressure, must be discharged so that the system can return to an equilibrated state. Tension can arise either from internal sources such as intense wishes and emotional pain or from external danger situations. Tension relief is sought without any concern about or regard for the consequences of the discharge-seeking behavior, which is often at odds with societal mores. This is a primary operating principle within the primary process unconscious.

Points of view: The set of ordering principles consisting initially of the dynamic, structural and economic points of view that Freud used to describe psychological phenomena comprehensively. Later the genetic and adaptive points of view were added. Each point provides a different perspective from which one can view psychological issues. The points of view are useful in considering clinical observations on an abstract level. See *structural*, *dynamic*, *economic* and *genetic points of view*.

Primary process: A type of thought characteristic of the Unconscious. It is irrational and consists of condensations, displacements, symbolization and absence of negation. It is primitive in nature and is related to the unmodified expression of the drives as dictated by the pleasure principle. The illogical nature of the manifest content of dreams and of overt psychoses is an example of primary process thought.

Reality principle: In the course of development, the discharge of tension that operates in accord with the pleasure principle eventually gives way to the necessities that govern life in a social context. Other people are seen as having needs and feelings. Actions are seen as having consequences. Logic prevails as postponement, delay and inhibitions govern the mode of behavior.

Repression barrier: Originally described by Freud as part of the topographic model. It was the result of defensive forces in the System Preconscious that opposed the intrusion of forces in the System Unconscious. Freud modified this concept when he developed the tripartite model in 1923. The repression barrier was then conceived as the collection of defenses within the ego that opposed the intrusion of the forces of the id.

Secondary process: A type of thought that is rational and part of the Preconscious. It is related to the reality principle in that it contains elements that make delay of immediate discharge and postponement of action possible in both thought, language and behavior.

Selfobject: Originally, the caretaker during childhood that fulfills the function of meeting psychologically essential selfobject needs. Objects that provide the selfobject needs are experienced in terms of their need-fulfilling function rather than as entities in their own right. Originally hyphenated, Kohut decided to remove the hyphen from the term self-object in 1977 (Cocks 1994). He did this to convey the sense that the object is not experienced as being separate from the self in terms of the psychological function it provides.

Selfobject needs: Essential psychological experiences originating in childhood that continue in varying form throughout life. These include the need to idealize, the need to be affirmed, valued and validated, and the need for a sense of commonality and kinship with another human being. These needs are part of the narcissistic configurations Kohut describes.

Selfobject transference: A term describing the self's experience of the need-fulfilling selfobject. In the selfobject transference the selfobject is experienced in terms of the specific psychological function it provides for the self rather than in terms of its own unique qualities.

Structural point of view: One of several ordering principles Freud used in his attempt to describe psychological phenomena. The structural point of view conceives of the mind as an apparatus composed of three agencies: ego, id and superego, and describes the relationship between them. In classical Freudian theory this relationship is one of conflict.

Superego: One of the agencies of the mental apparatus. It is a concept that describes the internal moral prohibitions, attitudes and standards that guide the personality. It forms through the internalization of parental attitudes and behavior.

Transference: A concept first developed by Freud to describe the relationship of one system within the topographic model to another system within the same model. In Freud's original conceptualization, transference is the intrusion of the Unconscious into the Preconscious. Since his original formulation, the concept has taken on many additional meanings. Most commonly now, 'transference' is used to describe the experience, in the present, of relationships that have their origin with the objects of childhood.

Transmuting internalization: Kohut's concept of psychological structure-building, modeled on Freud's concept of internalization following loss. For Kohut, degrees of the idealization of the idealized object are re-internalized when the object fails in its idealizing selfobject function. The minute loss to the optimal frustration precipitates the process of transmuting internalization.

Vertical split: First referred to by Freud as a split in the ego, the vertical split draws upon the tripartite model to explain the defense of disavowal. It refers to a rent in the structure of the ego or the self that serves to keep perception and conception apart.

Chronology

1913: Born 3 May, Vienna.
1932: Graduates from Doblinger Gymnasium, June.
1937: Father dies, November.
1938: Witnesses Freud's departure from Vienna, June. Receives medical degree from University of Vienna, November.
1939: Leaves Vienna for England, March.
1940: Leaves England for the United States, February. Arrives in Chicago, March.
1941: Resident in neurology at the University of Chicago Hospitals.
1945: Becomes United States citizen, July.
1947: Assistant professor of psychiatry at the University of Chicago, School of Medicine.
1948: Marries social worker Betty Meyer, October.
1950: Son, Thomas August, born, March. Graduates from the Institute for Psychoanalysis, Chicago, October.
1953: Faculty, Institute for Psychoanalysis.
1957: 'Introspection, Empathy, and Psychoanalysis' presented at the twenty-fifth anniversary celebration of the Institute for Psychoanalysis, Chicago, November.
1963–4: President, Chicago Psychoanalytic Society.
1965–73: Vice-President, International Psychoanalytical Association.
1966: 'Forms and Transformations of Narcissism' published.
1968: Gives Sigmund Freud Lecture at the Psychoanalytic Association of New York: 'The Psychoanalytic Treatment of Narcissistic Personality Disorders,' December.
1971: *Analysis of the Self* published. Diagnosed as having leukemia, October.

1973: Chicago Conference on 'Psychoanalysis and History,' honoring sixtieth birthday, June.
1977: *The Restoration of the Self* published.
1979: 'The Two Analyses of Mr. Z' published.
1981: At Fourth Annual Conference on the Psychology of the Self, University of California, Berkeley, October, delivers 'On Empathy.' Dies 8 October, Billings Hospital, Chicago. Son Thomas presents 'Introspection, Empathy and the Semi-circle of Mental Health,' November.
1984: Posthumous publication of *How Does Analysis Cure?*

Bibliography of the work of Heinz Kohut

PAPERS

1949
'August Aichhorn – Remarks after His Death,' in P. Ornstein (ed.) *The Search for the Self*, vol. 1, pp. 131–3. New York, International Universities Press, 1978.

1951
(a) 'The Psychological Significance of Musical Activity,' *Music Therapy*, vol. 1, pp. 151–8.
(b) 'Discussion of *The Function of the Analyst in the Therapeutic Process* by Samuel D. Lipton,' in P. Ornstein (ed.) *The Search for the Self*, vol. 1, pp. 159–66. New York, International Universities Press, 1978.

1952
'Book Review of *Psychanalyse de la musique* (1951) by André Michel,' in P. Ornstein (ed.) *The Search for the Self*, vol. 1, pp. 167–70. New York, International Universities Press, 1978.

1953
'Discussion of "Natural Science and Humanism as Fundamental Elements in the Education of Physicians and Especially Psychiatrists" by Henry von Witzleben,' in P. Ornstein (ed.) *The Search for the Self*, vol. 1, pp. 171–6. New York, International Universities Press, 1978.

1954
'Discussion of "*Eros and Thanatos*: A Critique and Elaboration of Freud's Death Wish" by Iago Galdston,' in P. Ornstein (ed.) *The Search for the Self*, vol. 1, pp. 177–85. New York, International Universities Press, 1978.

1955
(a) 'Some psychological effects of music and their relation to music therapy,' *Music Therapy*, vol. 5, pp. 17–20.
(b) 'Book Review of *The Haunting Melody: Psychoanalytic Experiences in Life and Music* (1953) by Theodor Reik,' in P. Ornstein (ed.) *The Search for the Self*, vol. 1, pp. 187–90. New York, International Universities Press, 1978.
(c) 'Book Review of *Beethoven and His Nephew: A Psychoanalytic Study of*

Their Relationship (1954) by Edith and Richard Sterba,' in P. Ornstein (ed.) *The Search for the Self*, vol. 1, pp. 191–3. New York, International Universities Press, 1978.

1956
(a) 'Discussion of "Modern Casework: The Contribution of Ego Psychology" by Annette Garrett,' in P. Ornstein (ed.) *The Search for the Self*, vol. 1, pp. 195–200. New York, International Universities Press, 1978.
(b) 'Discussion of "The Role of the Counterphobic Mechanism in Addiction" by Thomas S. Szasz,' in P. Ornstein (ed.) *The Search for the Self*, vol. 1, pp. 201–3. New York, International Universities Press, 1978.

1957
(a) 'Reporter "Clinical and Theoretical Aspects of Resistance" on Panel: American Psychoanalytic Association New York, December 1956 Meeting,' *Journal of the American Psychoanalytic Association* 1957, vol. 5, pp. 548–55.
(b) '*Death in Venice* by Thomas Mann: A Story about the Disintegration of Artistic Sublimation,' in P. Ornstein (ed.) *The Search for the Self*, vol. 1, pp. 107–30. New York, International Universities Press, 1978.
(c) 'Observations on the psychological functions of music,' in P. Ornstein (ed.) *The Search for the Self*, vol. 1, pp. 233–53. New York, International Universities Press, 1978.
(d) 'Book review of *The Arrow and the Lyre: A Study of the Role of Love in the Works of Thomas Mann* (1955) by Frank Donald Hirschbach,' in P. Ornstein (ed.) *The Search for the Self*, vol. 1, pp. 255–7. New York, International Universities Press, 1978.
(e) 'Discussion of "Some Comments on the Origin of the Influencing Machine" by Louis Linn,' in P. Ornstein (ed.) *The Search for the Self*, vol. 1, pp. 259–61. New York, International Universities Press, 1978.
(f) 'Discussion of "A Note on Beating Fantasies" by William G. Niederland', in P. Ornstein (ed.) *The Search for the Self*, vol. 1, pp. 263–5. New York, International Universities Press, 1978.

1958
'Discussion of "Looking over the Shoulder" by Morris W. Brody and Philip M. Mechanik,' in P. Ornstein (ed.) *The Search for the Self*, vol. 1, pp. 267–9. New York, International Universities Press, 1978.

1959
'Introspection, Empathy, and Psychoanalysis: An Examination of the Relationship between Mode of Observation and Theory,' in P. Ornstein (ed.) *The Search for the Self*, vol. 1, pp. 205–32. New York, International Universities Press, 1978.

1960
(a) 'Reporter "The Psychology of Imagination" on Panel: American Psychoanalytic Association Philadelphia, April 1959,' *Journal of the American Psychoanalytic Association* 1960, vol. 8, pp. 159–66.
(b) 'Childhood Experience and Creative Imagination: Contribution to Panel on the Psychology of Imagination,' in P. Ornstein (ed.) *The Search for the Self*, vol. 1, pp. 271–4. New York, International Universities Press, 1978.
(c) 'Beyond the Bounds of the Basic Rule: Some Recent Contributions to

Applied Psychoanalysis,' in P. Ornstein (ed.) *The Search for the Self*, vol. 1, pp. 275–303. New York, International Universities Press, 1978.
(d) 'Discussion of "Further Data and Documents in the Schreber Case" by William G. Niederland,' in P. Ornstein (ed.) *The Search for the Self*, vol. 1, pp. 305–8. New York, International Universities Press, 1978.

1961
'Discussion of "The Unconscious Fantasy" by David Beres,' in P. Ornstein (ed.) *The Search for the Self*, vol. 1, pp. 309–18. New York, International Universities Press, 1978.

1962
'The Psychoanalytic Curriculum,' in P. Ornstein (ed.) *The Search for the Self*, vol. 1, pp. 319–36. New York, International Universities Press, 1978.

1964
(a) 'The Position of Fantasy in Psychoanalytic Psychology: Chairman's Introductory Remarks to the Symposium on Fantasy,' in P. Ornstein (ed.) *The Search for the Self*, vol. 1, pp. 375–7. New York, International Universities Press, 1978.
(b) 'Some Problems of a Metapsychological Formulation of Fantasy: Chairman's Concluding Remarks to the Symposium on Fantasy,' in P. Ornstein (ed.) *The Search for the Self*, vol. 1, pp. 379–85. New York, International Universities Press, 1978.
(c) 'Franz Alexander: In Memoriam,' in P. Ornstein (ed.) *The Search for the Self*, vol. 1, pp. 387–8. New York, International Universities Press, 1978.
(d) 'Values and Objectives,' in P. Ornstein (ed.) *The Search for the Self*, vol. 1, pp. 389–93. New York, International Universities Press, 1978.

1965
(a) 'Autonomy and Integration,' in P. Ornstein (ed.) *The Search for the Self*, vol. 1, pp. 395–403. New York, International Universities Press, 1978.
(b) 'Discussion of "Correlation of a Childhood and Adult Neurosis: Based on the Adult Analysis of a Reported Childhood Case" by Samuel Ritvo,' in P. Ornstein (ed.) *The Search for the Self*, vol. 1, pp. 405–7. New York, International Universities Press, 1978.

1966
(a) 'Discussion of "Termination of Training Analysis" by Luisa G. de Alvarez de Toledo, Leon Grinberg, and Marie Langer,' in P. Ornstein (ed.) *The Search for the Self*, vol. 1, pp. 409–22. New York, International Universities Press, 1978.
(b) 'Discussion of "Some Additional Day Residues of the Specimen Dream of Psychoanalysis" by Max Schur,' in P. Ornstein (ed.) *The Search for the Self*, vol. 1, pp. 423–5. New York, International Universities Press, 1978.
(c) 'Forms and Transformations of Narcissism,' in P. Ornstein (ed.) *The Search for the Self*, vol. 1, pp. 427–60. New York, International Universities Press, 1978.

1968
(a) 'The Evaluation of Applicants for Psychoanalytic Training,' in P. Ornstein (ed.) *The Search for the Self*, vol. 1, pp. 461–75. New York, International Universities Press, 1978.

(b) 'The Psychoanalytic Treatment of Narcissistic Personality Disorders: Outline of a Systematic Approach,' in P. Ornstein (ed.) *The Search for the Self*, vol. 1, pp. 477–509. New York, International Universities Press, 1978.
(c) 'Introspection and Empathy: Further Thoughts about Their Role in Psychoanalysis,' in P. Ornstein (ed.) *The Search for the Self*, vol. 3, pp. 83–102. New York, International Universities Press, 1990.

1970
(a) On Leadership [1969–70],' in P. Ornstein (ed.) *The Search for the Self*, vol. 3, pp. 103–28. New York, International Universities Press, 1990.
(b) 'On Courage [early 1970s],' in P. Ornstein (ed.) *The Search for the Self*, vol. 3, pp. 129–81. New York, International Universities Press, 1990.
(c) 'From the Analysis of Mr. R. [early 1970s],' in P. Ornstein (ed.) *The Search for the Self*, vol. 3, pp. 183–222. New York, International Universities Press, 1990.
(d) 'Narcissism as a Resistance and as a Driving Force in Psychoanalysis,' in P. Ornstein (ed.) *The Search for the Self*, vol. 2, pp. 547–61. New York, International Universities Press, 1978.
(e) 'Discussion of "The Self: A Contribution to Its Place in Theory and Technique" by D.C. Levin,' in P. Ornstein (ed.) *The Search for the Self*, vol. 2, pp. 577–88. New York, International Universities Press, 1978.
(f) 'Scientific Activities of the American Psychoanalytic Association: An Inquiry,' in P. Ornstein (ed.) *The Search for the Self*, vol. 2, pp. 589–614. New York, International Universities Press, 1978.

1971
'Peace Prize 1969: Laudation,' in P. Ornstein (ed.) *The Search for the Self*, vol. 2, pp. 563–76. New York, International Universities Press, 1978.

1972
(a) 'Thoughts on Narcissism and Narcissistic Rage,' in P. Ornstein (ed.) *The Search for the Self*, vol. 2, pp. 615–58. New York, International Universities Press, 1978.
(b) 'Discussion of "On the Adolescent Process as a Transformation of the Self" by Ernest S. Wolf, John E. Gedo, and David M. Terman,' in P. Ornstein (ed.) *The Search for the Self*, vol. 2, pp. 659–62. New York, International Universities Press, 1978.

1973
(a) 'Psychoanalysis in a Troubled World,' in P. Ornstein (ed.) *The Search for the Self*, vol. 2, pp. 511–46. New York, International Universities Press, 1978.
(b) 'The Future of Psychoanalysis,' in P. Ornstein (ed.) *The Search for the Self*, vol. 2, pp. 663–84. New York, International Universities Press, 1978.
(c) 'The Psychoanalyst in the Community of Scholars,' in P. Ornstein (ed.) *The Search for the Self*, vol. 2, pp. 685–724. New York, International Universities Press, 1978.

1974
(a) 'Letter to the Author: Preface to *Lehrjahre auf der Couch* by Tilmann Moser,' in P. Ornstein (ed.) *The Search for the Self*, vol. 2, pp. 725–36. New York, International Universities Press, 1978.

(b) 'Remarks about the Formation of the Self: Letter to a Student Regarding Some Principles of Psychoanalytic Research,' in P. Ornstein (ed.) *The Search for the Self*, vol. 2, pp. 737–70. New York, International Universities Press, 1978.

1975

(a) 'Originality and Repetition in Science,' in P. Ornstein (ed.) *The Search for the Self*, vol. 3, pp. 223–9. New York, International Universities Press, 1990.
(b) 'The Self in History,' in P. Ornstein (ed.) *The Search for the Self*, vol. 2, pp. 771–82. New York, International Universities Press, 1978.
(c) 'A Note on Female Sexuality,' in P. Ornstein (ed.) *The Search for the Self*, vol. 2, pp. 783–92. New York, International Universities Press, 1978.

1976

(a) 'Creativeness, Charisma, Group Psychology: Reflections on the Self-Analysis of Freud,' in P. Ornstein (ed.) *The Search for the Self*, vol. 2, pp. 793–843. New York, International Universities Press, 1978.
(b) 'Preface to *Der falsche Weg zum Selbst, Studien zur Drogenkarriere* by Jurgen vom Scheidt,' in P. Ornstein (ed.) *The Search for the Self*, vol. 2, pp. 845–50. New York, International Universities Press, 1978.
(c) 'Reflections on the Occasion of Jean Piaget's Eightieth Birthday,' in P. Ornstein (ed.) *The Search for the Self*, vol. 3, pp. 231–4. New York, International Universities Press, 1990.

1978

(a) 'Conclusion: The Search for the Analyst's Self,' in P. Ornstein (ed.) *The Search for the Self*, vol. 2, pp. 931–8. New York, International Universities Press, 1978.
(b) 'Letters to Eric Heller,' in P. Ornstein (ed.) *The Search for the Self*, vol. 2, pp. 908–27. New York, International Universities Press, 1978.
(c) 'Self Psychology and the Sciences of Man,' in P. Ornstein (ed.) *The Search for the Self*, vol. 3, pp. 235–60. New York, International Universities Press, 1990.
(d) 'Reflections on *Advances in Self Psychology*,' in P. Ornstein (ed.) *The Search for the Self*, vol. 3, pp. 261–357. New York, International Universities Press, 1990.
(e) 'Introductory Remarks to the Panel on "Self Psychology and the Sciences of Man,"' in P. Ornstein (ed.) *The Search for the Self*, vol. 3, pp. 387–93. New York, International Universities Press, 1990.

1979

(a) 'The Two Analyses of Mr. Z,' in P. Ornstein (ed.) *The Search for the Self*, vol. 4, pp. 395–446. New York, International Universities Press, 1990.
(b) 'Four Basic Concepts in Self Psychology,' in P. Ornstein (ed.) *The Search for the Self*, vol. 4, pp. 447–70. New York, International Universities Press, 1990.
(c) 'Remarks on Receiving the William A. Schonfeld Distinguished Service Award,' in P. Ornstein (ed.) *The Search for the Self*, vol. 4, pp. 471–4. New York, International Universities Press, 1990.
(d) 'Remarks on the Panel on "The Bipolar Self,"' in P. Ornstein (ed.) *The Search for the Self*, vol. 4, pp. 475–81. New York, International Universities Press, 1990.

1980
(a) 'Greetings,' in P. Ornstein (ed.) *The Search for the Self*, vol. 4, pp. 483–8. New York, International Universities Press, 1990.
(b) 'Selected Problems in Self Psychological Theory,' in P. Ornstein (ed.) *The Search for the Self*, vol. 4, pp. 489–523. New York, International Universities Press, 1990.

1981
(a) 'On Empathy,' in P. Ornstein (ed.) *The Search for the Self*, vol. 4, pp. 525–35. New York, International Universities Press, 1990.
(b) 'Introspection, Empathy, and the Semicircle of Mental Health,' in P. Ornstein (ed.) *The Search for the Self*, vol. 4, pp. 537–67. New York, International Universities Press, 1990.

1950
Kohut, H. and Levarie, S. 'On the Enjoyment of Listening to Music,' in P. Ornstein (ed.) *The Search for the Self*, vol. 1, pp. 135–58. New York, International Universities Press, 1978.

1963
Kohut, H. and Seitz, P. 'Concepts and Theories of Psychoanalysis,' in P. Ornstein (ed.) *The Search for the Self*, vol. 1, pp. 337–74. New York, International Universities Press, 1978.

1978
Kohut, H. and Wolf, E. 'The Disorders of the Self and Their Treatment: An Outline,' in P. Ornstein (ed.) *The Search for the Self*, vol. 3, pp. 359–85. New York, International Universities Press, 1990.

BOOKS

1971
Analysis of the Self, New York, International Universities Press.

1977
The Restoration of the Self, New York, International Universities Press.

1984
How Does Analysis Cure?, Chicago and London, University of Chicago Press.

UNPUBLISHED LECTURE SERIES

1960
Kohut, H. and Seitz, P. (ed.) (1960) 'Kohut's Unpublished Course P. 200, 300, "Psychoanalytic Psychology,"' in Kohut Archives, located at the Chicago Institute for Psychoanalysis.

PUBLISHED LECTURE SERIES

1974
Elson, M. (ed.) (1987) *The Kohut Seminars on Self Psychology and Psychotherapy with Adolescents and Young Adults*, New York and London: W.W. Norton.

1972–6
Tolpin, P. and Tolpin, M. (1996) *The Chicago Institute Letters of Heinz Kohut*, Hillsdale, NJ, Analytic Press.

PUBLISHED CONVERSATIONS AND CORRESPONDENCE

1923–81
Cocks, G. (1994) *The Curve of Life: Correspondence of Heinz Kohut 1923–1981*, Chicago and London, University of Chicago Press.

1981
(a) 'The Psychoanalyst and the Historian [January 29, 1981],' in C. Strozier (ed.) *Self Psychology and the Humanities: Reflections on a New Psychoanalytic Approach* (1985), pp. 215–21. New York and London, W.W. Norton.
(b) 'Idealization and Cultural Selfobjects (February 12, 1981),' in C. Strozier (ed.) *Self Psychology and the Humanities: Reflections on a New Psychoanalytic Approach* (1985), pp. 224–31. New York and London, W.W. Norton.
(c) 'On the Continuity of the Self and Cultural Selfobjects [February 26, 1981],' in C. Strozier (ed.) *Self Psychology and the Humanities: Reflections on a New Psychoanalytic Approach* (1985), pp. 232–43. New York and London, W.W. Norton.
(d) '"One Needs a Twinkle of Humor as a Protection against Craziness" [March 12, 1981],' in C. Strozier (ed.) *Self Psychology and the Humanities: Reflections on a New Psychoanalytic Approach* (1985), pp. 244–53. New York and London, W.W. Norton.
(e) 'Civilization versus Culture [May 7, 1981],' in C. Strozier (ed.) *Self Psychology and the Humanities: Reflections on a New Psychoanalytic Approach* (1985), pp. 254–60. New York and London, W.W. Norton.
(f) 'Religion, Ethics, Values [June 6, 1981],' in C. Strozier (ed.) *Self Psychology and the Humanities: Reflections on a New Psychoanalytic Approach* (1985), pp. 261–2. New York and London, W.W. Norton.
(g) '"Stranger Take Word to Sparta: Here We Lie Obeying Her Orders" [July 16, 1981],' in C. Strozier (ed.) *Self Psychology and the Humanities: Reflections on a New Psychoanalytic Approach* (1985), pp. 263–9. New York and London, W.W. Norton.

General bibliography

Aichhorn, A. (1935) *Wayward Youth*, New York, The Viking Press.
Atwood, G. and Stolorow, R. (1984) *Structures of Subjectivity*, Hillsdale, NJ, The Analytic Press.
—— (1993) *Faces in a Cloud* (rev.), Northvale, NJ, Aronson.
Bacal, H. (1985) 'Optimal Responsiveness and the Therapeutic Process,' in A. Goldberg (ed.) *Progress in Self Psychology*, vol. 1, pp. 202–26. Hillsdale, NJ, The Analytic Press.
Basch, M. (1995) 'Kohut's Contribution,' *Psychoanalytic Dialogues*, vol. 5, no 3, pp. 367–73.
Baum, L.F. (1900) *The Wonderful Wizard of Oz*, G.M. Hill.
Beebe, B. and Lachmann, F.M. (1994) 'Representation and Internalization in Infancy: Three Principles of Salience,' *Psychoanalytic Psychotherapy*, vol. 11, pp. 127–65.
Beebe, B., Jaffe, J. and Lachmann, F. (1993) 'A Dyadic Systems View of Communication,' in N. Skolnick and S. Warshaw (eds) *Relational Perspectives in Psychoanalysis*, pp. 61–8, Hillsdale, NJ, The Analytic Press.
Cocks, G. (1994) *The Curve of Life: Correspondence of Heinz Kohut 1923–1981*, Chicago and London, University of Chicago Press.
Eidelberg, L. (1959) 'The Concept of Narcissistic Mortification', *International Journal of Psycho-Analysis*, vol. 40, pp. 163–8.
Ferenczi, S. (1930) 'Autoplastic and Alloplastic Adaptations,' in *Final Contributions*, p. 221. New York, Basic Books, 1995.
Freud, A. (1946) *The Ego and the Mechanisms of Defense*, New York, International Universities Press.
Freud, S. (1900) *The Interpretation of Dreams*, Standard Edition (*SE*), vols 4 and 5, pp. 1–63. London, Hogarth Press.
—— (1905a) *Three Essays on the Theory of Sexuality*, *SE*, vol. 7, pp. 125–245. London, Hogarth Press.
—— (1905b) 'Fragment of an Analysis of a Case of Hysteria,' *SE*, vol. 7, pp. 7–122. London, Hogarth Press.
—— (1911) 'Psychoanalytic Notes on an Autobiography of a Case of Paranoia (Dementia Paranoides),' *SE*, vol. 12, pp. 3–82, London, Hogarth Press.
—— (1912) 'Recommendations to Physicians Practising Psychoanalysis,' *SE*, vol. 12, pp. 111–29. London, Hogarth Press.

—— (1913) 'On Beginning the Treatment (Further Recommendations on the Technique of Psycho-analysis),' *SE*, vol. 12, pp. 123–44. London, Hogarth Press.
—— (1914) 'On Narcissism: An Introduction,' *SE*, vol. 14, pp. 69–102. London, Hogarth Press.
—— (1915) 'Instincts and Their Vicissitudes,' *SE*, vol. 14, pp. 111–40. London, Hogarth Press.
—— (1917) 'Mourning and Melancholia,' *SE*, vol. 14, pp. 239–58. London, Hogarth Press.
—— (1920) 'Beyond the Pleasure Principle,' *SE*, vol. 18, pp. 7–64. London, Hogarth Press.
—— (1921) 'Group Psychology and the Analysis of the Ego,' *SE*, vol. 18, pp. 67–143. London, Hogarth Press.
—— (1923) 'The Ego and the Id,' *SE*, vol. 19, pp. 23–66. London, Hogarth Press.
—— (1930) *Civilization and Its Discontents*, *SE*, vol. 21, pp. 59–145. London, Hogarth Press.
Galdston, I. (1955) '*Eros and Thanatos*: A Critique and Elaboration of Freud's Death Wish,' *American Journal of Psychoanalysis*, vol. 15, pp. 123–34.
Glover, E. (1931) 'The Therapeutic Effect of the Inexact Interpretation: A Contribution to the Theory of Suggestion,' *The Technique of Psychoanalysis*, pp. 353–66. New York, International Universities Press, 1955.
Goldberg, A. (1980) 'Self Psychology and the Distinctiveness of Psychotherapy,' *International Journal of Psychoanalytic Psychotherapy*, vol. 8, pp. 57–70.
Goldberg, A. (ed.) (1978) *The Psychology of the Self: A Casebook*, New York, International Universities Press.
Hitschman, E. (1956) *Great Men: Psychoanalytic Studies*, New York, International Universities Press.
Hoffman, I. (1991) 'Discussion: Toward a Social Constructivist View of the Psychoanalytic Situation,' *Psychoanalytic Dialogues*, vol. 1, pp. 74–105.
Kleeman, J. (1967) 'The Peek-a-Boo Game: Part I. Its Origins, Meanings, and Related Phenomena in the First Year,' *The Psychoanalytic Study of the Child*, vol. XXII. New York, International Universities Press.
Kohut, H. (1951) 'Discussion of *The Function of the Analyst in the Therapeutic Process* by Samuel D. Lipton,' in P. Ornstein (ed.) *The Search for the Self*, vol. 1, pp. 159–66. New York, International Universities Press.
—— (1954) 'Discussion of *Eros and Thanatos*: A Critique and Elaboration of Freud's Death Wish by Iago Galdston,' in P. Ornstein (ed.) *The Search for the Self*, vol. 1, pp. 177–85. New York, International Universities Press, 1978.
—— (1956) 'Discussion of "Modern Casework: The Contribution of Ego Psychology" by Annette Garrette,' in P. Ornstein (ed.) *The Search for the Self*, vol. 1, pp. 195–200. New York, International Universities Press, 1978.
—— (1957a) '*Death in Venice* by Mann: A Story about the Disintegration of Artistic Sublimation,' in P. Ornstein (ed.) *The Search for the Self*, vol. 1, pp. 107–30. New York, International Universities Press, 1978.
—— (1957b) 'Observations on the Psychological Functions of Music,' in P. Ornstein (ed.) *The Search for the Self*, vol. 1, pp. 233–53. New York, International Universities Press, 1978.
—— (1957c) 'Book review of *The Arrow and the Lyre: A Study of the Role of Love in the Works of Thomas Mann* by Frank Donald Hirschbach,' in

P. Ornstein (ed.) *The Search for the Self*, vol. 1, pp. 255–7. New York, International Universities Press, 1978.

—— (1957d) 'Discussion of "Some Comments on the Origin of the Influencing Machine" by Louis Linn,' in P. Ornstein (ed.) *The Search for the Self*, vol. 1, pp. 259–61. New York, International Universities Press, 1978.

—— (1959) 'Introspection, Empathy and Psychoanalysis: An Examination of the Relationship between Mode of Observation and Theory,' in P. Ornstein (ed.) *The Search for the Self*, vol. 1, pp. 205–32. New York, International Universities Press, 1978.

—— (1960) 'Beyond the Bounds of the Basic Rule: Some Recent Contributions to Applied Psychoanalysis,' in P. Ornstein (ed.) *The Search for the Self*, vol. 1, pp. 275–303. New York, International Universities Press, 1978.

—— (1966) 'Forms and Transformations of Narcissism', in P. Ornstein (ed.) *The Search for the Self*, vol. 1, pp. 427–60. New York, International Universities Press, 1978.

—— (1968) 'The Psychoanalytic Treatment of Narcissistic Personality Disorders: Outline of a Systematic Approach,' in P. Ornstein (ed.) *The Search for the Self*, vol. 1, pp. 477–509. New York, International Universities Press, 1978.

—— (1971) *Analysis of the Self*, New York: International Universities Press.

—— (1973) 'The Future of Psychoanalysis,' in P. Ornstein (ed.) *The Search for the Self*, vol. 2, pp. 663–84. New York, International Universities Press, 1978.

—— (1977) *The Restoration of the Self*, New York, International Universities Press.

—— (1979) 'The Two Analyses of Mr. Z,' in P. Ornstein (ed.) *The Search for the Self*, vol. 4, pp. 395–446. New York, International Universities Press, 1990.

—— (1981a) 'On Empathy,' in P. Ornstein (ed.) *The Search for the Self*, vol. 4, pp. 525–35. New York, International Universities Press, 1990.

—— (1981b) 'Introspection, Empathy and the Semicircle of Mental Health,' in P. Ornstein (ed.) *The Search for the Self*, vol. 4, pp. 537–67. New York, International Universities Press, 1990.

—— (1984) *How Does Analysis Cure?*, eds A. Goldberg and P. Stepansky. Chicago and London, University of Chicago Press.

—— 'Kohut's Unpublished Course P. 200, 300, "Psychoanalytic Psychology"' (1960), ed. P. Seitz, in Kohut Archives located at the Chicago Institute for Psychoanalysis.

Kohut, H. and Levarie, S. (1950) 'On the Enjoyment of Listening to Music,' in P. Ornstein (ed.) *The Search for the Self*, vol. 4, pp. 135–58. New York, International Universities Press, 1978.

Kohut, H. and Seitz, P. (1963) 'Concepts and Theories of Psychoanalysis,' in P. Ornstein (ed.) *The Search for the Self*, vol. 1, pp. 337–74. New York, International Universities Press, 1978.

Kohut, H. and Wolf, E. (1978) 'The Disorders of the Self and their Treatment: an Outline,' in P. Ornstein (ed.) *The Search for the Self*, vol. 3, pp. 359–85. New York, International Universities Press, 1990.

Lachman, F.M. and Beebe, B. (1991) 'Three Self Psychologies – or One?', in A. Goldberg (ed.) *The Evolution of Self Psychology: Progress in Self Psychology*, vol. 7, pp. 167–74. Hillsdale, NJ, The Analytic Press.

—— (1992) 'Representational and Self Object Transferences: A Developmental Perspective,' in A. Goldberg (ed.) *New Therapeutic Visions: Progress in Self Psychology*, vol. 8, pp. 3–15. Hillsdale, NJ, The Analytic Press.
—— (1995) 'Self Psychology: Today,' *Psychoanalytic Dialogues*, vol. 5, no. 3, pp. 375–84.
Lichtenberg, J. (1983) *Psychoanalysis and Infant Research*, Hillsdale, NJ, The Analytic Press.
—— (1989) *Psychoanalysis and Motivation*, Hillsdale, NJ, The Analytic Press.
Linn, L. (1958) 'Some Comments on the Origins of the Influencing Machine,' *Journal of the American Psychoanalytic Association*, vol. 6, pp. 305–8.
Mitchell, S. (1988) *Relational Concepts in Psychoanalysis*, Cambridge, MA, Harvard University Press.
Mitchell, S. (ed.) (1995) 'Self Psychology after Kohut: A Polylogue,' Special issue of *Psychoanalytic Dialogues*, vol. 5, no. 3.
Ornstein, P. (1990) 'Introduction: The Unfolding and Completion of Heinz Kohut's Paradigm of Psychoanalysis,' in P. Ornstein (ed.) *The Search for the Self*, vol. 3, pp. 1–83, New York, International Universities Press.
Ornstein, P. and Ornstein, A. (1995) 'Some Distinguishing Features of Heinz Kohut's Self Psychology,' *Psychoanalytic Dialogues*, vol. 5, no. 3, pp. 385–91.
Shane, M. and Shane, E. (1993) 'Self Psychology after Kohut: One Theory or Many?' *Journal of the American Psychoanalytic Association*, vol. 41, pp. 777–98.
—— (1994) 'Self Psychology in Search of the Optimal: A Consideration of Optimal Responsiveness; Optimal Provision; Optimal Gratification; and Optimal Restraint in the Clinical Situation,' Presented at the 17th Annual Conference on the Psychology of the Self, Chicago.
Stern, D. (1985) *The Interpersonal World of the Infant: A view from Psychoanalysis and Developmental Psychology*, New York, Basic Books.
Stolorow, R. (1995) 'An Intersubjective View of Self Psychology,' *Psychoanalytic Dialogues*, vol. 5, no. 3, pp. 393–9.
Stolorow, R. and Atwood, G. (1992) *Contexts of Being*, Hillsdale, NJ, The Analytic Press.
Stolorow, R., Brandchaft, B. and Attwood, G. (1987) *Psychoanalytic Treatment*, Hillsdale, NJ, The Analytic Press.
Tausk, V. (1919) 'On the Origin of the "Influencing Machine" in Schizophrenia,' *Psychoanalytic Quarterly*, vol. 2, pp. 519–56 (1933).
Terman, D. (1988) 'Optimum Frustration: Structuralization and the Therapeutic Process,' in A. Goldberg (ed.) *Learning From Kohut: Progress in Self Psychology*, vol. 4, pp. 113–25. Hillsdale, NJ, The Analytic Press.
Tolpin, P. (1988) 'Optimal Affective Engagement: The Analyst's Role in Therapy,' in A. Goldberg (ed.) *Learning from Kohut: Progress in Self Psychology*, vol. 4, pp. 160–8. Hillsdale, NJ, The Analytic Press.
Wolf, I. (1996) Personal communication.

Index

addictions 50, 73
aggression *see* narcissistic rage
Aichhorn, A. 12
alter-ego/twinship transference 88
ambitions: based on grandiose self 61; exhibitionism as root of 118
analyzability 176
anxieties: disintegration 188; in narcissistic disorders 65, 94–5, 114; in neurosis 114
autonomy 165

Basch, M. 198
Beebe, B. 200
biological principles in psychoanalysis 22, 106, 196–7
bipolar self *see* self, bipolar
borderline states 48, 121; transference in 47–8

case material 80–5, 96–103, 122–33, 181–5; *see also* Kohut, H.
castration anxiety 159; *see also* oedipal phase; Oedipus complex
childrearing *see* parental responsiveness
classic psychoanalytic theory *see* drive-defense theory
classical analysis: empathic failures in 138, 170; *see also* drive-defense analysts; interpretation; technique; therapeutic factors; therapeutic goals; therapy
cognition, role in structure-building 191

cohesiveness, development of 89
compensatory structures 107, 110, 156–8
configurations *see* structures
connectedness *see* empathic connectedness
corrective emotional experience 168, 170
countertransference 80; enslavement feelings 96
creativity, narcissism transformed into 62
cure *see* therapeutic factors; therapeutic goals

defect *see* deficits, developmental
defense 178–81: vs. area of progressive neutralization 41; deficits underlying 180; against failed selfobjects 180; healthy aspects of 181–5; misidentification of 170; repression barrier 57–8; *see also* disavowal; repression; resistance
deficits, developmental 28, 50–2, 170; treatment of 107; *see also* selfobject needs; structures
dehumanization, trauma of 188
delusions 36
dependence *see* selfobject needs
depression underlying defective self 196
desexualization *see* neutralization
developmental arrest *see* deficit; drive fixations

developmental lines *see* narcissism
developmental processes *see* therapeutic factors
diagnostic classification 121–2
disappointment *see* frustration
disavowal 92, 203
disintegration anxieties *see* anxieties, disintegration
dream content: disintegration in traumatic states 114; wish-fulfillment in neuroses 114
drive fixations, role of self in 111
drive-defense analysts: misinterpretation of rage 113; misinterpretation of selfobject transference 169–70; nonresponsiveness of 113, 137–8; selfobject failures of 138
drive-defense theory: biases 106, 162; and biological principles 22, 106, 196–7; interface with Kohut's ideas 40–3, 197, 199; Kohut's additions to 40, 56; Kohut's course on 19–43; Kohut's departure from 4, 50, 106, 162, 196; narcissism pathologized by 106; structural theory 56; and therapeutic atmosphere 170
drives, Kohut's view of 196
drives (component): as breakdown of fractured self 112, 120, 196; elicited by empathic failures 116

ego-ideal 42–3, 61, 73
Eissler, R. 12
empathic connectedness 190, 191; disintegration anxiety prevented by 188; need for 188
empathic failures: in classical analysis 138, 170; drives elicited by 116
empathy 6, 186–9; conceptions and developmental levels of 186–91; development of 17; Freud on 17; as instrument of observation 70, 186; narcissism transformed into 62; vs. neutrality 5; 'On Empathy' (Kohut, H.) 5, 6, 186, 190, 192, 197; as optimal frustration 173; sadistic 187, 191; vs. truth values 16
exhibitionism: based on grandiose self 61; sexualized 120

exhibitionistic narcissism: as root of ambitions 118; work enhanced by 90
experience-near theory: vs. classical theory 105, 170; vs. experience-distant theory 105–6, 170, 204
explanation *see* interpretation

fragmentation 46, 65
free association 53
Freud, A. 12, 63
Freud, S.: on empathy 17
frustration, optimal 27, 29, 71, 201, 205; empathic response as 173; need-disruption-repair and 174; vs. traumatic 58
frustration, traumatic 56; alleviation via empathy 173

Galdston, I. 48
Gedo, J. 10, 11
Gitelson, M. 8
Goldberg, A. ix, x, 10, 13
grandiose self 36, 51, 60, 63, 66, 70, 86–103, 204; activated by narcissistic injury 74–5; ambitions based on 61; exhibitionism based on 61; integration into personality 61, 63, 86–7, 94–5; remobilization of 90
grandiosity *see* grandiose self; idealized parental imago; mirror transference
Guilty Man 117

Hitschman, E. 53
humor, and acceptance of transience 62
hypochondria 36
hypochondriacal anxiety 114; as objectless state 34

idealization 42; restitutive 46
idealized objects: search for approval and leadership from 73; traumatic loss of or disappointment in 76
idealized parental imago 51, 66, 70–85, 204; developmental arrest of 69; disturbances of 72–4;

integration into personality 61, 63; as projected narcissism 60; re-internalization of 60–1, 71
idealizing transference 76; clinical illustration 80–5; countertransference to 80; disruption of and transmuting internalization 79; reactions to disruption 78; resistance to 77; technique following disruption 78; types of 75–6
ideals 61; based on idealized parental imago 61; narcissism as root of 42–3
insight *see* therapeutic factors
internalization, transmuting 43, 71, 167, 207; disruption of idealization and 79; vs. nontransmuting 199, 200; origin of concept 199
interpretation: rage following 113; of resistance 96; role in treatment 18, 138, 189; therapeutic factors in 18, 171–2, 189; *see also* therapy
interpretation, explanation component: cognitive element of 191; dynamic and genetic elements of 174–7; relation to understanding component 189, 191
interpretation, inexact 172–3
interpretation, understanding component 172–5, 177, 189

Kohut, H., clinical work and practice of 190, 202; case material 74, 91–2, 107–10, 122–5, 190; evolution of 16, 141–52, 170; response to therapeutic failures 16, 170
Kohut, H., life of 2–3, 13, 14, 104, 195, 208–9; death 186; self-reflections 170; trauma 15
Kohut, H., personality of 7–9, 12, 14, 104–5, 190, 195, 196; mirroring needs 15; and mother 14
Kohut, H., theoretical views of: criticism of 197–201; development of self psychology 16, 54; early work 44; evolution of 3–4, 16, 54–5, 104–5, 118, 153–4, 170; *see also* drive-defense theory

Kohut, H., works of 13, 210–16; 'Concepts and Theories of Psychoanalysis' 41–3; course on Freudian theory 19–43; 'On Empathy' 5, 6, 186, 190, 192, 197; 'Two Analyses of Mr. Z' 141–52, 170; writing style 194–5
Kohutian analysis *see* therapy

Lachmann, F. M. 200
Linn, L. 52
Lipton, S. 47

Mann, T. 44–6
mental health *see* therapeutic goals
merger transference 88
mirror transference 89; analyst's acceptance of 95–6, 100; countertransference to 96; disruption of 90; types of 88–91; *see also* grandiose self; transference, alter-ego; transference, merger
mirroring needs 61
mortality, acceptance of 62
mother–child relations *see* mirroring; parental responsiveness
music 46–7, 51

narcissism: bias against 106; definitions 59; disrupted infantile 60, 68–9; forms and transformations 59–63, 68–9; legitimized by Kohut 60, 107; neutrality toward 59, 170; vs. object love 59, 107; as restitutive 48; separate developmental lines 42, 59, 68–9, 107
narcissistic behavior disorders: bipolar self and 122; use of action vs. fantasy for restitution 122
narcissistic constancy 90
narcissistic disorders, anxieties in 65, 94–5
narcissistic disorders, treatment of: phases of 77; resistance to 77
narcissistic injury 74–5; in classical analysis 138–70; elicits drives 116; *see also* narcissistic rage

Index

narcissistic needs 194; analyst's acceptance of 95, 170; sexualization of 73–5
narcissistic personality 65, 122; bipolar self and 122; differential diagnosis 65; self cohesiveness vs. fragmentation 65
narcissistic rage 46; as breakdown of assertiveness 112, 115, 120; caused by narcissistic injury 115; following analyst's selfobject failure 138; following unempathic interpretation 113; misinterpretation of 113; as product of disintegrating self 115; repressed masochism caused by 41
narcissistic self 60; *see also* purified pleasure ego
narcissistic transferences 64; *see also* transference, selfobject
Nazis, disregard for victims' humanity 188
needs *see* narcissistic needs
neglect: guilt elicited by 188; inability to articulate 188
neologisms 35
neurosis, structural 33; anxiety in 114
neurosis, transference 65
neutrality 170; impossibility of 5, 162–3; vs. nonresponsiveness 137; toward narcissism 59, 170
neutralization 41; vs. repression 57
neutralization, area of progressive 57; vs. barrier of defenses 57–8; transmuting internalization leads to 57–8
nonconflictual structures 41

object hunger *see* selfobject needs
object relatedness: loss of, in psychosis 34; *see also* empathic connectedness; therapeutic factors, selfobject attunement
objects (true) *see under* selfobjects
oedipal material: in analysis 133–4, 159–61; new vs. transference 134, 159; without anxiety 134
oedipal phase 133–6, 160; cohesive self as prerequisite for 134; joy in 134, 135; parental responses to 134–5, 160, 161
Oedipus complex: abnormality of 136, 161; empathic failures as cause of 136, 160, 161
omnipotence, transformed into pride 62
omniscience *see* idealized parental imago
'On Empathy' (Kohut, H.) 5, 6, 186, 190, 192, 197
optimal frustration *see* frustration, optimal
Ornstein, A. 10
Ornstein, P. 10
overindulged persons 28

paranoid delusions, based on deadness vs. conflict 52
parental responsiveness 87, 188; during oedipal phase 134–6
passage through object 71, 199; *see also* internalization, transmuting
passivity, as life-sustaining facade 181–5
perversions: defend against depression 116; enfeebled self and 112, 121; exhibitionism 120; as sexualized selfobject relationship 116; voyeurism 120
phobia: oedipal as nucleus of neurosis 35; preoedipal as nucleus of psychosis 35, 36
psychoanalysis: history of 20; *see also* therapy
psychoanalysts *see* drive-defense analysts
psychoanalytic theory *see* biological principles in psychoanalysis; drive-defense theory; Kohut, theoretical views of
Psychology of the Self: A Casebook (Goldberg, A.) 13
psychopathology: addictions 50, 73; borderline states 47–8, 121; classification of 121–2; exhibitionism 120; narcissistic behavior disorders 122; narcissistic disorders 65, 77, 94–5; neurosis 33,

65, 114; paranoid delusions 52; phobia 35, 36; psychosis 33–5, 38, 121; schizoid personality 34; *see also* grandiose self; hypochondria; perversion; symptoms
psychosexual fixations: role of self in 111
psychosis 33–5, 121; vs. neurosis 33, 38
psychotic regression 33–4
psychotic symptoms, and sustenance of object relations 35, 38
purified pleasure ego 36; *see also* narcissistic self

rage *see* narcissistic rage
reality testing, developed via optimal frustration 27
repair 174
repression *see* defense
repression barrier 57–8; vs. area of progressive neutralization 41
resistance 170, 178–81; as healthy 181; interpretation of 96; as self preservation vs. drive repression 180–1; to selfobject transference 77; technique and 77; *see also* defense

sadism 187, 191
schizoid characters 34
Schweitzer, A. 53
scientific attitude 48–9
Seitz, P. 19, 55–8
self: as affect container 113; definition 122; nature of 65; role in drive fixations 111; undefinability 139–40, 199
self, bipolar 61, 118, 119–20, 177; compensatory nature of 119; criticism of 198, 199; in narcissistic disorders 122, 126; skills and talents in 119; tension arc of 119
self, pathology of 170; depression underlying defective self 196; and drive fixations 111
self cohesiveness, development of 89
self defect *see* deficits, developmental

self preservation, primacy of 180
self psychology *see* Kohut, theoretical views of
self psychology, post-Kohutian 200
self structuralization, stages of 112
self-interest *see* narcissism
selflessness, virtue of 106
selfobject needs 72, 170, 206; vs. classical transference 51; normality of 165, 168, 170; *see also* idealized parental imago; mirroring needs
selfobject transference *see* transference, selfobject
selfobjects 4, 36, 46, 206; defenses against 180; vs. objects 71–2
self-soothing functions, disorders of 73, 74
self-state dreams 46
sexuality: drive vs. self psychology view of 116; as result of disrupted affection 112; *see also* perversion
sexualization of narcissistic needs 73–5
sleep, going to 51
splitting, vertical 92–5, 207
spoiled persons 28
structural deficits 28, 50–2, 170; in superego 73; treatment of 107; *see also* selfobject needs
structural theory 56
structure-building 71–2, 177; limits of 176; role of cognition in 191; *see also* internalization
structures: compensatory 107, 110, 156–8; defensive 107; fragility of new structures 35; nonconflictual 41; secondary 157
superego, deficits in 73, neutralized 43
symptoms 35; delusions 36, 52; paranoia 52; psychotic 35, 38; *see also* anxieties; hypochondria; psychopathology

Tausk, V. 52
technique 166, 169, 177, 201–2; acceptance of mirror transference 95–6; acceptance of selfobject transference 170; disruption of

selfobject transference and 78–9, 90–1, 166; human responsiveness vs. friendliness 77; nonresponsiveness repeats selfobject trauma 138; *see also* interpretation; neutrality
tension regulation disorders 73, 74
therapeutic atmosphere in drive-defense vs. self psychology 170
therapeutic factors 164, 177, 181, 201–2; acceptance of narcissistic needs 95, 170; cognition 191; corrective emotional experience 168, 170; of inexact interpretations 172–3; insight into threats to self 181; need-disruption-repair 174; selfobject attunement 165, 167, 168, 172, 189; selfobject failures via transference 139, 166–7; transmuting internalization vs. insight 51, 167, 168; undoing denial of need and dependence 51; working through 79, 92, 164; *see also* internalization; interpretation
therapeutic goals 125–6, 156–8, 167–8, 177; autonomy 165; compensatory structures 107, 110, 125–6, 156–8; creative narcissistic expression 110, 177; for injured vs. disorganized self 155; Kohutian vs. classical 59, 155–8; limits of 121; realization of skills and talents 156, 177; structure-building 71–2, 176–7, 191
therapy 170, 177, 189; interpretive phase of 112; limitations of 121, 176; merger phase of 112, 191; oedipal stage of 159–60; stages of 112, 123–6, 172; *see also* analyzability; drive-defense analysts; interpretation; technique
Tolpin, P. 10
Tragic Man 117
transference: alter-ego/twinship 88; in borderline states 47–8; conceptions and types of 23, 25–6, 48, 50, 56; defense vs. need 47–8; merger 88; narcissistic 64 (*see also* transference, selfobject); vs. non-transference 40–2, 47; technical 23 transference; selfobject 50, 51, 121, 170, 207; as nonrepetition 121; working through disruption of 79; *see also* idealizing transference; mirror transference
transference-like experiences 2, 63
transience 62
transmuting internalization *see* internalization, transmuting
trauma 56; integration prevented by 63; parental emptiness as worst 188; repeated by analytic nonresponsiveness 138; role in psychopathology 56
tripartite model 56
truth values vs. empathy 16
twinship transference *see* transference, alter-ego

understanding *see* empathy; interpretation, understanding component

values: anti-narcissism 60, 106, 107; selflessness 106; truth vs. empathy 16; Western morality biases 106
vertical splitting 92–5, 207
visual relatedness 89; *see also* mirroring
voyeurism, sexualized: as response to failed idealized selfobject 120
vulnerability, narcissistic 45

Western morality, biases of 106
wisdom vs. narcissistic delusions 62
wish vs. tension 50
Wolf, E. ix, x, 7–18
work, defensive aspects of 90